Inventing Value

Value is central to the market sectors of the contemporary economy, yet the best-established theories of value fail to expose how it operates and how it is manipulated for profit. This book begins to reconstruct the theory of value. In one sense, it argues, value is a personal assessment of worth, but those assessments draw deeply on normative standards. The book examines those standards and how they are formed, transformed and supported by the construction of new social structures. The empirical evidence comes from contemporary financial examples: the mortgage-backed securities that caused the global crash of 2008, how venture capitalists secure outrageous valuations for so-called unicorn companies and the rise of Bitcoin. The result is a theory that shows how value is invented by value entrepreneurs in pursuit of their interests and thus provides a new basis for criticising the role of value in the commodity economy and the finance sector.

DAVE ELDER-VASS'S experience as a government economist, a corporate IT manager and a sociologist at Loughborough University gives him a unique insight into the contemporary economy. His previous books include *Profit and Gift in the Digital Economy* (2016) and *The Reality of Social Construction* (2012).

T0370730

Inventing Value

The Social Construction of Monetary Worth

DAVE ELDER-VASS
Loughborough University

CAMBRIDGE
UNIVERSITY PRESS

Shaftesbury Road, Cambridge CB2 8EA, United Kingdom

One Liberty Plaza, 20th Floor, New York, NY 10006, USA

477 Williamstown Road, Port Melbourne, VIC 3207, Australia

314–321, 3rd Floor, Plot 3, Splendor Forum, Jasola District Centre, New Delhi – 110025, India

103 Penang Road, #05–06/07, Visioncrest Commercial, Singapore 238467

Cambridge University Press is part of Cambridge University Press & Assessment, a department of the University of Cambridge.

We share the University's mission to contribute to society through the pursuit of education, learning and research at the highest international levels of excellence.

www.cambridge.org
Information on this title: www.cambridge.org/9781009199322

DOI: 10.1017/9781009199353

First published 2022
First paperback edition 2024

A catalogue record for this publication is available from the British Library

Library of Congress Cataloging-in-Publication data
Names: Elder-Vass, Dave, author.
Title: Inventing value : the social construction of monetary worth / Dave Elder-Vass.
Description: [New York] : Cambridge University Press, [2022] | Includes bibliographical references and index.
Identifiers: LCCN 2021061907 (print) | LCCN 2021061908 (ebook) | ISBN 9781009199339 (hardback) | ISBN 9781009199322 (paperback) | ISBN 9781009199353 (epub)
Subjects: LCSH: Value. | Money.
Classification: LCC HG223 .E43 2022 (print) | LCC HG223 (ebook) | DDC 338.5/21–dc23/eng/20220104
LC record available at https://lccn.loc.gov/2021061907
LC ebook record available at https://lccn.loc.gov/2021061908

ISBN   978-1-009-19933-9   Hardback
ISBN   978-1-009-19932-2   Paperback

To Mam and Dad

Contents

Figures

Acknowledgements

This book was made possible by the generous provision of a Political Economy Research Fellowship by the Independent Social Research Foundation (ISRF). I would like to thank the ISRF for their support and for the vibrant interdisciplinary community of heterodox scholarship they have created. I particularly thank the ISRF's recently retired director of research, Louise Braddock, for going out of her way to help me make connections and obtain important material.

This work has improved vastly as a result of the support, advice and criticism provided by many people over the last five years, often through commenting on draft papers during the tortuous process of turning my ideas into this book, but also through many fascinating conversations, both face to face and virtual. My thanks go to Bruce Carruthers, Nathan Coombs, Dean Curran, Olivier Favereau, Harvey Frost, Emma Greeson, Ito Jimenez, Steve Kemp, Wolfgang Knöbl, Clive Lawson, Tony Lawson, Sarah Manski, Alistair Milne, Jamie Morgan, Line Nyhagen, Doug Porpora, Steve Pratten, Tim Rutzou, Aaron Sahr and Thomas Thurnell-Read. Various anonymous readers and referees also made important contributions, above all those at Cambridge University Press, but also those at a number of journals. No doubt I have forgotten many others who also helped, for which I apologise.

I also thank the Hamburg Institute for Social Research and the Cambridge Realist Workshop for inviting me to a number of discussions that helped to test and develop my ideas. Many audience members have made useful and stimulating comments on relevant papers, both there and at conferences held by the International Association for Critical Realism (IACR), the Society for the Advancement of Socio-Economics (SASE) and the Finance and Society Network.

I would like to thank John Haslam at Cambridge University Press and his team for the exceptional quality of their work in publishing not only this but also my earlier books with them.

Once again, my greatest thanks are reserved for my wife, Alisa, for her unwavering support and encouragement, and also for her help in the struggle to find an appropriate title for this book.

Finally, I would like to thank several journals and their publishers for permission to reprint material that has appeared previously in the articles listed below. None of them are reproduced in full, but sections have been reused across various chapters of the book.

'A history of Bitcoin – told through the five different groups who bought it', *The Conversation* (28 August 2018). © 2018, The Conversation Trust (UK) Limited.

'No price without value', *Cambridge Journal of Economics* (2019) 43(6), 1485–1498. © 2019, Dave Elder-Vass.

'Assets need audiences: How venture capitalists boost valuations by recruiting investors to asset circles', *Finance and Society* (2021) 7(1). © 2021, Dave Elder-Vass.

'Book Review: *The nature of social reality: issues in social ontology* by Tony Lawson', *Journal of Critical Realism* (2021) online in advance of print. © 2021, Informa UK Limited.

1 | *Introduction*
Inventing Value

This book begins the task of reconstructing the theory of value. Value is central to the commodity and asset sectors of the contemporary economy: nothing can be bought or sold, whether goods, services or assets, without a belief about what it is worth. Given the enormous influence of market economies in our social world, value thus plays a key role in determining events and outcomes in contemporary society. Yet the best-established theories of value are radically inadequate to the task of explaining the role that value plays. On the one hand, mainstream economics sees value as the equilibrium price produced by the forces of demand and supply, but most prices are not in equilibrium and this model ignores many of the most important forces that influence them. This is much more than just an explanatory problem, since the model of equilibrating markets is central to the legitimation of the current economic system: without it the economic emperor has no clothes. On the other hand, critiques of the contemporary economy have been heavily influenced by the notion of value as the amount of socially necessary labour embedded in a product, drawn from Marx, which is equally untenable. This version of value theory has dominated critical political economy, not only in its Marxist variants but also more subtly through its influence on concepts such as *value creation* and *value extraction*. We need a more coherent concept of value so that we can expose how value actually operates in our economy and the increasingly problematic ways in which it is being manipulated for profit.

In their place, this book develops a theory of value that returns to its historical roots and to our common-sense understandings: value is, deceptively simply, *what an item is worth*. The book draws on recent work in valuation studies and in the French tradition of the economics of conventions, but also goes beyond that work by reintroducing explicit consideration of the role of social structures in shaping value, thus also re-structuring contemporary work on value. Our sense of the value of a thing is personal, but also draws deeply on normative standards of value, and a coherent understanding of value must therefore examine those normative standards and how they are formed, transformed and supported. The book's empirical focus is on the value of financial assets, and on the ways in which that value is *constructed* – or indeed *invented* – by actors in the finance sector pursuing their own interests. The very existence of financial assets depends on them being perceived as having value, and that perception in turn depends on the existence of distinctive structures that I have called *asset circles* and *asset complexes*, theorised for the first time in this work.

This introductory chapter outlines the argument of the book and positions it both politically and intellectually.

Theories of Value

The first step we must take in this journey is to confront the contentious concept of *value* itself. Existing understandings of economic value are dominated by two traditions of economic thought. On the one hand, we find the mainstream marginalist tradition in economics, which tends to ignore explicit mentions of value, but in practice treats it as identical to the notion of equilibrium price – the price a commodity would have if demand and supply for it were in balance. In a sense, value is an objective quantity for the marginalists: at any one time, every commodity is seen as having a single price for all, determined by the larger forces of the market. On the other hand, we find Marxist understandings of value as the product of labour. For Marx, value is also an objective property of commodities, determined by the amount of social necessary labour time required to produce them, and it sits at the heart of his critique of capitalism, which is concerned with how the value produced by labour is appropriated by the ruling class. Chapter 2 rejects both of these understandings of value but also explores how the Marxist approach has seeped into and distorted other progressive attempts to get to grips with the problem of value. The concepts of *value creation* and *value extraction*, common in these discourses, rest on a Marxist-influenced productionist concept of value that is no more sustainable than the orthodox Marxist version. These discourses are at their strongest when they ignore the idea that value is created by production and instead frame decisions about the economy in terms of what we might call the *social value* of its products, recognising that value is not an objective but a normative quality. Indeed, despite their facades of objectivity, I suggest, both the Marxist and marginalist accounts have normative undercurrents and there is a good reason for this: value *is* fundamentally a normative concept.

Chapter 3 develops this insight by building on a more promising recent literature on value. In practice, as the French conventions theorists have pointed out, talk of value functions in the economy as a set of justifications for prices (Boltanski & Esquerre, 2016, p. 37). There is, therefore, a sense in which value is subjective – each of us forms our own opinion of the value of a thing. However, this is not a purely individualistic subjectivity: the opinions of value we form are shaped by social forces, mediated through what I call *lay theories of value*. A lay theory of value is an everyday argument about a factor that affects the price that ought to be paid for a certain type of thing. When we form an opinion of the value of a thing, we usually take account of several such theories. The theories themselves are fundamentally normative, in at least two respects. First, they are theories about the price at which something *ought* to be bought and sold. Second, they are socially shared theories. Not only do we learn about them from each other, but we also learn which theories are socially accepted and in what circumstances from our interactions with each other. We may deploy such theories in making decisions about transactions, but also sometimes in negotiating prices, and only those theories that others also accept can be deployed successfully in negotiations.

One part of the study of value, then, must be to examine how it is that some lay theories of value rather than others become established as norms. This is often strongly influenced by what we may call *value entrepreneurs*, or *inventors* of value, typically producers or suppliers of goods who do discursive work – often in the form of advertising and marketing – to persuade potential customers to adopt favourable valuation conventions and apply them to their products. Because value depends on what we think about it, value entrepreneurs can invent value if they can shape what we think, creating reasons – reasons that would not otherwise have influenced us – for us to value goods more highly. Most obviously, this strategy is widely adopted by the producers of so-called luxury goods. These lay theories of value have a significant influence on the prices that purchasers are willing to pay for goods, and also on the prices that sellers are prepared to accept, but prices are not entirely determined by our theories of value. Rather, these are one important group of causal factors amongst others, and Chapter 3 also discusses how we should think of the relationship between value and price in a context where other factors also influence price outcomes.

When we turn more specifically to value in the finance sector, in Chapter 4, we find that lay theories of the value of financial assets are closely linked to beliefs about future returns from those assets. For most investors, the significant benefit from buying a financial asset is that it entitles the holder to a stream of income, often in the form of payments such as interest or dividends and the price that is realised when the asset is subsequently resold. Conventional accounts of financial value suggest that we can forecast these payments, sometimes giving a range of probabilities to different possible outcomes, then calculate the present value of the stream of income. But all such forecasts are inherently uncertain, and so beliefs about the value of financial assets depend upon stories: fictions, as Jens Beckert calls them, that are made up about those future returns (Beckert, 2016).

At one level, those stories work in much the same way as our understandings of value more generally: they depend on persuading investors to accept certain lay theories of value (also known as valuation conventions) and to accept that a given asset should be valued on the basis of a particular theory or set of theories. During the internet stock boom of the very early twenty-first century, for example, value entrepreneurs argued that companies would be able to convert visitors to their websites into profit in the long term and therefore that the more visitors a company had to its site, the higher it should be valued, regardless of how much profit (or, usually, loss) it was making in the short term. Many investors were persuaded of this theory of value, and persuaded to apply it to the stocks of a series of so-called new economy companies, many of which subsequently collapsed under the weight of their losses (Thrift, 2001).

The chapter draws on the work of John Maynard Keynes and André Orléan on financial valuation conventions, Pierre Bourdieu's work on symbolic value and Jens Beckert's work on fictional expectations to build an explanation of how financial value is invented. The stories that are told about financial value are central to this explanation, but stories do not weave this magic in the abstract, as some accounts of the influence of discourse seem to imply. On the contrary, their influence depends on who tells them and on whom they are told to. Some groups or classes of financial actors have enormous discursive, social, political and/or economic power, giving them the capacity to construct more influential narratives: the power to sell promises, to become successful financial value entrepreneurs. The power of those promises is squared in the realm of financial assets, because not only their value but also the very existence of the assets themselves depends on what we think about them. Financial value entrepreneurs not only invent or manipulate the discourses about how we should value their assets but also invent the assets themselves, and the discourses that construct them as being assets at all. But those promises have to be sold *to* someone to have any effect. An audience must be persuaded by the story, and in particular a group of investors must be created that is willing to take the story and its connection to a particular asset seriously enough to consider buying the asset. In other words, these stories work in part by constructing what I call *asset circles* for the financial asset concerned. Only once a group has been created that takes the asset seriously as a potential investment does it become important on what basis – on the basis of what lay theories – those potential investors are prepared to value the asset.

Chapter 5 develops the concept of asset circles and outlines the structural elements of the book's approach to value in general and financial value in particular. As a type of norm, lay theories of value are backed by structures that I call *norm circles* (Elder-Vass, 2010b). Assets, however, are more complex. Unlike ordinary goods and services, but like money, financial assets cannot *exist* without a belief that they can be redeemed or sold on at some point in the future, and so they depend on a further layer of social construction. The chapter develops the argument through the parallels between financial assets and money. Both depend for their very existence on social structures. In the case of money I call these *monetary complexes*, which include both a monetary infrastructure and also a *monetary circle*: a group of social actors that are willing to accept the particular monetary instrument concerned in payment. Without a monetary circle, money is worthless, indeed it is not even money. Similarly, I argue that the existence of financial assets depends on structures that I call *asset complexes*, which in turn consist of a combination of an asset circle – a group of investors open to buying the asset – and an asset infrastructure – the technology and institutions that record the existence of the asset and make it tradable. Both norm circles and asset complexes are themselves subject to influence from structures such as banks and other finance sector organisations, and the discursive structures through which those organisations exert some of their influences.

Financial Value in Practice

The second, more empirically oriented, part of this book is about these processes of influence. It discusses how asset circles are constructed and how their members are persuaded to apply particular lay theories of value to the assets they are interested in. Having introduced these concepts in the first four substantive chapters, the next three use material from publicly available sources to apply the argument to three different classes of financial assets. All three are cases where value remains in doubt, either because the assets are relatively new or because their valuation has been in crisis. First, I discuss venture capital, which constructs high valuations for companies with highly uncertain futures in order to launch them onto the stock exchange; second, the cryptocurrency Bitcoin, where the entire valuation system still remains in doubt, and may yet collapse; and third, mortgage-backed securities and related derivatives – the precarious assets, invented and then constructed as safe by leading investment banks, that brought about the 2008 crisis.

My cases are all drawn from the riskier end of the spectrum of financial assets. In a sense the advocates of each of these groups of assets are seeking to borrow the discourses and theories of value that underpin the valuation of financial assets at the safer end of the spectrum – assets such as shares in well-established companies with steady divided flows, state-issued money and government bonds – and apply them to quite different types of asset. The very uncertainty of these cases makes the work that is done to persuade potential investors more apparent.

In Chapter 6, I begin with the case of venture capital, which in some ways is the simplest case because venture capitalists are not trying to introduce a whole new class of assets; rather, they are trying to invent value for new examples of a familiar asset class. Venture capitalists buy stakes in private companies and seek to develop them into larger companies that can be sold on, often by floating them onto the public stock exchange, ideally as unicorns – private companies valued at over a billion dollars – so that they can sell their stake at a large profit. In doing so they aim to create a new financial asset – public shares in the company they have invested in – but in a context where shares in companies more generally are a familiar asset within a well-established institutional and discursive context.

While venture capitalists seek to develop the revenues of the businesses they buy, arguably their largest contribution is to build an asset circle for the company's stock and to spin a set of narratives about its value. The chapter traces this process through its typical stages, beginning with the business plans that form the basis for an initial investment by the venture capitalists – works of fiction that create a narrative about the business's revenue prospects. Ultimately, however, venture capitalists have little interest in the revenues of the companies they back, except as a means to a very different end: the possibility of selling its shares at a profit. They thus gradually construct an asset circle, beginning with other venture capitalists who are persuaded to join in subsequent funding rounds, and then on to other major institutional investors when it is time to launch the stock on the public exchanges. At each stage narratives are constructed that connect the business being promoted to existing theories of corporate value and existing schemes of categories. At each stage every possible effort is also made to associate the business with existing institutions possessing the symbolic capital required to consecrate its value in the eyes of potential investors. Finally, in some of the most successful cases for venture capitalists, the initial public offering (IPO) of shares provides a test of both the size of the asset circle that has been established and the success in establishing narratives that justify a value for it – and, if successful, positions the venture capitalists for their payday. Venture capitalism is thus a complex of practices and organisations that builds businesses but also constructs their valuations, drawing on but also developing the wider culture of valuation that prevails in the finance sector.

Unlike venture capitalists, the advocates of Bitcoin have invented a whole new class of assets from scratch, and done so outside the framework of established financial institutions. Bitcoin is an electronic currency, based on a blockchain: a cryptographically secured distributed database of previous transactions. Chapter 7 investigates how this new type of asset has come to be regarded as having value. What kinds of discourse have been deployed? What valuation conventions have been invoked or developed? Which audiences have these discourses been addressed to? What forums have been used to address these audiences? How have they been persuaded to join the asset circle for Bitcoin? These discourses have functioned largely outside the mainstream financial system and yet they have succeeded in constructing a purely virtual asset as valuable. This provides an illuminating comparison with the more mainstream cases. It shows the processes of narrative construction very clearly, in a context where existing financial power was largely absent, demonstrating both the potential and the limitations of such situations.

Bitcoin began life not as a financial asset but as a form of money. Its early advocates were not trying to create an asset circle but a monetary circle for Bitcoin: a group of social actors willing to accept Bitcoin in payment. Their early narratives were thus strongly oriented to the strengths of Bitcoin as a means of payment, but these narratives have encountered significant resistance. Although they remain in circulation, and continue to provide motivation for some Bitcoin buyers, there is a sense today in which they are merely the ideology of Bitcoin, while most owners of Bitcoin now hold it as an investment, a financial asset. More recent narratives of Bitcoin's value have become increasingly oriented to its potential as an investment, and gradually the original *monetary* circle has been supplemented and arguably largely supplanted by an *asset* circle: actors who regard it as a potentially valuable investment.

Because Bitcoin does not generate a revenue stream, other than the possibility of selling it on in the future, it is in some respects a particularly pure form of financial asset: one whose value depends entirely on the belief that it could be sold on in the future at a profitable price. Its valuation conventions are therefore also separated entirely from beliefs about such revenue streams and instead depend very much on beliefs about future price changes – an example of what Keynes referred to as the "beauty contest" model of financial markets (Keynes, 1973, pp. 154–155). In this model, potential buyers and sellers of an asset value it on the basis of what they think other buyers will be willing to pay for it in the future. In such contexts, asset prices are notoriously volatile. At the same time, however, there remain "hodlers" of Bitcoin who continue to hold it for more ideological reasons, providing a relatively stable minimum membership of its asset circle and thus insulating it from total collapses in value.

The contrast between Bitcoin and the topic of the third case study could hardly be greater. Chapter 8 deals with the rise and fall of structured securities built from subprime mortgages in the early twenty-first century. These were relatively new products, which "sliced and diced" low quality mortgage debt to create new securities that were often given AAA risk ratings and purchased in large numbers by major financial institutions. While the early backers of Bitcoins were complete outsiders, the inventors of these new securities were some of the most powerful actors in the global financial system: the US investment banks. While the dominant discourses have tended to dismiss Bitcoin as a dangerous unstable invention of cranks, until 2008 they presented mortgage-backed securities as one of the great innovations of modern finance. Yet they turned out to be equally unstable and in 2008 their value collapsed, threatening to bring the world financial system down with them.

While the narratives of Bitcoin's value were built on its innovative nature as a new kind of asset, the most important narratives of the value of these new kinds of securities positioned them as just another variation of an already familiar form of financial assets: fixed-income securities such as government and corporate bonds. Considerable care and indeed power were devoted to having them rated by the same credit agencies that rated those bonds and therefore to having them positioned in the market as equivalent to those bonds. A security backed by subprime mortgage repayments could therefore receive the same AAA rating as the safest bonds, which made them investible by the most conservative mutual funds and investment managers. Rather than constructing a new asset circle for these new kinds of asset, the investment banks constructed a narrative that inserted them into a class of assets that was already backed by an asset circle with a huge amount of investment funds at its disposal.

The success of this insertion in turn depended on the enormous multifaceted structural power of the investment banks. Their political power had enabled them to push back regulation of financial innovation since the 1980s, making it possible for them to sell risky new products with little or no regulatory intervention, and indeed they continued to employ that power to protect these assets from regulation until the crisis unfolded. Their discursive power – their symbolic capital, in Bourdieu's terms – meant that potential investors were willing to trust their narratives of safety and equivalence for these new products. And their economic power enabled them to manipulate the ratings system to secure the high ratings from the credit agencies that were required to make these securities acceptable to major institutional investors. Their power to construct value for these securities made them enormous profits, but also had a devastating impact on the global economic system when the narrative could no longer be sustained.

On the one hand, these case studies begin to illustrate the sheer diversity of the financial assets that can be constructed as valuable and of the actors inventing their value. On the other hand, they reveal the similarities between the structures of value in all of these different cases. In every case the process depends on the construction of narratives of value that encourage potential buyers to see the financial instrument concerned as an investible asset, shape how they categorise the instrument and thus influence the valuation conventions or lay theories of value they are willing to apply to them. None of this is natural or inevitable, and the assets the process constructs are utterly dependent on the complex of institutions and discourses that sustain these narratives. When the narratives are cast into doubt, so are the assets upon which our entire contemporary financial system is based.

Financial Value versus Social Value?

The explosion of financial assets over the last few decades has transformed the world's leading economies. The finance, insurance and real estate sectors now account for 21 per cent of US national income – double its level in 1947 (Howells & Morgan, 2020, p. 11; Witko, 2016). The financial services sector alone constitutes 8 per cent of the formal economy of the United States and 7 per cent in the United Kingdom (Rhodes, 2019, p. 8). Beyond its sheer scale, it plays a pivotal role in the wider economy, with substantial power over the flow of funds to other sectors, and in politics, where it is often able to influence policy in its interests, not only through lobbying but also through the regular exchange of personnel between the sector and the top echelons of government. One measure of that influence was the progressive loosening of financial regulations, allowing rampant financial innovation with little regard for the risks it created until in 2008 it generated the greatest crash in living memory.

One of the central mysteries of contemporary society is how the financial sector has managed to accumulate so much wealth and power. The heart of the answer is its capacity to create financial assets – stocks, bonds, options, derivatives and the like – which investors are prepared to buy. These assets have been naturalised: they have come to be seen as unproblematic objects with value in their own right and thus as just one more commodity that it is perfectly reasonable to buy and sell for profit. Yet in reality they are nothing more than promises, typically promises to deliver a revenue stream if certain conditions are satisfied, and highly tenuous promises at that. The value of these assets, to put it differently, is socially constructed: it depends on the beliefs of investors about their value, which depend in turn on the stories that are told in order to encourage those beliefs.

The naturalisation of financial assets thus obscures an extraordinary set of structures that lie behind the acceptance of such promises by investors. Once we look behind the veil of naturalisation, we can see both the layer upon layer of promises but also the possibility at each layer of things going wrong. These are mountains of promises, where a slippage of any one stratum could bring the whole edifice crashing down, as we saw in 2008. Perhaps what is most extraordinary of all is that a massive portion of our economy has been built on top of this mountain of promises, and that the institutions that construct the mountain extract enormous revenues from their power to sell them, while those revenues are also naturalised, as profits from supposedly productive activity. Yet it is far from clear what the social benefits of the process are, if there are any, and if so whether they justify the enormous risks created for the rest of our economic system.

This book aims to peel back some of these layers, to reveal how these promises are created and sold and how this process produces the apparent value of financial assets. We cannot rely on conventional economics to explain this. Its models of supply and demand take the naturalisation of financial assets for granted and as a consequence they obscure rather than illuminate the fundamental drivers of the prices of financial assets. To put the point as simply as possible: financial assets have value only because they are believed to have value, and mainstream economics hardly scrapes the surface of how such beliefs are established.

This book develops and applies an alternative, sociologically influenced account of how those beliefs are constructed. It argues that the value of assets such as money, shares and derivatives is socially constructed: it is experienced as an individual belief but it depends on collective normative structures that shape those beliefs. The demand for financial instruments is thus created by narratives that generate expectations of future value, by institutions that bolster these expectations, and by persuading other financial actors to accept them as facts. While such values are often stabilised, they are potentially highly precarious, generating massive risk for our economic system.

We must also ask whether these are the kinds of values that ought to be governing our economic and thus our social lives. As Mariana Mazzucato and indeed many other critics of mainstream economics have argued, there are different kinds of values and monetary value is often not a good measure of the *social* value of the different options facing us as a society (Mazzucato, 2018). Unlike many material goods and personal services, financial assets do not meet directly material human needs. No doubt they sometimes help investors to meet such needs in the future, notably through providing opportunities to invest savings, funding pensions and underpinning the provision of insurance, but there are other ways of meeting our genuine needs that may avoid the risks and the savage inequality that result from relying on investment markets. The issues are complex, but we are entitled to ask whether the buying and selling of financial instruments creates social value at all, or ultimately generates greater social costs than any benefits it may deliver.

It is difficult to obtain a balanced answer to questions like these because of the enormous power of the finance sector to repress such discourses in the public sphere. The playing field is sloped vertiginously against critics of the financial institutions, for a host of reasons. One is the revolving door between senior political positions and lucrative positions in the finance sector that places financiers in positions of governmental authority and creates a sense of common interest between politicians and finance (notably the many former Goldman Sachs bankers in recent US administrations: Dealbook, 2017). Another is the ways in which the discourse of mainstream economics portrays the success of the banks and other financial institutions as a reasonable reward for responding to a set of markets that simply and neutrally express the needs of the wider economy and society. This discourse implies that the prices of the financial assets on which their power depends are an objective reflection of the social value of their contribution and serves to legitimate financial markets and financial profits. This argument in turn has led to the modification of national accounting principles to treat the profits of the finance sector as part of the national income (Assa, 2018). Combined with the obsession of the political media with so-called economic growth, this means that politicians who are measured in part by their ability to deliver growth in national income have an incentive to support growing profits in the finance sector. The consequence is that the sector ends up being treated by politicians as untouchable and by mainstream economists as a triumph of the market model (until it collapses, and even then the qualifications are temporary).

And yet, if the prices of financial assets are a product, not of meeting a genuine social need, but at least partly of processes through which finance sector actors use their market power, their discursive power and their political power to invent and shape the value of financial assets, then the whole basis of the glorification and safeguarding of the sector must be called into question. If the values of financial assets are a means for finance sector actors to profit at the expense of wider society rather than a means for them to provide for the needs of wider society, we must ask whether this is what is best for us collectively and be prepared to rethink the place of finance in our society. The better we can understand how these processes work, the better placed we are to determine what sort of political response is appropriate. This book is a step towards understanding those processes better.

Taking a Realist Perspective

The argument builds on work from a range of disciplines, most notably economic sociology, heterodox economics and political economy, and in particular on excellent recent work in the study of finance and valuation. In recent years academics have engaged with the micro-sociological basis of financial markets, the performativity of economic theory, financialisation, asssetisation and indeed the global financial crisis, all of which are relevant to this project. Nevertheless, work on financial valuation has been seen as one of the most pressing absences in contemporary economic sociology (Carruthers & Kim, 2011, p. 253). Although work on financial valuation has started to flourish since Carruthers and Kim's survey, it has typically been limited by its orientation to micro level action and interaction and relative neglect of social structural forces. That focus is often a result of the pragmatist perspective of its authors: a perspective that has been seen as shaping the field (Barman, 2015, p. 12). On the other hand, work in the political economy of finance has tended to focus on macroeconomic questions without connecting them to microsociological understandings of the human actions that contribute to them.

Some of this work is also limited by its disciplinary orientations. I reject the division of labour, often attributed to Talcott Parsons, in which sociology deals with "the social" and economics with "the economic" as if these were two different realms of reality. They are not. The economy is not merely embedded in the social, as some economic sociologists have argued: it is inherently social itself. Economic events are social events. More recent economic sociology has pushed the boundaries of the economic questions to which sociological methods can be applied but it still seems to fall short of offering alternative approaches to issues such as the causal explanation of price determination that are considered core to economics. While sociologists are increasingly offering partial explanations of price determination, they generally avoid offering comprehensive explanations that take account of both the kinds of causal factors discussed by economists and those introduced by sociologists. Too many of them continue to concede economic matters to the economists. By contrast, I take the view that economic events should be explained in just the same way as other social events and therefore that sociologically inflected approaches must be taken to even the core questions of economics. That does not mean that I am pursuing a sociological imperialism, in which economics is to be taken over by sociology; on the contrary, it means that I regard disciplinary boundaries in the social sciences as obstacles to proper explanation. Rather than expanding one discipline at the expense of another, we need to break down the boundaries between them. That perspective is also reflected in what is perhaps an unconventional approach to sociology itself, seeing it as concerned with providing causal explanations, and not just interpretations, of social events.

These perspectives arise in part from my broader philosophical commitment to a critical realist approach to the social sciences. For critical realists, all events are understood as multiply-determined by the interacting causal powers of many different entities at varying levels of structure. More specifically, both individual action and social structures are seen as causally significant for social events and outcomes, and this book's argument goes beyond the existing literature primarily through its attention to the structures involved in valuation in general and financial valuation in particular. There is already work in the field that sees familiar structures such as financial institutions and indeed their discursive influence as causally significant. I go further, though, by also seeking to analyse the distinctive structures that are involved in the very nature of value and financial value, and how they are in turn influenced by those more familiar structures. The relevant aspects of critical realist theory are introduced where they are essential to understanding the substantive argument, notably a discussion of causality in open systems in Chapter 3 that leads in to an explanation of the influence of value on the determination of prices, and an explanation of the realist approach to structures, mechanisms and emergent causal powers in Chapter 5, where the deeper structures behind financial valuation are examined.

Some readers may be surprised to find a book that claims value is socially constructed also invoking a realist philosophy of causation, as realism and constructionism have often been seen as conflicting with each other. However, as I and several other critical realists have argued at length, realism and a moderate version of constructionism are not merely compatible but complementary (Elder-Vass, 2012; Sayer, 2000, pp. 81–102; C. Smith, 2010, pp. 119–206). For realists, social construction is a real causal process, driven in part by specific intentional actors, under the influence of a range of social structures, mediated through the production of discursive structures and producing causal consequences for potentially identifiable affected audiences. Once we recognise that social construction is thoroughly compatible with a realist social ontology, we need to explain the mechanisms behind social construction and the role played by both active agency and social power in those mechanisms. These questions are obscured by vaguer and sometimes superficially more radical constructionisms that ascribe construction simply to discourse or language in general rather than to active agents along with their interests and the power at their disposal (Elder-Vass, 2012, pp. 3–14). Social construction operates *through* language and discourse, but language and discourse are not its driving forces (Elder-Vass, 2011).

This causal approach is anathema to more extreme versions of constructionism. There are several parts to it. First, we must pay attention to the processes in which constructions are developed but also to the actors who often play active causal roles in them. Second, we must attend to the interrelationship between these discourses and the wider institutional context. And third, these discourses do not function by hanging vaguely in the air and generally affecting the symbolic atmosphere, but rather by having specific effects on specific audiences. For example, a credit rating is a symbolic category assigned to an asset – it is a social construction, in that it depends on how we think about it, and there is a set of discourses that tend to stabilise belief in these ratings as reliable guides to investment quality. Nevertheless, the actual assignation is done by a specific actor, the rating agency, and as we will see in Chapter 8 it is subject to manipulation and influence, for example, from the bank commissioning the rating. Finally, it has its effect by persuading a specific audience, in this case institutional investors who use credit ratings as inputs to their investment decisions. This attention to audiences is perhaps the most distinctive element of the book's argument, and applying it to the case of financial assets leads to the concept of asset circles, which is its most distinctive conceptual contribution. Beyond this ontological and explanatory innovation, the crucial benefit of a realist constructionism is that it allows us to see, from the realist perspective, that the construction of financial value is to a large extent a product of power, exercised by social actors who shape what is constructed in their own interests, and from the constructionist perspective, that it could be constructed differently.

One implication of the critical realist approach is that we need to approach the task of explaining social phenomena by combining two complementary methods: retroduction and retrodiction. Retroduction means picking out one key causal mechanism and examining how it operates across a range of circumstances. Retrodiction, on the other hand, is oriented to giving a fuller explanation of a narrower set of events by identifying the significant causal mechanisms involved in their causation and examining how they interact to produce the event(s) concerned (Elder-Vass, 2010b, pp. 48, 72–73; Lawson, 1997, pp. 24, 221). Among other things, the early chapters of the book retroduce specific mechanisms and structures of general relevance to the explanation of value and financial value. To identify a mechanism, we generally need to look across multiple cases and recognise something that they have in common, understanding the complexity of each case while also looking for elements of repeatability (Rutzou & Elder-Vass, 2019). Likewise, to test a retroductive explanation we need to transplant it to other potentially parallel cases and examine whether something adequately similar can be seen there. Each explanation of a particular mechanism or structure then becomes a building block that can be combined, tentatively, with others to build retrodictive explanations of actual events. The later chapters illustrate the operation of the mechanisms identified in the early chapters, in interaction with others, by giving retrodictive accounts of the cases concerned: by looking at how a range of different powers and mechanisms interact in them.

This book, then, applies the realist methods of retroduction and retrodiction to develop constructionist explanations of value and financial value that recognise the active roles played by interested actors including powerful social institutions. It introduces novel concepts that help us to understand the structural forces at work in the realm of value and thus reconstructs the theory of value in a form that helps us to understand that the value of financial assets, far from being the natural and desirable outcome of neutral market processes, is actively manipulated by powerful financial institutions in pursuit of ever-expanding profit and power.

2 | How (Not) to Think about Value

The concept of value is deeply embedded in debates about the economy, yet it is also deeply problematic. There are many different ways of understanding *value*, including many that are not directly concerned with economic questions, and we must begin by establishing some clarity over which versions we are engaging with. This chapter will argue, however, that even the best-established *economic* understandings of value are radically unsatisfactory. It is therefore essential, before outlining a more coherent understanding of value, to clear some ground by explaining what is wrong with the established approaches. This chapter criticises three in turn: the theory of value implicit in the marginalist tradition in economics, Marx's labour theory of value and the notion of value at work in more popular discourses of *value creation* and *value extraction* such as the recent work of Mariana Mazzucato. This discussion, however, is not intended as a comprehensive critique of these traditions, but rather as a means to mark out the space that the argument of this book aims to occupy.

Some versions of the concept of value, such as aesthetic value in culture and numeric value in mathematics, are largely outside the scope of this book, as are moral *values* as such, although I will argue that conceptions of economic value are often deeply normative. Even in economic discourse, however, there are multiple versions of the concept in circulation. The marginalist tradition thinks of value as an idealised version of market price, as what I will call *equilibrium value*: the price that a good would have if demand and supply for every good in the market was simultaneously balanced out to produce an optimum price for them all. The Marxist tradition thinks of value as *labour value*: the amount of labour time required to produce a good. The value creation/extraction trend reaches towards a more important notion of value that I will call *social value*, but the pervasive influence of Marxist thinking on the left has led to this being conflated with something like labour value, leading to confused arguments about the role of value.

One part of my argument is that some of these versions have damaged our collective capacity to think about how the economy should operate; another is that the Marxist and marginalist versions have encouraged unreasonable expectations about the role that a theory of value can play in our understanding of the economy. We must therefore consider not only the content of different concepts or theories of value but also the purposes that they have been employed for. In many cases these purposes have been misconceived. A coherent theory of value can do important things for us, but it cannot provide a universal theory of how the economy does or should operate, and yet both the marginalists and Marx have positioned their understandings of value as providing such theories. The more recent work on value creation and extraction does not overreach quite as far because it focuses on ethical questions about how the economy should operate rather than explanatory questions about how the economy actually does operate. Yet it still assumes that the same concept of value can be used to address both explanatory questions and two fundamental political questions about how we should operate our economy: what should be produced? and how should the benefits arising from production be distributed? These are important questions, but reducing them to questions of value when the concepts of value being used are as inadequate as those criticised in this chapter makes it harder, not easier, to resolve them.

Marginalism and Value

The basic framework of mainstream economics can be traced back to the late nineteenth century marginalist or neoclassical revolution in economics led by Walras, Jevons and Menger (Elder-Vass, 2016, p. 72; Mirowski, 1991, p. 193). This system of thought was in part a reaction against classical theories of value and makes little overt use of the term *value*. As Mirowski points out, one key book in the tradition is called *The Theory of Value* (Debreu, 1959), and yet Debreu and subsequent marginalists tend to see value theory as nothing more than "a synonym for price theory" (Mirowski, 1991, p. 141) and value as nothing more than a synonym for price (e.g. Varian, 2010, p. 27).

According to marginalist theory, price is determined by the balancing of demand and supply in a market. Let me summarise the theory briefly and crudely (for a little more detail see Elder-Vass, 2016, pp. 74–77; or for much more, a textbook such as Varian, 2010). Demand depends on assessments by potential purchasers of the *utility* of an item. Utility is roughly synonymous with how useful an item would be to the purchaser or how much benefit they believe they would obtain from owning it. The idea is that each potential purchaser takes a view on how much they would be willing to pay for the item, given its utility. On the other side, potential suppliers are motivated by the possibility of making profits, and so they are willing to supply at any price that exceeds their (marginal) relevant costs of production (which may vary depending on the quantity that they produce). In this theory, price is a variable that adjusts dynamically to balance the quantity of the item that is produced and sold. According to the theory, it should settle at a level where all buyers who are happy to buy at that price are able to do so while all suppliers who are happy to sell at that price are able to do so. If the price was a little higher, suppliers would want to sell more but there would be less purchasers willing to pay the price, hence some goods would remain unsold so suppliers would drop the price. If it was a little lower, there would be more willing purchasers but less suppliers willing to sell at that price and some buyers would be unable to obtain the product so suppliers would raise the price. Marginalists argue that the price will adjust to eliminate such imbalances until it reaches an equilibrium level and in practice they see the equilibrium price of a good as its value. Although they rarely put it in these terms, we may say that they have a theory of value as the *equilibrium value* of a good.

This is an objectivist theory of price or value in the sense that it sees value, understood as equilibrium price, as one quantity that is the same for all market participants for any given product. Granted, that quantity may vary dynamically over time, but at any one time it is taken to be set at one and the same level for all participants by market forces rather than being particular to an individual, and the marginalist theory is taken to be a scientific theory of the processes by which it is set.

It is more common to see the marginalist theory described in the literature as *subjectivist*, for two reasons. The first is relational: by comparison with the labour theory of value it lacks the supposedly objective referent of labour value for its theory of price. The second is the role played in it by the concept of utility. In a sense the utility of a thing for a person is its value to them, and although utility is not expressed in monetary terms or indeed given a unit of measure at all, it is conceived of as a subjective ordering. For any given individual, different choices have lesser or greater utility than each other, and at some point utility is translated into a willingness to pay a specific amount for an item. So utility is not the same thing as value, but it is tempting to see a theory of subjective value here: as if the monetary value of a thing to a person was determined by its utility to them. The theory then might seem similar to that advanced in this book, not least because it implies that different people may put different subjective values on the same thing and these plural valuations then interact in the process of price determination. Although there are parallels, there are also important differences. Earlier I suggested that utility is "roughly synonymous with how useful an item would be" but this was rather too specific – utility in the marginalist model (like value in mine) is influenced by *any* factor that affects the attractiveness of the item to the potential purchaser. But rather than proceed to consider what these factors might be and how they are influenced, the more sophisticated marginalists have emptied the concept of any substantive content at all and see it "only as a *way to describe preferences*" (Varian, 2010, p. 54). What this means is that utility is not actually a quantity or a mechanism in its own right that influences valuation, but simply a reflection of how much someone is willing to pay for something. If someone is willing to pay more for A than for B, then that means that A has more utility for them than B, and utility has no other empirical content than this. The consequence is that the concept of utility does not provide us with a subjective theory of value after all – utility, for the neoclassical tradition, is just an empty conceptual structure that is used to support the argument that different people are willing to pay different amounts for the same thing. To be strictly fair, the marginalists do not generally claim that it does provide a theory of value, but they are often read as if the concept of utility means that they have a theory of what lies behind demand. They do not: utility does not provide a theory of subjective value but rather a placeholder for its absence.

Although it is presented, even today, as a theory of price, the marginalist theory is really a theory of price as an ideal rather than as an empirical phenomenon. As Orléan puts it, "In Walras, equilibrium price ... functions as a norm" (Orléan, 2014, p. 47). One part of what Orléan means here is that in many commodity exchanges it is implausible to see the actual price that is paid for an item as an equilibrium price for a market as a whole. Even at one and the same time, for example, we will often find different people in a similar context paying different prices for equivalent items. According to neoclassical theory, such differences should be eliminated by arbitrage – the practice of people exploiting price differences by buying where prices are low and selling where prices are high until the price difference is eliminated, but in practice there are often systematic forces maintaining price differentials for the same product (Elder-Vass, 2016, p. 77; Kirman & Vriend, 2000). I have personally observed, for example, identical pieces of furniture on sale at radically different prices at stores oriented to different demographics within a few miles of each other – where the more expensive store is able to rely on a lack of information about competing prices that arises in part from the social stratification between their customers and those of the cheaper store. In Kirman and Vriend's study of a wholesale fish market in Marseilles, price dispersion for equivalent products was sustained over the long term as a result of loyalties between buyers and sellers (Kirman & Vriend, 2000). If there was really such a thing as an equilibrium price for these items in these periods, it was not the same thing as the actual prices being advertised or paid, but some sort of regulative concept: a notional price at which marginalist theory says goods ought to be exchanged. While Marx, as we shall see, had a theory of *value* as a non-empirical phenomenon distinct from actual prices, the marginalists, ironically, have a theory of *price* as a non-empirical phenomenon that is also distinct from actual prices! No doubt many mainstream economists have moved beyond the cruder versions of marginalism, but the mainstream remains flawed whenever it continues to pursue formalisations that rest on the assumption that price equilibrium is achieved.

If the neoclassical model is so weak as a theory of price, we might wonder why it has been so successful in securing the adherence of academic economists for so long. No doubt there are a number of reasons, but one is that the marginalist theory of price, despite the claims for its scientific status, actually functions more as a normative theory of value after all. Equilibrium price, in most markets, is not the

actual price at which goods exchange but the price at which marginalist theory says goods *ought* to exchange. The subtext remains
strongly ethical. Equilibrium prices, according to the theory, balance
the interests of producers and consumers, providing what is seen as a
kind of fairness between classes, and also a kind of fairness between
different consumers. By ignoring any other considerations of justice
and the fact that actual prices rarely match theoretical equilibria, this is
taken to imply that the market delivers a fair price, a just price, an
ethically proper price, and not just an ethically neutral causal outcome.

One reason for the continuing popularity of this theory of value is
thus that it legitimates capitalism, or at least a commodity system, as
an economic system. It shifts responsibility for its many negative
outcomes to a vast impersonal mechanism that is positioned as generating the best possible outcome overall, thus excusing those cases
where it produces more harmful outcomes as merely side effects of
optimising the system as a whole. Both decisions about what is produced in the economy and how incomes are distributed are seen as
being optimised by the working of the market. In effect, the marginalist
model implies that the equilibrium value of a good is equal to its *social
value* (a concept I return to below).

That legitimation falls apart once we recognise that price determination in practice does not fit the theory. Not only do prices rarely
match theoretical equilibrium values, but there is a whole host of other
flaws in the model. First, not all things with social value are produced
for exchange, or exchanged. This was a key focus of my previous book,
which stressed the continuing importance of the gift economy in its
many guises, and services provided by the state also escape the model
(Elder-Vass, 2016). But this is also the point of classic arguments about
public goods such as clean air, education that increases the long-term
productivity of students, and public health services that protect everyone by being freely accessible to the poor who would otherwise carry
diseases that infected others of all social classes. These goods have a
social value that is not reflected in their prices and so commodity
systems tend to fail to produce as much of them as is socially desirable.
Second, not all things produced for exchange do have social value, or
at least whether they have it is legitimately contentious – do guns and
bombs have social value, for example? Third, the creation of negative
social value is often not captured by the market – externalities such as
pollution, for example, are not priced unless government regulation

imposes a cost for creating them. Fourth, because only demand that is backed up by the ability to pay affects market prices, the model has a built-in assumption that it is fair to allocate goods in a way that is determined by the existing distribution of wealth and income – the things that rich people want get produced because they can afford to pay for them, but not the things that poor people need.

The marginalists, however, tend to ignore these inconvenient truths, and argue that even if the world does not deliver *exactly* what the model promises, it is close enough for the model to stand as an ethical justification for the market system – and thus for equilibrium prices to be fair values in exchange (for a comprehensive debunking of marginalist claims, see Keen, 2011). Indeed, some are even prepared to argue that the real world must be brought closer to the model in order to achieve the ideal output it predicts, through, for example, neoliberal privatisation and marketisation projects. Even problems that other theorists have seen as market failures, according to neoliberals, are best solved by extending rather than regulating markets, as seen most strikingly in the "unfolding disaster of carbon trading", in which climate change is (not) addressed by allowing firms to trade the right to pollute in markets (Lohmann, 2010, p. 91).

In the end, the marginalist tradition shares some fundamental characteristics with the Marxist tradition to which it is so strongly opposed. It presents itself as a scientific theory, but the phenomenon it purports to explain – in this case equilibrium price – is not an empirical phenomenon at all. It neglects a vast range of causal factors that influence real prices. It purports to be value-neutral, but draws on covert normative resources to support highly political conclusions. And ultimately it rests on an unsustainable notion of value as an objective quality.

Marx and Value

Although I will argue that it shares these features with the marginalist tradition, in many other respects Marx's labour theory of value is radically different. Marx's theory is the most developed version of the classical tradition of value theory against which the early marginalists defined themselves. Although it is much less influential in economics faculties and policy-making circles than mainstream economics, it remains important because variations on the Marxist perspective continue to attract and, I will argue, confuse critics of the economic and financial systems, including both committed Marxists and others who have been influenced more loosely by Marxist ideas (discussed in the section "Value Creation and Value Extraction?"). This section (which draws on my earlier book: Elder-Vass, 2016, pp. 61–69) will briefly explain Marx's labour theory and then discuss why it is problematic, focusing on those issues that are most relevant to the larger argument of the book. While there are contemporary debates over the proper interpretation of the theory amongst Marxists who continue to search for ways to make it work, these tend to be rather obscure and technical, so I will only touch on them briefly.

For Marx, as for earlier political economists, the theory of value sought to reveal the "inner structure or order" behind economic phenomena (Heilbroner, 1988, p. 105). He presented his work as a scientific account of the laws of motion of capitalist society, with his labour theory of value as the centrepiece. The definitive statement of his theory of value can be found in the first chapter of the first volume of *Capital* (Marx, 1954). He begins with the commodity: an item produced for sale on the market. Every commodity, he argues, has two essential factors, which he calls its use value and its exchange value (although he usually just calls exchange value "value"). The use value of a commodity is simply the usefulness it has for us as a result of the ways in which its physical properties enable it to be used. While the use value of different commodities of the same type can be compared quantitatively, such as the length of two different pieces of linen, the use values of different kinds of commodity are qualitatively different and thus quantitatively incommensurable. Yet commodities of different kinds can be exchanged for each other, and in doing so a value equation is made between them – x litres of corn is treated as equivalent to y kilos of iron, for example. Therefore, Marx argues, "the exchange values of commodities must be capable of being expressed in terms of something common to them all, of which thing they represent a greater or less quantity" (Marx, 1954, p. 45). Ignoring other plausible candidates such as money, he argues that the only property that all commodities have in common is "being products of labour" (Marx, 1954, p. 45) (see Cutler, Hindess, Hussain & Hirst, 1977, p. 58). The magnitude of value of a commodity, he concludes, is "the quantity of the value-creating substance, the labour, contained in the article", measured by its duration (Marx, 1954, p. 46). Marx recognises that different commodities are, however, products of different kinds of labour, and in order to make them quantitatively comparable we must abstract from this difference, and compare them in terms of the amount of "human labour in the abstract" contained in them (Marx, 1954, p. 46).

Marx inherited the broad outlines of the labour theory of value from the English economist David Ricardo (McLellan, 1980, pp. 39, 89). One of his major innovations, however, was to apply the same theory to the value of labour power (McLellan, 1980, pp. 90–91). He argued that, just as the value of a commodity was determined by the amount of labour required to produce it, the value of labour power was determined by the amount of labour required to reproduce it: in other words, by the labour power required to produce the commodities needed to sustain the worker in the long term (including the cost of raising new workers, which was borne by the worker's family) (Marx, 1954, pp. 167–168, 188). That cost in turn was contingent on social standards, and could be measured by the normal wage paid to a worker (Marx, 1954, p. 168). This in turn gave Marx a way to explain the profits made by the capitalist who employed the worker to produce the commodities: as long as the worker was made to work longer than was required to pay her wages, then the value of goods produced by the worker was greater than the value of her labour power, and *surplus value* was created in the process of production – the total value was expanded, and the capitalist (typically) appropriated this surplus value as profit. This gave Marx an account not only of how the rewards of the productive worker were determined but also those of the capitalist entrepreneur, and both accounts were based on the same theory of value that explained the ratios at which different commodities were exchanged. Hence the theory of value could provide the basis for a larger theory of the operation of the capitalist system as a whole, including, most notably, Marx's theory of the falling rate of profit.

For the purposes of this book, the first major problem with this argument concerns the relation between Marx's concept of value and the concept of price. Marx insists that value is distinct from price (e.g. Marx, 1954, p. 104), but if value is not the same thing as price, we are entitled to ask what exactly value *is*. Marx gives us a theory of what *determines* the exchange value of an object – the amount of socially necessary abstract labour required to produce it – but without an indication of how value might appear as an empirical phenomenon in its own right, exchange value has no other *meaning* in this system than the amount of labour required to produce the commodity. To say that this is *determined* by the amount of labour required is merely circular.

Marx did attempt to find a way to reconcile the theory of value with a theory of price, in his work in volume 3 of *Capital* on what has come to be known as the transformation problem (Marx, 1959, Chapter VIII–X), although his failure to publish this work in his lifetime suggests that he never resolved the issue to his own satisfaction. Nevertheless, this attempt does also suggest that, consistent with his objective of developing a scientific theory of capitalism, he saw the concept of value as having an explanatory role in a theory of actual prices. The transformation problem has been the focus of extensive debate for over a century. It has been suggested that the consensus until the 1970s was that it invalidated Marx's theory of value, but more recently a number of attempts have been made to overcome it (Foley, 2000; Mohun & Veneziani, 2017). Some, such as Dumenil and Foley's "New Interpretation", give up on the attempt to reconcile value and prices and instead reposition Marx's value theory as a statement about exploitation that only holds, and only needs to hold, at the level of the system as a whole (Foley, 2000). Others, such as the Temporal Single System Interpretation, employ complex algebraic reasoning to defend Marx's conclusions, but can only do so by accepting that values are influenced by prices, which seems to abandon Marx's central argument (Kliman & McGlone, 1999; Mohun & Veneziani, 2017).

It is possible that Marx did not see the gap between value and price as a problem because he took for granted a concept of value that was already in general circulation. As Mirowski explains,

it became common to postulate a distinction between intrinsic value, naturally determined and fundamentally stable, and market price, an epiphenomenon of the myriad conjunctures of the historically specific market. In effect, equivalence was thought to hold sway for intrinsic values, whereas market price was relegated to the subordinate function of clearing the market (Mirowski, 1991, p. 154).

It seems likely that this discursive framing of value informed Marx's thinking, so that there is a sense in which value (perhaps adjusted for profit equalisation as the discussion of the transformation problem in Volume III suggests) was taken to equate to the *normal* or equilibrium price of a commodity. Orléan tells us something similar: "Classical economists... think of value not as something associated with prices, as they are fashioned by market forces at each instant, but instead as a regulative concept that governs their movement over the longer term" (Orléan, 2014, p. 47). If this were so, we could read Marx as saying that value, as normal price, is determined non-circularly by the socially necessary quantity of labour, even though actual prices may deviate in the short term for a variety of reasons. Indeed in places it seems that value does correspond in Marx's system to some sort of notion of normal price (Mirowski, 1991, p. 177). However, this does not solve the problem, except in a world of very stable prices, because we would now need to specify the concept of a normal price in empirical terms – is it, for example, an average price? Over what period? In what geographical space? In practical terms this solution generates more questions than it answers, and certainly more than Marx answers. Ultimately, then, Marx's concept of value has no clear empirical referent.

The second major issue is that the labour theory of value is an objectivist theory, in the sense that it treats value as a quantity that exists independently of the beliefs of participants and that can therefore be discovered and explained by a scientific theory. This is a foundation stone in Marx's attempt to develop a scientifically based critique of capitalist society. As Dolfsma puts it, "the value of an object was ... supposed to inhere in objects" (Dolfsma, 1997, p. 401). Or as Orléan puts it, this is a *substance* theory of value, which sees "value as the consequence of a substance, or quality" of goods themselves (Orléan, 2014, p. 12). Mirowski argues that classical political economists, including Marx, were searching for "a value substance" that was generated in the process of production, and then "conserved in the activity of trade to provide structural stability to prices" (Mirowski, 1991, p. 142). For Marx, that substance was abstract human labour. Labour time is taken to be able to influence exchange value because each commodity has "human labour in the abstract ... embodied or materialised in it" (Marx, 1954, p. 46). Marx constantly repeats the point that labour isn't just used to produce the commodity but is actually "contained in the article" (Marx, 1954, p. 46), another belief he took over from Ricardo (Arthur, 2001, p. 217). Many contemporary Marxists continue to insist that labour is somehow present as substance (perhaps an "immaterial substance" (Ehrbar, 2007,

p. 237)) in the commodities it has produced, thus providing an object-ive basis, within the commodities themselves, for their exchange value (e.g. Ehrbar, 2007; Engelskirchen, 2007). This idea is designed to solve the problem that price is clearly determined at the time of exchange, but a labour theory of value requires that *value* be the outcome of the process of production and not the process of exchange: another idea that remains a staple of mainstream Marxism (e.g. D. Harvey, 2011, p. 101). But the idea that labour is somehow contained in an object it has produced is bizarre. Labour is a process, not a substance, and although it may reconfigure the substance of an object, it does not and cannot introduce any new labour substance into it. Value, con-ceived of as a residue of labour in a commodity, is purely a figment of the value theorist's imagination.

The problem only gets worse once we recognise that is not concrete but abstract labour that Marx takes to determine value (Elson, 1979, pp. 135–138, 159). The entire theory depends on abstracting from specific kinds of labour to produce a kind of standardised measure of labour time that is adjusted for differences in the type of work done. Otherwise, like use values, the different kinds of labour are qualita-tively different and thus quantitatively incommensurable. But Marx fails to explain why it is *valid* to abstract from the qualitative differ-ences of different kinds of labour when he has argued that it is *not* valid to abstract from the qualitative differences of different kinds of use value (Cutler et al., 1977, p. 58; M. Harvey & Geras, 2013, pp. 37–38). These adjustments are also problematic because Marx ends up using wage rates to determine the relative value of different kinds of work, again allowing value to be determined in part by price, when his theory seems to require that value is independent of price. But it is hard to see how he could sustain this. As Cutler and his co-authors have pointed out it is only at the point of exchange that some sort of equivalence is or could be established between the different kinds of labour that have contributed to producing different commodities (Cutler et al., 1977, p. 89). The implication is that abstract labour cannot be a substance that is a part of a commodity but is merely a measure derived from the prices at which goods exchange, which is of course exactly opposite to the result that Marx is trying to establish. Mirowski sums up these issues by arguing that Marx "simultaneously argued for two contradictory versions of the labor theory of value": the substance theory and one that allows the amount of abstract labour in a product and thus its value to be determined by technological and market conditions at the time of exchange (Mirowski, 1991, pp. 180–181).

The very idea that there could be such a substance is highly problematic (Elder-Vass, 2016, p. 65), but so is the use that Marx makes of this argument. Marx's framing of his theory of value as objective and scientific was intended to position his work in a wider discursive context in which science and ethics were seen as rigidly separated and where the authority of science could be employed to clothe his work in greater legitimacy. Hence, he claimed to have eliminated moral claims and qualities entirely from his analysis.

Yet, as Geras has shown, Marx's project is in reality deeply ethical (Geras, 1985; Harvey & Geras, 2013). One of the labour theory of value's primary functions in Marx's work is to underpin his theory of exploitation: to sustain the claim that workers do not receive the full value of what they produce under capitalism. While this is expressed by Marx as a technical or factual claim, its practical function in political economy is to sustain an ethically based condemnation of capitalism under the cover of a supposedly scientific theory (Elder-Vass, 2016, pp. 67–69). From this perspective, Marx's theory of value starts to look like a theory of *just* prices. It is, first, a theory of the just price of labour: that workers ought to receive the full value of their product. And second, it is a theory of the just price of commodities: that commodity prices ought to reflect the amount of (socially necessary) labour expended to produce the item concerned. In Marx's terms, workers under capitalism do not receive the full product of their labour, but Marx's theory of exploitation seems to depend on an implicit theory of just values in a system beyond capitalism, and the political appeal of his system depends in part on this ethical subtext.

Ultimately, then, Marx's theory of value remains hanging in mid-air. His concept of value has no clear empirical referent, though it may be related to a notion of normal price that is difficult to operationalise outside a world of stable prices. It is based on an ontologically incoherent assumption about the preservation of labour input as a kind of value substance in the commodity. And it carries an ethical payload that derives from a notion of just price in some ideal future economy that cannot be realised in our current economy (and perhaps ought not to be, under any system: Elder-Vass, 2016, pp. 68–69).

Value Creation and Value Extraction?

While Marx's labour theory of value as such is only endorsed these days by a sub-set of committed Marxists, it is important to understand why it is problematic because it has also shaped the discursive environment more widely amongst critical thinkers. This has led to the emergence of confused and misleading versions of the concept of value and unrealistic expectations of what it can do for us. This chapter engages with this issue by discussing the work of Mariana Mazzucato on value creation and value extraction (Mazzucato, 2018). Mazzucato is by no means the only writer who has used these or similar terms, although it is perhaps more common to talk in terms of *wealth* creation and extraction, which avoids ties to the concept of value (e.g. Sayer, 2015, p. 31; Shaxson, 2018, pp. 3–4). The concepts have also penetrated into the more popular management literature but they arguably morph there into a more superficial argument where even though the term *value* is used, it is seen in practice as a synonym for monetary revenue. When Strebel and Cantale, for example, "define value extraction as the capturing of value from other stakeholders" they mean *monetary* revenue obtained at some other actor's expense (Strebel & Cantale, 2014). I will focus here on Mazzucato's use of the concepts of value creation and value extraction because she provides a particularly clear version of the discourse and her clarity helps us to see why it is problematic.

Mazzucato is concerned with some fundamental political questions about how we should operate our economy, and employs the concepts of value creation and value extraction to address two questions in particular: what should be produced? and how should the benefits arising from production be distributed? Her work is excellent in many ways, making very clear how inadequate "the market" is as a solution to these questions and how important it is that states are able to make provision for social needs. I will return to the latter issue in the section "Social Value" but first we must focus on how she employs the concept of value.

Mazzucato does not explicitly advocate any particular theory of value but she does make it central to her argument (Mazzucato, 2018, p. 18). She also gives some clear indicators of the broad kind of value theory she favours when she criticises marginalist economic theory and suggests a desire to recover a more classical understanding of value:

'value', a term that once lay at the heart of economic thinking, must be revived and better understood. Value has gone from being a category at the core of economic theory, tied to the dynamics of production ... to a subjective category tied to the 'preferences' of economic agents (Mazzucato, 2018, p. 272).

Her particular focus is on "value creation", which she defines as "the ways in which different types of resources (human, physical and intangible) are established and interact to produce new goods and services", and on "value extraction", which she defines as "activities focused on moving around existing resources and outputs, and gaining disproportionately from the ensuing trade" (Mazzucato, 2018, p. 6). She links the idea of value creation, or wealth creation, to popular discourses that have been used to justify the wealth of entrepreneurs, but seeks to question that usage, saying that "we need a radically different type of narrative as to who created the wealth in the first place – and who has subsequently extracted it" (Mazzucato, 2018, p. xvi). Myth-making about value creation, she argues, "has allowed an immense amount of value extraction, enabling some individuals to become very rich and draining societal wealth in the process" (Mazzucato, 2018, p. xviii).

Her definitions link closely to the classic (but problematic) distinction between productive (value-creating) and unproductive (value-extracting) activities, and she devotes much of her chapter on the history of value to how different thinkers have drawn the boundary between them. As she says, "the touchstone was generally what kind of activity was thought to further the common good", although different thinkers offered different criteria of which activities fulfilled this requirement (Mazzucato, 2018, p. 22). Value creation, on this account, would seem to be the process of furthering the common good, and value extraction the process of undermining the common good, but there is a further element to her definition of value extraction: the notion of gaining disproportionately. The implications are confused. What if someone gains disproportionately from doing something socially useful – is that value extraction? What if someone does something socially harmful but does not gain from it – is that value extraction? Is it, in other words, the disproportionate gain or the socially worthless character of the activity that makes something value extracting? We can also doubt her criteria of which activities are socially useful and which are not. After all, a great deal of material production consists of "moving around existing resources" into new configurations. Does that make assembly of mechanical products from pre-manufactured parts, for example, unproductive and thus a source of value extraction?

There are several problems here. The first is that her argument (like its precursors) conflates two different problems: the problem of what activities are socially desirable and the problem of what rewards people deserve from their contribution to those activities. There are important things to be said about both problems but they are not the same problem, and the confusions implicit in her definition of value extraction are a consequence of trying to use the same concept to address both.

The second is that the whole argument about value creation and extraction rests on implicit assumptions about the nature of value that are largely absorbed from the Marxist tradition. The argument assumes that value is something invariant that is created in the process of producing goods and services, preserved and transported unchanged as those goods and services circulate through the economic system and then appropriated by someone through the act of taking a share of the monetary income that arises from the sale of those goods. In other words, although she doesn't attribute the creation of value entirely to labour, Mazzucato's argument about value creation still has too much in common with elements of the labour theory of value that are untenable for all the reasons discussed in the previous section and indeed elsewhere.

Let me break this down more carefully. Once we have rejected the labour theory of value it is clear that there is no invariant thing embodied in goods and services that we could call value. Value, rather, is some sort of social relation, and can vary as a result of factors that are independent of the object produced or the material service delivered. Take, for example, Mazzucato's suggestion that the touchstone of what is productive, and thus the touchstone of value creation, is what serves the common good (the argument is similar if we choose a different social relation as the touchstone of value). If this is the case, then whether a given activity produces value is not determined by the activity itself but by the social benefits it delivers and those benefits may vary independently of whatever occurred at the time of the productive activity. If it is even conceptually possible to measure such value, the amount of value would depend on the size of the social benefit, and not at all, for example, on the character or amount of labour done to produce it. Rather, *it is the fact that the output is used to serve the common good that makes the labour productive and the product valuable.* Value in the sense of serving the common good is not created and then carried through the system to a point of realisation but only comes about as a result of the realisation.

Furthermore, if value is not something that appears at the moment of production and then circulates unchanged, it is not then available for other actors to skim off in an act of value extraction further along the process. In saying this, I am not denying that there are actors who profit unreasonably from the roles that they play in the economic system. The point, rather, is that talk of value extraction, while it may be expressive and it may therefore be politically effective in drawing attention to the problem, cannot be connected to a coherent theory of value that in turn can be used to theorise the wider workings of the economic system or indeed the ways in which these actors profit. The term functions well enough as a way of expressing disapproval for certain economic activities but it tells us nothing about what lies behind the profits these actors appropriate.

Social Value

Towards the end of her book, however, Mazzucato starts to use the term *value* rather differently. In her conclusion she argues that "rather than focusing on which activities are inside or outside the production boundary, today we can work to ensure that all activities – in both the real economy and in the financial sector – promote the outcomes that we want" (Mazzucato, 2018, p. 278). Given that she earlier identified value creation with activities inside the production boundary and value extraction with those outside it, this seems to signal a different orientation. She goes on to say,

The concept of value must once again find its rightful place at the centre of economic thinking. More fulfilling jobs, less pollution, better care, more equal pay – what sort of economy do we want? When that question is answered, we can decide how to shape our economic activities, thereby moving activities that fulfill these goals inside the production boundary so they are rewarded for steering growth in the ways we deem desirable (Mazzucato, 2018, p. 281).

Now the logic has been reversed in a way that resembles my argument earlier – it is no longer what is productive that determines what has value, but instead we are to call things productive that generate value, and value itself is to be identified with the pursuit of a range of social goals for the economy. I call this *social value*, to distinguish it from the earlier understanding of value as something that is created in production and extracted later in the economic process. Although Mazzucato doesn't say so, these are clearly different concepts of value. The concept of social value is explicitly normative: it arises from carrying out economic activities that achieve desirable social goals. It is not created by the activity of production and transformed unchanged through the economic process, but rather depends on the use that is made of goods and services. A pile of bricks might have greater social value when used to build a public hospital rather than a prison for a repressive government, for example, or when it is used to build apartments for twenty ordinary families rather than a mansion for a billionaire. This version of value theory is far more useful, and indeed reflects the powerful core argument of Mazzucato's work: that social value rather than market forces should guide many of the most important decisions about our economy.

Social value, however, cannot be definitively measured or determined, and is always open to debate. Is it more important to increase spending on public health services or on education? Do we need more police or less? Should we prioritise public transport or digital networks? We cannot expect to find a theory of social value that can answer these questions for us as if they could be read off from a scale. Evaluations of social value are questions on which there are multiple potentially valid perspectives. A coherent approach to assessing social value will need to balance the range of different people's needs and assessments of social value through a democratic process of consultation and negotiation – something like Habermas's deliberative democracy (Habermas, 1996). Nor can we assess the relative social value of meeting competing needs in the abstract, but only by learning from our experience. It is therefore rational to see social expenditure as an evolving rebalancing of priorities in the light of experience and not as a calculation from first principles on any given occasion. Mazzucato's argument, in other words, leads us back towards something like the social democratic approach to public expenditure that was enormously important in the twentieth century but has been in retreat due to the rise of neoliberalism since the 1980s.

The concept of social value can also be applied to the commodity economy as a way of making sense of priorities in regulating it – as we see in Mazzucato's call for less pollution and more equal pay, for example. On one hand, commodity systems do contribute to the welfare of the population, for example through the production of food or housing for private sale, although we may doubt whether the more extravagant versions deliver as much social value as their prices imply. But, on the other, there are also things produced for private sale that we might judge have no social value at all, or far less than their price, such as cigarettes and weapons, for example. The well-known range of market failures, such as its inability to price in externalities (deaths resulting from lung cancer or shootings, for example) or the social value of public goods, and the influence of wealth on allocation and pricing, mean that regulation is essential, and the concept of social value expresses the need to take social priorities into account in correcting for the inadequacies of commodity systems.

A social concept of value is therefore ethically and politically significant, but it does not offer us the sort of analysis of how the commodity economy actually works that both Marx and the marginalists aimed at. If a theory of value is to help to explain how the economy works, it will need to be a different kind of theory of value than any of these. Nor does the concept of social value help us much with the other important (though neglected) sector of our contemporary economies: the gift sector (Elder-Vass, 2016, pp. 32–35). The gift sector is not guided by the monetary considerations that seem to dominate concepts of value in the commodity sector and to a lesser extent the public sector of the economy. The gift sector is ruled by care for others and by work that is done to develop and sustain social relationships. If there is a kind of value at work here it is not one of the three discussed in this chapter – equilibrium value, labour value or social value.

Social value, then, is important, but it does not offer us the kind of all-encompassing theory, one that can be placed "at the core of economic theory", that Mazzucato is looking for (Mazzucato, 2018, p. 272). Mazzucato is a sure-footed guide to the importance of ethical questions in the politics of the economy, but her account of value has little to tell us about how the commodity economy actually works.

Reflecting on her ambitions brings us to a central question for theorists of value: what can we reasonably expect a theory of value to do for us?

Why Theorise Value?

The value theorists whose work has been considered in this chapter have big ambitions for the theory of value, but their theories are ultimately unable to deliver on those ambitions. Does that mean, as Mazzucato seems to think, that what we need is a better theory of value that *is* capable of delivering them, or does it mean that we have been asking too much of theories of value? Is it really viable to have a single theory that provides both the core of an explanation of how the contemporary economy works and also answers a whole series of ethical and/or political questions about the economy? What role, in other words, can and should the concept of value actually play in economics and political economy?

The theories we have looked at have attempted to fulfil some or all of a range of purposes:

1. An explanation of how the economy works
2. A basis for critique of the economy
3. A basis for determining what should be produced
4. And a basis for determining the distribution of income
5. All the way through to a complete politics of the economy

For marginalist purists, for example, the equilibrium theory of price provides (1) a comprehensive explanation of how the commodity economy works, or at least (2) a comprehensive explanation of how the economy *should* work in the absence of government interference, and thus a basis for rejecting such interference. It (3) not only explains how the price system determines what is produced but also provides a justification (the concept of Pareto optimality) for the actual allocation of resources to productive tasks in the commodity system, and (4) the same argument is taken to justify the distribution of income that results from a system of perfect markets. This in turn (5) leads to a politics, whose latest iteration is neoliberalism, that says the economy must be run on purely market principles.

For many Marxists, the labour theory of value provides (1) a comprehensive theory of the dynamics of the capitalist economy, and (2) a basis for critiquing capitalism as inherently exploitative. (3) Its implications for the distinction between productive and unproductive labour provide a criterion for determining what sort of economic activities should and should not be pursued. (4) Although it is not explicit, the labour theory of exploitation seems to imply that incomes should be distributed (at least prior to full communism) in proportion to each individual's labour contribution to production. (5) And the labour theory of value is at the heart of Marx's politics and in particular the demand that capitalism be overthrown to end the exploitation of labour.

Mazzucato is much less assertive about what her approach to value *can* deliver, but retains the ambition that a unified theory of value should (1) provide the core of a theory of how the economy works and (2) of how it should be changed. She (3) retains the productive/unproductive distinction as a criterion of what economic activities should be undertaken, and in the end roots that distinction in what I have called the social value of their outputs. She (4) uses the concept of value extraction to critique the distribution of incomes and seems to want a theory that can root social value and/or questions of its distribution in some other kind of value. Finally, (5) although her political conclusions are arguably less far-reaching, she sees value theory as underpinning the need for public expenditure, regulation and intervention in the commodity economy.

It is easy to see how attractive it is to have a unified theoretical system built around a single core concept that appears to explain everything important about how the economy works and how it should be changed. But all of those above are fundamentally flawed: they employ ultimately incoherent arguments about value that cannot provide satisfactory solutions to either the question of how the economy works or the question of how we should change it. But is this only a feature of these *particular* theories of value, or is it a necessary feature of *any* theory that aims to fulfil all of these purposes through a single concept of value? There are at least two ontological reasons to think that it is a necessary feature.

The first relates to the explanatory ambitions of these theories. Economic systems are complex open systems, in which many different causal factors interact (Lawson, 2003). Sometimes, and for some purposes, we may be able to identify a subset of these factors that have a decisive influence, but even when this is the case that influence will always remain open to change as the causal context changes. While both the marginalist and Marxist models have been elaborated in ways that are intended to make them more realistic, in both cases the core argument remains too focused on a single mechanism – equilibration in markets in the marginalist case, and the exploitation of wage labour in the Marxist case – to provide us with coherent explanations of how a complex system like our contemporary economy works.

The second reason is that we cannot reduce ethical questions to explanatory questions (Elder-Vass, 2010a). Questions about what should be produced and how much income different people should receive are not reducible to questions about the facts or mechanisms of economic processes. Rather, they can only be answered by reference to our ethical values, and because different people have different values as well as different interests, they can only be resolved satisfactorily through processes of debate and agreement (Elder-Vass, 2010a). That is not to say that explanatory theory is irrelevant to these issues, because we need to understand how things work and what consequences they tend to bring about before we can evaluate them ethically, but it does mean that we can never simply derive ethical conclusions from explanatory theories.

No single theory of value, therefore, will ever be able to fulfil all of the roles that these authors want it to. What, then, should we expect from theories of value? First, I suggest, we should recognise that value in economics is not a single unified phenomenon, and that we might need multiple concepts of value to reflect different aspects or types of value. Of those examined above, only the social concept of value seems worth preserving, as it lies at the heart of public decision-making about the economy, but social value is clearly an ethical concept that has little to tell us about the explanatory questions that earlier theories of value sought to address. This book argues that value is also at the heart of how the commodity economy works – but value of a very different kind than the three examined above. We will therefore need at least one more concept of value to enable us to analyse its causal role in the economy, and the next chapter seeks to outline just such a concept.

Second, we should expect successful explanatory theories to be less ambitious than the marginalist or Marxist theories of value. Causation in the economy is the outcome of many interacting mechanisms, and theories of value will only illuminate a subset of those mechanisms. They may give us insight into important processes, but neither theories of value nor any other economic theory will ever provide us with a single master key to unlock all the secrets of the economy, capitalist or otherwise.

Third, if a theory of value does give us insight into important processes, it may also create opportunities for critique of those processes, but it will not lead directly and inexorably to necessary ethical conclusions. When we know how a process works and what outcomes it tends to produce we can question whether it should work differently or indeed whether it should be allowed to operate at all, but our answers to those questions will also depend on how we evaluate the interests of the various affected individuals and thus on further ethical premises.

Conclusion

Value is not an objective quantity, a number that can be determined scientifically if only we have the right theory. Neither the Marxist theory of value as a product of labour nor the marginalist theory of value as a product of price equilibration in the market is viable, and both fail at the same two points. First, they claim to explain a phenomenon with empirical relevance to the operation of the economy and yet their theories *are not* theories of such phenomena. Neither exchange value as Marxists understand it nor equilibrium price as the marginalists understand it equates to actual prices paid in the market or to any other observable or measurable empirical phenomenon. Nor can either tradition demonstrate how their favoured concepts of value causally determine prices, profits or any other actual phenomenon of economic importance (although I will argue that demand and supply considerations, and labour costs, are often *amongst* the many factors that interact to cause price outcomes). Neither, then, is a scientific theory of an objective phenomenon and this brings us to the second point at which both fail. Rather than scientific theories of how some economically relevant phenomenon is actually determined, both are covertly normative theories of how prices *ought* to be set in some sort of ideal economy. This makes them performative contradictions: they are normative theories that deny they are normative theories.

Despite their failings, these theories have profoundly influenced contemporary discourse about value. Political interventions continue to draw on concepts such as value creation and value extraction as if these were based on a coherent concept of value. But the idea that value is an invariant quality of goods and services, created when they are produced, that flows through the system and ends up being extracted by someone, remains unsatisfactory even if we detach it from the labour theory of value. We need to move on from seeing value as the basis for complete theories of the economy and of the politics of the economy, and start to recognise the limits to what a theory of value can achieve, and indeed the need for multiple theories of different kinds of value.

In particular, we need to distinguish between ethical arguments about what should be produced, and how people should be rewarded, on the one hand, and explanatory questions about the causation of economic events on the other. Mazzucato does provide us with part of the answer to these questions towards the end of her book when she invokes what I have called *social* value as a criterion of what should be produced. Nevertheless, we also need a different kind of theory and a different concept of value to analyse how value functions in the commodity economy.

This book develops or synthesises such a theory as part of a critical explanatory account of value and the role that it plays in the contemporary commodity system. It will argue that objectivist understandings of value have stood in the way of taking a valid critical position that proceeds from how value actually operates in the contemporary economy. Far from being fixed, value is highly mutable and major concentrations of social power have emerged that sustain themselves by manipulating value at our expense. This is true in the commodity economy, where branding, status goods and heritage and other status narratives are widely used to extract super profits from buyers, and it is even more true in the financial economy, where an increasing proportion of financial instruments are sustained at bizarre valuations by the discursive and institutional power of those inventing the assets and the narratives that sustain their valuations.

3 | *Value and Price*

This chapter starts to develop an alternative theory of value. It begins by introducing the notion of value as a normative concept. In contrast with the obscurities of the dominant theories of value, I will argue that the basic nature of value is surprisingly simple and indeed thoroughly familiar from everyday discourse: the economic value of a thing is the price it *ought* to exchange at. Of course, there may be many different views of what that price should be, and many different arguments to consider in judging it. But to say that the value of a thing is defined in this way does not mean that there is only *one* price that is its value for everyone, as objectivist theories of value assume. It simply means that whenever someone holds a belief or makes a statement about the economic value of a thing, it is a belief or statement about the price it ought to exchange at. When we talk about the value of something in the context of exchange, we are talking about what it is *worth*, about what a fair price for it would be. Although each of us forms our own opinion of the value of a thing, however, there are social forces that tend to produce convergence in those opinions. Value is thus normative – doubly normative, as it is influenced by assessment of what is a just price, and these assessments themselves depend on social norms about valuation. The chapter explains these normative assessments in terms of what I call *lay theories of value*, which are norms about the fair price of commodities.

What, though, is the purpose of explaining this kind of value? Value in this sense is purely a feature of systems of commodity exchange, and it is significant, in particular, because it is a moment in the process of establishing a price for a commodity. The primary purpose of theorising it is therefore to contribute to a theory of the causal determination of commodity prices, which then have enormous further significance in commodity economies because of the influence they have on incomes and on the determination of what gets produced and how resources are allocated to this process. This approach, then, prioritises the study of how value actually functions in the economy rather than the construction of legitimising or delegitimising discourses like those that orient the marginalist and Marxist accounts respectively. That does not exclude critical applications of the theory, but such applications must be built on theory that is explanatorily coherent in the first place, rather than by constructing supposedly explanatory theory on the basis of ideological premises.

The chapter, then, will examine how value contributes to price determination, but that does not imply that value alone *determines* price, because like all other events, pricing events are not determined by any single mechanism. They are determined in open economic systems and so we need to see them as the outcome of many interacting forces, of which value claims form one important group. The second section of the chapter introduces the critical realist view of causation that enables us to make sense of this role for theories of value.

The argument then builds critically on contributions that have been made by recent valuation theorists, particularly the economics of conventions school and recent sociological work on valuation as a process. Indeed, significant parts of the argument are synthesised from this work and the chapter therefore interleaves discussion of these traditions with development of my substantive account of value. Despite their important contributions, however, some work in these traditions has neglected considerations of social structure, power and the audiences for valuation discourses. The last part of the chapter reintroduces these.

Value Is a Normative Concept

It is generally accepted that the economic concept of value bears some relationship to the concept of price, although the nature of that relation is controversial. Aspers and Beckert, for example, see it as the amount of money that someone is willing to pay for an item (Aspers & Beckert, 2010, p. 8). The International Valuation Standards Council asserts that "value is not a fact but an opinion", "a hypothetical price" based on "an estimate of the benefits that would accrue to a particular party from ownership" (International Valuation Standards Council, 2013 paragraph 8). In a similar vein, Boltanski and Esquerre say that value "serves as the justification for prices" (Boltanski & Esquerre, 2016, p. 37). As Boltanski puts it,

Value talk only happens in situations in which there is a problem with the price. The notion of value is used when there is a situation in which a price ought to be criticized or justified … So what is the function of 'value'? It is the justification of the price, plain and simple (Boltanski, Esquerre & Muniesa, 2015, p. 78).

The implication is clear: value is a normativised expectation about price, an expectation about the price that an item ought to sell at. Of course, there may be many different views of what that price should be, and many different arguments to consider in judging it. But to say that the value of a thing is defined in this way does not mean that there is only one price that is its value for everyone. It simply means that when a lay actor holds a belief or makes a statement about the economic value of a thing, it is a belief or statement about the price it ought to exchange at. Here the term *ought* denotes an ethical claim, strongly related to questions of fairness in exchange or just price.

In the Western academic tradition, early discussions of value such as those in Aristotle and Aquinas adopted this notion of the just price as the standard of value (Heilbroner, 1988, pp. 108–109; Mirowski, 1991, pp. 110, 146). This concept did not denote a single fixed price, but rather "the outcome of a myriad of imponderable considerations tethered to the individual case and the specific context" – a "reflection of social relations" (Mirowski, 1991, p. 110). This notion of the just or reasonable price, however, was not merely academic, but rather was embedded in lay discourse and practice. This is brilliantly illustrated in Edward Thompson's classic paper "The Moral Economy of the English Crowd in the Eighteenth Century" (Thompson, 1971). Thompson discusses food riots in eighteenth-century England, showing that they were more or less universally responses to soaring food prices, in particular the price of wheat and bread, in a context where the poor would typically spend half their income on wheat or bread – and often more when the price rose. Frequently these "riots" took the form of crowds insisting that farmers, millers, bakers or merchants sell their stocks at what the crowd considered a fair price, "a traditional 'moral' price set by the crowd" (Thompson, 1971, p. 126). This price might vary from time to time and place to place, but it was a price at which the working poor could afford to feed their families, a price that reflected the social entitlement to a reasonable subsistence that they saw as the moral counterpart to their role in the economy (also see Hann, 2010, p. 190).

There are intriguing parallels between Thompson's moral economy and recent work on fairness in behavioural economics. Kahneman, Knetsch and Thaler, for example, conducted an extensive telephone survey of what their Canadian respondents saw as fair and unfair pricing practices (Kahneman, Knetsch & Thaler, 1986). They found that prices that have been established for some time generally come to be accepted as fair, but deviations from these prices are potentially problematic. In particular, although raising prices was generally considered acceptable when it was done in response to rising costs, it was unacceptable when it was done in order to exploit market shortages. Prices, in other words, are the subject of social norms, and there are strong parallels between Thompson's historical cases and contemporary pricing norms. As numerous game theory experiments and empirical studies have shown, many transactors are also prepared to back their disapproval of unfair pricing practices with retaliatory action (Fehr & Gächter, 2000). This tendency may contribute to prices being "sticky" since sellers are often aware that they can be penalised for price increases by buyers shunning their goods, whereas there are rarely penalties for failing to reduce prices.

These examples point towards an unashamedly normative conception of economic value, and thus one that may draw on wider moral values. On one hand, value is normative in the sense that the principles employed in assessing fair value are social norms: they are largely learned from social interaction and influenced by normative pressures about what ways of valuing things are appropriate. On the other, it is normative in the ethical sense that it is a belief about the fair or just price of a thing. Unlike the objectivist accounts of value discussed in the previous chapter, no attempt is made here to disguise the normative foundations of the concept in a technical theory that purports to expunge normativity. This does not mean, however, that we must collapse the moral and economic *concepts* of value into each other – on the contrary, we must keep them analytically distinct so that we can examine the relations between them. We may usefully divide valuations, for example, into different "regimes of value" (Appadurai, 1988), or "orders of worth" (Boltanski & Thévenot, 2006). Evaluations of things or services in the context of non-economic regimes of value may contribute to our assessments of their economic value, but these continue to be assessments against different standards. We may evaluate a product on aesthetic grounds, for example, as part

of the process of taking a view on its economic value. What is distinctive about economic value is that it is an assessment of the fair price of a
thing against a monetary standard of exchange.

Perhaps the most striking difference between these different forms of
valuation is that economic value is necessarily expressed in quantitative form. Even in barter, valuation implies judging the relative worth
of two commodities in quantitative terms, but in modern society
economic valuation is overwhelmingly quantified in terms of money.
Sometimes monetary valuation may evoke or stand for a sense of what
else one could do with the money involved, but even where this is the
case, economic values are assessed in monetary terms. Indeed, the role
of money as a quantitative measure of value is generally seen as one of
its key social functions.

Price in an Open Economic System

An adequate theory of price would look very different from the marginalist model discussed in Chapter 2. One reason is that the
marginalist model assumes a causal closure, in which price is the
outcome of interactions between atomistic agents who adjust to each
other purely on the basis of price changes, isolated from other causal
factors. Such conditions rarely (if ever) occur in the social realm
(Lawson, 2006, pp. 494–497). Real economic systems are open
systems. Events that occur in open systems are influenced by multiple
causal mechanisms or powers that may interfere with each other and
alter each other's effects (Faulkner, 2007). Hence it is an error to
explain any real social phenomenon such as price determination in
terms of a single mechanism – price equilibration in this case. Although
a *tendency* to price equilibration through demand and/or supply
adjustments (as opposed to an assumption that equilibrium prices are
actually achieved) is often causally relevant to the determination of
prices, a large range of other factors are also significant, and any
coherent theory of price must recognise that the mix and strength of
causal influences will vary depending on the actors and structural
characteristics in each case or group of cases (Elder-Vass, 2016,
pp. 78–81). As has been argued at length elsewhere, we need a critical
realist ontological framework to account for causal processes in such
systems (Elder-Vass, 2010b; Lawson, 2003). Let me briefly summarise
what this involves by focusing on a subset of the framework:

a) actual events are the outcome of multiple interacting causal powers
(Bhaskar, 1975, pp. 110–111; Elder-Vass, 2010b, p. 47);
b) causal powers are produced by mechanisms: repeatable processes
that depend on the structure and composition of the entities possessing the power concerned (Elder-Vass, 2012, pp. 17–18);
c) because events are the outcome of multiple interacting powers,
individual causal powers do not produce exceptionless empirical
regularities but rather tendencies for a given type of outcome to
follow, tendencies that may be defeated by other interacting causal
powers (Fleetwood, 2001).

From this it follows that explanation in the social sciences should
aim to identify the causal powers that interact to produce social events,
and that this requires us to conduct two related explanatory processes,
known as:

i) *retroduction*: a movement "from a conception of some phenomenon
of interest to a conception of some ... type of thing, mechanism,
structure or condition that, at least in part, is responsible for the
given phenomenon" (Lawson, 1997, p. 24). I take this to require the
identification and explanation of the mechanism that produces a
given type of causal power (Elder-Vass, 2010b, p. 48); and
ii) *retrodiction*, which entails the identification of the set of causal
contributors to states of affairs (Lawson, 1997, p. 221), or more
specifically the identification of the set of causal powers that inter-
acted to produce an event (Elder-Vass, 2010b, p. 48). As Bhaskar
puts it, "To completely account for an event would be to describe
all the different principles involved in its generation". However, he
goes on to say that "a complete explanation in this sense is clearly a
limit concept" and in practice it is only viable to consider the most
significant contributions to any given event or type of event
(Bhaskar, 1975, p. 111).

Taken literally, retrodiction seems to suggest that we should spend our
time constructing detailed explanations for every single event of interest to us; in practice, however, this too is a limit concept. While it may
sometimes be necessary to conduct detailed investigations of individual
cases, we can often perform what I call *retrodictive generalisation*. This
is the relatively familiar explanatory practice of identifying the
common causal factors to be found across a group of cases that are

in some way related. Good explanatory work, however, also requires what I propose to call *retroductive generalisation*: when we have identified a specific mechanism, we will often find that it is a particular concrete variation of a more abstract but more widely occurring mechanism. Both are important moments of the explanatory process.

The theory of value developed in this book is concerned with retroducing a mechanism or rather a group of similar mechanisms that contribute, along with other factors, to causing price outcomes. In this explanatory context, some of the mechanisms theorised in the marginalist tradition may also remain relevant (Elder-Vass, 2016, pp. 78–81). Price setting may be affected, for example, by concerns over the effect on demand of raising prices too high, or the availability of substitutes. But these are only a small subset of the causal factors influencing pricing, and factors that may be undermined by others. For example, many producers are able to insulate themselves from the effect of cheaper substitutes on the price they can charge by developing preferential attachment in their customers (Callon Méadel & Rabeharisoa, 2002; Chamberlin, 1956, pp. 56–57, 71). Apple, for example, uses its marketing strategies to create a sense that its products are cooler and more usable than the alternatives and as a consequence is able to sell them at a higher price than competing products (Elder-Vass, 2016, pp. 123–129; McGuigan, 2009, p. 124).

Alongside mainstream economics there are several heterodox traditions, and sometimes we can turn to these for more plausible explanations of economic phenomena (Keen, 2011, pp. 444–459; Lawson, 2006). Heterodox economics, unfortunately, has had relatively little to say about price, the main exception being work in the post-Keynesian tradition. Post-Keynesians argue that prices are not adjusted constantly in response to market forces, or determined by marginal costs of production, but instead set by producers "in advance of trade" by adding a mark-up to average costs of production (Downward & Lee, 2001, p. 474). They then adjust the price only rarely, usually in response to cost changes. At least some post-Keynesians also recognise that pricing occurs in open systems where many causal forces interact, and therefore other factors must also be taken into account (Downward & Lee, 2001, p. 473). We must, for example, ask what determines the mark-up, and the changes in prices when they do occur. These arguments work well as a critique of marginalist theories of price equilibration by identifying an important class of cases where equilibration does not occur, or is at best an occasional influence. They are, however, only a partial alternative to marginalist price theory. One reason is that the theory applies in some cases but not in many others. Stable cost-plus pricing may be the norm for manufacturing producers, but it is not for financial assets, auctions, large retail businesses with strong competitors, stock clearance, products made to fulfil one-off negotiated orders, automated pricing on sites such as amazon .com, state regulated prices, fine art showrooms or prices subsidised as loss leaders, for example (which is not to say that these cases fit the marginalist framework any better: most of them do not).

The strength of the open systems framework, however, is that it creates space for us to take account of not only these relatively familiar mechanisms but also a broad range of others, and my argument is that a significant set of those mechanisms are best explained using a reframed theory of value. In developing such a theory, I aim to identify one generalisable mechanism that must be taken into account alongside others in a vast range of explanations of specific price outcomes. This is a far more modest objective than that of Marxist or marginalist theories of value, both of which are built around the hope that the entire economy and its laws of motion can be boiled down to the effects of a few mechanisms described in their theories of value. That may be disappointing for some readers, but it represents a resetting of the ambitions of value theory to something that is both realistic and achievable.

Lay Theories of Value

A more effective overall theory of value must abandon ill-conceived attempts to identify the basis of the objective economic value of things, for the simple reason that things do not have an objective value. Instead, I argue that a coherent overall theory must be a theory of how we form our estimates of value, and this process is dominated by what I call *lay theories of value*. Lay theories of value are norms about prices – norms about what factors should influence prices and how. Any socially shared belief about a principle or standard that should influence the price of some type of commodity or asset is a lay theory of value. There are many such theories, though we are not accustomed to calling them that, and they are often (though not always) relatively simple, which is perhaps one reason they tend to fall under the academic radar. Unlike objectivist theories of value, they are typically partial in the sense that each theory addresses only one of the many factors that influences the value of a thing. Thus, for example, one common theory of value is that an item that is sub-standard, perhaps because it was constructed defectively, it has been damaged, it has deteriorated over time or it requires repair, should cost less than an equivalent item of the expected standard of quality. Another, and one that has been produced by many years of discursive work by the producers of "luxury" goods, is that an item that is associated with higher social status should cost more than one without such associations. In the later chapters, we will come across a wide variety of others.

Generally, the act of valuing a particular thing (whether by a potential buyer or a potential seller) will involve taking into account a number of these theories, rather than just one. One might use both of the theories introduced in the previous paragraph, for example, in forming a view on the value of a damaged luxury item. The mix of theories that a given actor employs in a given case will also depend on a number of further factors, such as the objective characteristics of the item to be valued, the context in which the valuation is done and the previous social experience that has influenced both which theories the actor is attached to and how they perceive and classify the item to be valued. One consequence is that different buyers and sellers may apply different mixes of theories of value to the same product, hence there can be wide variations between different people's assessments of value, and indeed the empirical evidence supports this (E. W. Zuckerman, 2012, p. 224). But the view advanced here also implies that we should routinely expect multiple theories of value to be in play for each actor, even when they are evaluating the price of a single product at a single moment in time.

In a sense, then, this book is developing a *second-order* theory of value, a theory of the everyday, largely non-academic first-order *theories of value* that are actually deployed by social actors in valuing items. Those first-order theories are about the quantity of money that a thing *ought* to exchange for – its fair, just or ethically proper price. Rather than an objective quantity, value is subjective in the sense that different people may have different understandings of the value of a thing, but this is not the subjectivity of the isolated atomistic individual of neoclassical theory. Rather, it is a subjectivity that is also social in the sense that individual judgements of value are shaped by *intersubjective* cultures of valuation (Aspers & Beckert, 2010, p. 24). Those cultures in turn take the more specific form of lay theories of value. Different lay theories of value, sometimes complementary and sometimes contradictory, may be advocated or supported by different and overlapping groups of people and the extent of their influence is a product of discursive struggles into which powerful actors invest considerable resources. Hence a second-order theory of value should pay attention to what factors influence the set of theories of value that is brought to bear in any given case and what affects the weightings that actors give to them. This is the retrodictive moment of the explanation.

In addition, we need to examine those lay theories themselves and how they come to be accepted by economic actors in the first place. This is the social constructionist element of the overall theory and also one of the retroductive moments of the explanation, identifying specific causal mechanisms behind assessments of value and how they operate. Value is socially constructed in the sense that it depends on the shared theories of value that actors believe in and employ, and because there are powerful social influences on which theories they accept. The social construction of value, I should stress, is entirely consistent with value also being real in the sense that it is causally significant (Elder-Vass, 2012). It is also entirely consistent with there being objective material factors that actors take into account in the process of valuation (E. W. Zuckerman, 2012, p. 227). In general, causality in the social world includes influences from human individuals, from wider social forces and from material objects (Elder-Vass, 2017a, 2017b), and this is equally true of processes of valuation.

Lay theories of value are fundamentally normative: they are standards that we take to be socially accepted, and they only work to the extent that they *are* socially accepted. We can therefore employ more general work on the sociology and social ontology of normativity to help us make sense of them. As I have argued at length elsewhere, any given norm is able to influence us when, and to the extent that, it is supported by a *norm circle* (Elder-Vass, 2010b, 2012; also see Chapter 5 below). A norm circle is a group of people who are committed to endorsing and enforcing a particular norm. We learn about a norm when we experience the action that these people take to endorse and enforce it, and that action encourages us to believe that we will face positive or negative social sanctions depending on whether or not we

conform to the norm in our own actions. Different norms have different but profusely overlapping norm circles, and normative change
operates by building up or eroding away the membership of the circles
that support particular norms. To say that lay theories of value are
socially constructed, then, means that there are norm circles that
support those theories, norm circles that encourage us to believe that
it is appropriate to apply those theories of value in certain sorts of
situation (I will discuss norm circles and their relation to lay theories of
value in more detail in Chapter 5).

This in turn means that to make sense of valuation we must understand not only the processes in which we *apply* lay theories of value but
also those processes that lead us to *adopt* some theories of value rather
than others in the first place: the structural processes through which
norm circles for theories of value develop (I will also return to this in
Chapter 5). As norms, lay theories of value are cultural and therefore
we would expect them to be linked to the other cultural commitments
of the actors concerned. This opens up potential connections with
empirical and theoretical work that might help to explain which lay
theories become established and in which groups of the population.
Thus, for example, the sorts of cultural affinities explored by Bourdieu
may impact the theories that particular actors hold – perhaps, for
example, rich people are more likely to see status goods as having
value since this is a theory of value that enables them to display their
sense of distinction (Bourdieu, 1984). Equally, it may be that commonly held theories of value fit into the classification of forms of
justification into different "orders of worth" that has been developed
by Boltanski and Thévenot and thus into a wider historical story about
how modern culture has developed and differentiated (Boltanski &
Thévenot, 2006).

While the origins of some lay theories of value may have long-term
historical roots, others are much newer. In the finance sector in particular, this book will argue that we can trace the invention and/or
development of new theories of value and identify at least some of the
social actors involved in advocating them and the processes through
which they build support for them. These theories of value influence
actual prices by influencing what prices the actors are prepared to
accept as fair and reasonable, and as a result of this they are the
constant target of a vast infrastructure generated primarily by sellers
to bias and exploit lay theories of value to their own advantage.

The Economics of Conventions

The concept of lay theories of value has a great deal in common with the concept of *conventions*, as understood by the French school of the economics of conventions. This tradition began by studying how judgements are made about the nature and value of things. The conventions theorists argued that we make such judgements by employing socially sanctioned general principles or "socio-cultural logics" that they call *conventions*, although they are also referred to by different authors as "orders of justification, quality conventions, or worlds of production" (Diaz-Bone, 2017, p. 241). The earliest work in the tradition considered how people classify others into socio-professional categories (Jagd, 2007, p. 76). This kind of categorisation or classification judgement has come to be known as *qualification*, and one of the important findings of the conventions school is that this is a key element of market processes. The notion of a market depends on the idea that different products are comparable, and the process of qualification identifies which class of products a particular item should be compared with, using what Desrosières calls "conventions of equivalence" (Diaz-Bone, 2017, p. 242). These judgements occur "in processes in which actors share a collective interpretation" (Diaz-Bone, 2017, p. 249). Conventions themselves are collectively shared standards or rules about how to make these judgements, which emerge and develop in the process of making judgements, but which tend to become widely accepted to the point where they are taken for granted by the actors (Diaz-Bone, 2017, p. 245). The conventions school applies this framework to a broad range of forms of qualification and valuation.

Perhaps the most influential work in this tradition is Boltanski and Thévenot's book *On Justification* (2006), which extends the theory of conventions to the broader sociological question of how people make judgements and resolve disagreements in all manner of social disputes about the "qualities and worth of objects, actions and persons" (Diaz-Bone, 2017, p. 245, fn 11). The authors argue that people use a range of forms of justification that they call "orders of worth", which invoke quite different kinds of values, and that many social disagreements are in effect disputes about which order of worth applies to a given question. Each order of worth, however, is a relatively well-established set of social norms, flowing from a larger, broader principle. They identify six "worlds", each governed by a different order of worth, including for example the civic world, where the higher common principle is commitment to collectives and the collective good (Boltanski & Thévenot, 2006, p. 185) and the industrial world, whose higher common principle is efficiency (Boltanski & Thévenot, 2006, p. 204).

Conventions are intersubjectively normative (Favereau, 2008) and there is thus a parallel between what I have called lay theories of value and the theory of conventions. However, there may also be differences. One concerns the question of field. Rather than economic value, Boltanski and Thévenot apply the tradition to broad questions of justification in disputes between people, and most of the economic applications apply conventions to the question of how the qualities of things are categorised – to questions, one might say, of use value rather than exchange value (Favereau, 2017). But there are other thinkers in the tradition who *do* apply the notion of convention to monetary valuation, in particular André Orléan, who has recently applied the economics of conventions to financial markets (Orléan, 2014).

Another and perhaps more decisive divergence between conventions and lay theories of value is over the question of granularity. Boltanski and Thévenot's orders of worth or justification are complex normative regimes organised around a central theme or principle, whereas lay theories of value are single, sometimes quite simple, norms about price. But it is not clear whether we should *define* conventions by the example of orders of justification, or see those orders as only one variety of convention. In the latter case, we could also have conventions at lower levels of granularity, which might approach the case of lay theories of value, and Orléan arguably takes a step in this direction. Having said that, this is not the usual way of deploying the concept of conventions.

This is apparent in the other prominent recent application of conventions theory to the question of monetary valuation: Boltanski and Esquerre's work on what they call the *enrichment economy*, an increasingly important segment of the economy supplying luxury goods whose value is enriched by (often rather dubious) narratives linking them to traditional heritages (see the section "Valuation as a Process" for more detail). Rather than investigate the specific theories of value at work here, however, they focus on macrosocial paradigms of value that they call "forms", identifying a new "collection form" that operates in the economy of enrichment by contrast to the "standard form" of the industrial economy and the "asset form" of the financial economy (Boltanski & Esquerre, 2016, p. 37). One reason, then, to distinguish lay theories of value from valuation conventions is to make clear that they operate at a much more detailed level of granularity than most (though not necessarily all) applications of conventions theory.

A third possible divergence, which may follow from the differences in granularity, is that conventions theorists tend to take the view that a single convention is primary with regard to any given outcome. They do recognise that multiple conventions, including valuation conventions, may operate in the same space (Chiapello, 2015, p. 14), but although different actors may deploy different conventions, negotiation is generally a contest over which will apply, rather than a balancing of different conventions (Boltanski & Thévenot, 2006). For Boltanski and Thévenot, for example, disputes are normally resolved by all parties accepting a single principle of justification, and although compromises are possible, they regard them as fragile and by implication as unusual (Boltanski & Thévenot, 2006, pp. 277–278). By contrast, I argue that multiple lay theories of value may interact even in the formation of a single actor's assessment of value, and yet more in processes of negotiation, and it is common for many of them – as well as other causal factors – to have an influence on price outcomes. This divergence may also be related to the somewhat monolithic understanding of normativity implicit in philosophical convention theory, which tends to see conventions as universally adopted in a given social space in order to resolve coordination problems. Everyone in the United Kingdom, for example, is expected to adopt the convention of driving on the left, whereas everyone in France is expected to adopt the convention of driving on the right. Each convention is equally capable of resolving the coordination problem of preventing head-on collisions, but only if it is adopted by everyone in the relevant space. By contrast, seeing lay theories of value as norms governed by profusely intersectional and competing norm circles that vary in size and influence allows us to see much more diversity in the normative structure of value.

Bearing in mind these possible differences, one could perhaps see lay theories of value as a variety of valuation convention, and I will sometimes use these terms interchangeably in the chapters that follow,

though I will tend to reserve *valuation conventions* for better established theories of value. Furthermore, the economics of conventions
supplies important resources for constructing a theory of value and
financial value. One of these is the concept of *reality tests*: "Reality
tests … settle disputes about qualities and worth of objects, actions,
and persons" (Diaz-Bone, 2017, p. 245, fn 11). In the context of their
work a reality test is the resolution of a dispute that settles which
order(s) of worth are to govern its outcome (Boltanski & Thévenot,
2006, p. 40). In the context of monetary valuation, agreeing a price for
an item is a reality test, a test that determines which lay theories of
value have most influence on a particular price (Boltanski & Esquerre,
2016, p. 37).

Prices

The term *price*, however, is ambiguous. On the one hand, the term is
often used to mean *realised price*: the amount that is actually paid in a
purchase transaction, and this is the sense in which I have used it in the
chapter so far. This is also the concept of price to which lay theories of
value are oriented in the sense that this is the outcome that discussions
about value seek to influence. On the other hand, however, the term is
also frequently used to mean *offer price* or *ticket price*: the amount at
which an item is offered for sale, frequently by showing that amount
on a price ticket (Aspers & Beckert, 2010, p. 27). In a way, the term
price is a misnomer for the latter concept, because price tickets are
actually a form of value claim, supported by a lay theory of value that
is particularly strong in many contemporary economies: the theory
that the price on a ticket is the price that *ought* to be paid. In most
supermarkets, for example, this theory reigns supreme and in many
countries it is almost unheard of for a customer to negotiate the ticket
price in a supermarket. Yet in other settings, price tickets are recognised as merely an opening step in a process of negotiation of the value
of the item (in the United Kingdom this includes second hand car
showrooms, although even here price negotiation is in retreat), and
in others there are no price tickets at all. This also illustrates another
important point about lay theories of value: their contextual specificity.
Like other kinds of norm, a theory of value that applies in one situation
may not apply in others, and social actors are expected to understand
the contextual parameters of theories of value.

Multiple theories of value may influence the process of exchange in at least two different ways. First, they may inform the parties' attitudes to the price without being explicitly articulated. For example, I may be presented with the opportunity to buy a certain item at price p, conclude on the basis of my own theories of value that the item is too expensive and decide not to buy it at all (or indeed decide it is cheap or fairly priced and proceed to buy it without further debate). But there is a second possibility: one or other of the parties may enter into a negotiation over the price, deploying theories of value to justify a higher or a lower level. The buyer may say, for example, "this price is too high because the product is damaged" and the seller may either reply within the terms of the same theory of value, for example, "actually those marks are not damage but a sign of the high quality of this item" or by deploying a different theory, for example, "but you are lucky this is already so cheap because this product is very rare". This does not necessarily lead to a single theory of value being accepted by all parties to the negotiation. Rather, various theories may all influence the outcome to various degrees, depending for example on the strength of attachment of the actors to them, their bargaining positions, familiar economic issues such as costs of production and alternative offers available in the market and the discursive strength of the theories being advocated (and thus the likelihood of the theory being accepted as legitimate by the other party). Prices, to put it another way, are multiply-determined by many interacting causal factors, and not just by theories of value, but the theories of value held by both buyers and sellers make an important contribution to the process of agreeing prices and to decisions about whether or not to buy.

Valuation as a Process

In recent years, economic sociologists have also become increasingly interested in valuation. Like the economics of conventions, this work is not confined to monetary valuation but rather sees it as sharing features with other forms of valuation (Helgesson & Muniesa, 2013, p. 2). There are significant overlaps between the argument of this book and work that has been done in this developing field of valuation studies. It shares my scepticism, for example, about the marginalist claim that economic value results from the balancing of supply and demand (Barman, 2015, p. 12) and instead tends to see value as a social construction (Barman, 2015, p. 10). On the other hand, it is often presented as having a pragmatist orientation (e.g. Barman, 2015; Muniesa, 2011) and as being focused on valuation as a process as if this were in conflict with value being a property.

Work in valuation studies often builds on the conventions tradition, although it usually cites sociological applications rather than the original economists, notably Boltanski but also Michel Callon (e.g. Callon et al., 2002). Another important influence has been the anthropologist Arjun Appadurai's work on commodities and the politics of value (Appadurai, 1988), which has some fascinating parallels with the conventions tradition. In particular, his concept of *regimes of value* has significant similarities to the notion of *orders of worth*. A *regime of value* is a normative complex "within which things are classified" and valued (Appadurai, 1988, pp. 13–15) and there can be multiple such regimes operating alongside each other. Gregory, for example, has introduced the idea of value-switching, in which the same item may move "from one value regime to another as, for example, when gold is purchased as a commodity, given as a gift to a daughter and passed on to descendants as a family heirloom" (Gregory, 2000, p. 110).

This is known as *value plurality*. Barman gives another application of value plurality, drawing on Boltanski and Thévenot but also on a number of sources from the valuation studies literature:

each and every market is understood to incorporate multiple orders of worth, including economic, social, political, and cultural value … For example, the determination of a good's economic value tends to result from the negotiation and translation of alternative orders of worth into an economic logic, as structured by broader political and institutional arrangements (Barman, 2015, p. 13)

This is an important argument: while the conventions tradition tends to emphasise the distinctness of orders of worth, sociologists of valuation have started to look at influences between them or cases of ambiguity (Stark, 2011). One way of expressing these influences, in my terms, would be to say that there are lay theories of economic value that relate it to other forms of value. Thus, for example, "a more aesthetically pleasing item should have a higher price", or "an item whose sale serves a good cause should have a higher price".

Other work in valuation studies has picked out theories or standards of value that are quite specific to particular types of commodity. For example, in a study of Dutch fiction book prices Franssen and Velthuis show that "consumers do not see prices as neutral outcomes of supply and demand and actively judge the fairness of prices against different social standards or orders of worth ... Prices ... must be seen as legitimate by consumers in order for markets to stabilize" (Franssen & Velthuis, 2016, p. 367). In the case of fiction books, it seems, what matters is not the aesthetic assessment of the writing, but rather the materiality of the book: "when it comes to prices, what is fair is intricately related to what is visible in terms of material properties of books" – customers expect to pay more for hardbacks, and more for larger format books and books printed on higher quality paper (Franssen & Velthuis, 2016, p. 377). In my terms, this is a retrodictive generalisation: the theory that the price of a book should reflect its material properties appears as a mechanism across a range of similar cases. There is also a sense here that lay valuation theories are strongly sensitive to what seems fair in terms of the wider normative background. Perhaps size and material quality are taken as indicators of the investment that publishers have made in a book and therefore that the price should reflect this – although in fact differences in size and material quality make a relatively small contribution to the cost of production. This hypothesis is a retroductive generalisation: the theory that the price of a book should reflect its material properties has been repositioned as a case of a more abstract lay theory of value, the theory that prices should reflect the cost, or at least the apparent indicators of cost, of a product.

There is also a considerable amount of work on the valuation of what we may loosely call luxury goods or status goods. Since Veblen's work on conspicuous consumption over a century ago it has been widely recognised that some goods are purchased in order to signal the high status of the purchaser rather than because of any inherent quality of the goods themselves (Veblen, 1899). In such cases the theories of value employed by the participants are very different than those employed for what Aspers calls "standard goods" (Aspers, 2009). Aspers argues that participants in status-oriented markets value goods on the basis of each other's identities – so that a high status art dealer, for example, can demand a higher price for an artwork because of her status in the market (Aspers, 2009, pp. 116–117). More generally, Karpik has identified a series of mechanisms that he calls *judgment devices*, which are used to assess the quality – and thus the value – of "singular goods": unique items that are individually priced rather than being instances of a type of item that are effectively all the same for valuation purposes, such as mass-produced goods. These judgment devices include personal networks, third party experts such as critics and guidebook writers, published rankings and appellations – quality indicators granted by independent third parties like those attached to bottles of wine (Aspers & Beckert, 2010, pp. 19–22; Karpik, 2010). Ultimately all of these mechanisms follow from a single more abstract theory of value: goods that enhance the apparent status of the purchaser should be valued more highly.

There are many variants of status and different goods may enhance status in different ways. The variant identified by Veblen was essentially wealth: in a society that values personal wealth a consumer can enhance their status by buying and conspicuously consuming something that other people know to be expensive. There are various prerequisites to attaining this – the item must be distinctive enough that others will recognise it, and its high cost must be well enough known for others to recognise it as a marker of wealth. This in turn generates a whole industry devoted to publicising expensive goods. The less wealthy, however, can still achieve other kinds of status recognition – recognition, in Bourdieu's terms, of their cultural rather than their economic capital (Bourdieu, 1984). At any one time, for example, some goods, but not others, are considered fashionable by those in certain cultural circles, and consumers can appear fashionable themselves within those circles by purchasing and displaying them – a major driver of the fashion industry and its vast expenditure on advertising. Even technology can be branded as "cool" with enough marketing effort (Elder-Vass, 2016, pp. 126–129).

Boltanski and Esquerre have documented a particularly interesting set of cases in their work on the enrichment economy. They argue that the appeal of luxury goods "stems from a kind of aura surrounding them, signifying that they are exceptional, the property of the elite" (Boltanski & Esquerre, 2016, p. 33), and that this aura is increasingly constructed though a process of "heritage creation", including "the fabrication of more or less fictional histories"

(Boltanski & Esquerre, 2016, p. 34) that *enrich* the objects concerned, in the sense of increasing their values. The value of these objects then comes to depend on "their accompanying narratives and genealogical reconstructions" (Boltanski & Esquerre, 2016, p. 44). I would add, though, that these narratives can only enrich objects in interaction with certain sorts of theories of value – the belief that an object with an associated sense of heritage should be valued more highly – and that the work that is done on building enrichment narratives for particular products *also* functions to legitimate this theory of value. All this work helps us to see that there is a family of lay theories of value that share the general feature that goods which enhance the apparent status of the purchaser should be valued more highly.

The field of valuation studies, then, and its cross-fertilisation with the economics of conventions, has provided rich resources for studying contemporary theories of value, and substantial support for the argument that we need to move beyond objectivist theories of value. Let me close this section, however, by expressing a concern about the influence of pragmatism in the field. Although valuation studies is by no means uniformly pragmatist and much of the work in this tradition is thoroughly compatible with other ontologies, including critical realism, occasionally the pragmatist orientation of some scholars becomes problematic (Elder-Vass, 2020). At one level, this pragmatist orientation manifests itself unproblematically as a focus of interest. Barman argues, for example, that it leads to a focus on "how value in a setting becomes produced" as opposed to concepts of value as inherent in an object or as a moral quality (Barman, 2015, p. 12), but she still thinks of value as a social construction (Barman, 2015, p. 10). Muniesa, however, takes things a step further, rejecting the entire debate over whether value is inherent or socially constructed and calling on us to replace "the very notion of value with the notion of valuation" as a form of action (Muniesa, 2011, p. 24). Muniesa may well be motivated in this by similar arguments to those I made about earlier theories of value in Chapter 2, but I would suggest that setting aside debates over the nature of value as such, as if the concept of value could be eliminated from studies of valuation, is an error. On the contrary, we can make much more sense of valuation processes if we recognise that value, and the theories of value deployed by ordinary actors, plays a central role in them.

Valuation and Power

We must also, however, look beyond the processes in which theories of value are deployed to the social forces that shape those theories of value in the first place. As Aspers and Beckert put it, research in valuation studies

has taken a perspective that is largely rooted in science studies and in cultural sociology. It is crucial to integrate political sociology much more strongly into this perspective, emphasizing the power-laden political struggles leading to the use of specific judgment devices... There is a *politics of classification* led by rent-seeking actors (Aspers & Beckert, 2010, p. 23)

I might word this a little differently: we must examine the power-laden political struggles leading to the use of specific theories of value; there is a *politics of valuation* led by rent-seeking actors (cf. the concept of the politics of value in Appadurai, 1988). But these formulations are very close: judgment devices include theories of value, and the politics of valuation overlaps strongly with the politics of classification. The core point is that certain economic actors, typically organisations, exert substantial power over valuation processes by influencing the predominant theories of value that we deploy and "also through the positioning of products under the *given* regime of devices prevailing in the markets" (Aspers & Beckert, 2010, p. 23).

We find similar themes in Bourdieu, with his concerns over how "unequal power relations, unrecognized as such and thus accepted as legitimate, are embedded in the systems of classification used to describe and discuss everyday life" (Johnson, 1993, p. 2), and also in the conventions tradition, which introduces the concept of valuation power (Eymard-Duvernay, 2011). As one conventions theorist puts it, "The politics of quantification and its critique is... the politics of choosing and thereby controlling the introduction and application of conventions and standards in markets and economic organizations" (Diaz-Bone, 2017, p. 248).

Often the organisations that produce and/or sell goods are able to exert significant power over this process, most obviously through advertising and marketing, but also by influencing government policies and media discourses related to the value of their products (Aspers & Beckert, 2010, p. 15; Beckert, 2016, p. 14). Many industries have also developed an infrastructure of supposedly independent third parties to bolster the theories of value that relate to their products. In the art market, for example, Bourdieu (1993) "emphasizes the role of critics and evaluators" in shaping assessments of the symbolic value of cultural goods (Lamont, 2012, p. 207) and their views on symbolic value strongly influence the economic value of those goods (Boltanski & Esquerre, 2016, p. 47). In this context, and no doubt many others, one very powerful theory of value is that products that are endorsed as having high cultural value by those who are consecrated as experts in the field should have a higher price.

As Aspers and Beckert imply in the quote with which I opened this section, too many scholars of valuation ignore the power of producers and third parties to influence lay theories of value, but it is perhaps even more common to forget the *publics* at which this power is directed, not as individuals but as the *audience* for the discursive work that is done to build support for specific theories and classifications. As normative devices, the causal influence of lay theories of value depends on the size, reach and strength of influence of the *norm circles* that support them, and the discursive power of these other actors is only effective when it succeeds in building those norm circles. The implication of this book, developed in the next chapter, is that valuation studies requires a broadening of perspective parallel to Stuart Hall's introduction of the active audience into research on media effects (Hall, 1973). Even Hall's version of the "old" media model, though, perhaps takes us only part of the way, since it is still essentially a story of top-down influence. Perhaps we need to look instead to parallels with the new media model, in which the public is no longer only a target of media influence but an independent population with its own beliefs and inputs to the process.

Conclusion

This chapter has argued that we need to think about the concept of value very differently than the writers discussed in the previous chapter. The value of a thing is not an objective quantity preserved unchanged from the moment of its production throughout its journey through the commodity system, nor is it a systemic quantity arising from the forces of price equilibration. Rather, it is the price that it ought to exchange at, and this is a subjective quantity in the sense that different individuals may take different views of it, but also a socially constructed quantity in the sense that in doing so they draw on socially or intersubjectively shared lay theories of value. The study of value needs to examine how these theories then feed into processes of determining prices and making exchange decisions, but we must also examine the shaping of these theories themselves and of beliefs about when and in what circumstances they apply. At the academic level, this gives us a single second-order framework for thinking about economic value: value claims are claims about what prices ought to be. At the lay level, there is a vast pool of theories of value that are deployed and contested in negotiations over price.

Lay theories of value are norms, the influence of which depends on the size and strength of the norm circles that support them, and that in turn is the subject of a complex politics of value, with interested and powerful actors seeking to invent and manipulate the theories of value that their publics hold. These theories of value play a fundamental role in influencing economic activity in contemporary society, not just at the level of individual transactions but far more widely. Thus, for example, all lay theories of value operate to legitimate the system of buying and selling in general by bolstering the idea that monetary exchange at certain prices is a fair way of transferring goods between economic actors.

One consequence of the perspective outlined here that distinguishes it radically from objectivist approaches is that it entails that different (though potentially overlapping) sets of theories of value may operate in different sectors of the economy, and indeed that different sets of actors may influence these theories in different ways in different sectors. No doubt we could examine a broad range of sectors, but this book will be focussing on just one: the valuation of financial assets, which is of particular interest partly because the products themselves, as well as their valuations, are socially constructed – or, indeed, invented – and partly because of the disproportionate impact of these inventions on the contemporary economy.

4 | *Theories of Financial Value*

Financial value, as I use the term in this book, is the monetary value of a financial asset: a belief or claim about what it is worth. Financial assets (also known as securities or financial instruments) are effectively contracts that entitle the holder of the asset to some form of future payment. They include, for example, *stocks* or *shares* in limited companies (also known as *equity*), government or corporate debt instruments with fixed payment streams (*bonds*) and various forms of *derivatives*, which are contracts that entitle the holder to a future payment based on the price of some other financial asset or indicator, including *options* to buy or sell some other asset at a fixed price at a fixed future date. Financial assets may be represented in ledgers, on paper certificates and/or in computerised records, but it is the legal entitlement to payment that is the asset rather than any material representation of it. They are therefore thoroughly socially constructed, in the sense that these entitlements depend utterly on there being a system of agreements about legal rights and material systems of recording such rights using systems of symbols. This in turn means that they are also heavily dependent on legal systems, and on the ways in which those legal systems have been manipulated over the centuries in the interests of the wealthy and powerful, as Katharina Pistor has recently argued (Pistor, 2019).

Most or all of what was said in the previous chapter about economic value in general also applies to financial value. But there are also further things we can say about financial value that arise from the distinctive nature of financial assets and thus the distinctive mechanisms that contribute to establishing their value. In particular, the point of purchasing a financial asset is usually that it is expected to provide the purchaser with future revenue streams – perhaps dividend payments from equity, or coupon payments from bonds, or redemption payments when a time-limited asset comes to maturity, or the proceeds from selling on the asset at some point in the future. Hence the value of a financial asset is in some way a reflection of that future revenue stream, but like anything else in the future, such revenue streams are inherently uncertain. As a result, the value of financial assets is particularly sensitive to opinions about the future, which in turn are profoundly influenced by discursive structures: socially preferred ways of talking, writing and thus thinking.

Academic understandings of financial value are dominated by the marginalist tradition of mainstream economics, and so this chapter begins by explaining the profound inadequacy of this approach to financial value. Unlike Chapter 2, there is no section on the equivalent Marxist theories. Marxists have many interesting things to say about the finance sector more generally, but their approach to financial value derives quite directly from the labour theory of value. The central point is that for Marxists value is a property of products that depends on the (socially necessary) amount of "productive" labour expended in their production, and they do not count labour in the financial sector as creating value at all (Lapavitsas, 2013, pp. 4, 11, 108, 127). Hence financial assets, on this account, cannot really have value. Instead, any revenue earned in the finance sector is seen as a deduction from real value produced or stored elsewhere in the economy, and the notion of financial value is an oxymoron. The entire finance sector, by implication, is parasitical on the rest of the economy. Logically, of course, Marxists could still have theories of the prices of financial assets, but they would have to be distinct from their theory of value. Hence Marxist theories of value cannot help us to explain how financial values, prices or profits are determined.

Instead, the chapter goes on to outline a theory of financial value based on more recent contributions from the literature, notably André Orléan's work on financial valuation conventions, Pierre Bourdieu's work on symbolic value and Jens Beckert's work on fictional expectations. It then engages a little more critically with recent work on the idea that economics plays a performative role in the finance sector. This chapter and the previous two provide a constructively critical review of the literature on value and financial value, but they also piece together what is in effect my theoretical hypothesis, which is supplemented with an ontological hypothesis in the next chapter and then tested by applying it to empirical cases in the later chapters of the book.

The Uncertain Value of Financial Assets

Mainstream economists embrace the idea that financial value is a function of future revenue streams. According to the standard textbook treatment, the value of a financial asset is the *net present value* of the stream of future payments that it provides access to. Some financial instruments such as government bonds provide a known and more or less guaranteed stream of payments, and in cases like these it is possible to predict the revenue for the entire life of the asset. But even in these cases it is usually assumed that purchasers prefer money today to the same amount of money at some point in the future, and so the present value of a revenue stream is not simply the total of all future payments. Instead, to calculate the present value of a revenue stream, future payments are discounted – they are reduced by an interest rate known as the discount rate (Varian, 2010, p. 192). So if, for example, the discount rate was 5 per cent per annum a payment of $100 in a year's time would be valued at $95 today and a payment of $100 in two years' time would be valued at a little over $90 today. Once all of the future payments that an asset's holder is entitled to have been discounted to present values, they can be added up to give the net present value of the asset itself.

The revenue streams from most financial assets, however, are rather uncertain. The long-term revenue streams from stocks or shares in a company, for example, depend on the level of dividend payment declared each year by the company, and this in turn depends on a range of factors including how profitable the company has been. Since the future profits of a company are uncertain, their future dividends are also uncertain. The mainstream deals with this by using what Orléan calls the "probabilistic postulate" (Orléan, 2014, p. 178). This involves treating returns at each future point in time as being ranged across a number of possible values, with a probability attached to each of the possible values, producing a probability distribution of possible returns. The hypothetical investors in this model then calculate the average of these possible outcomes and add up the averages for each expected future payment to provide a predicted net present value of the asset, and they also calculate the variability of the set of outcomes to give an indicator of the riskiness of the asset (Varian, 2010, pp. 236–237). Because investors are generally taken to be risk-averse, assets with a riskier revenue stream are taken to have a reduced value compared to assets with the same present value but a less risky revenue stream. Once this has been adjusted for, the marginalist theory predicts that asset markets will stabilise at a set of price levels where "all assets, after adjusting for risk, have to earn the same rate of return" (Varian, 2010, p. 244).

The marginalist view is that this stabilisation will occur because asset prices will move under the influence of supply and demand to a point where price equilibrium is achieved. While there are external factors that may lead to new assets being put on the market, much of the buying and selling of financial assets is a kind of recycling of existing assets to new owners, and so in this context both buyers and sellers are assessing prices on the same basis. Although different investors will often assess the value of a given asset differently, at the equilibrium point all those investors who think the net present value of the asset exceeds its current price will be holding it, while investors who disagree will not. If the price of an asset was higher, so the theory goes, then some asset holders would want to sell but there would be no others willing to buy and so the price would drop to a level where its price matched the adjusted net present value as assessed by the marginal investor (and vice versa if the price was lower). The marginalist theory of financial value is thus a variation of its theory of commodity values, with the same abstract forces of supply and demand operating, but different factors (expected monetary returns rather than the utility of consuming the item) influencing demand. The implication is that financial markets reconcile the varying assessments of value by different investors by finding an equilibrium price at which all investors can take positions consistent with their valuations.

One might expect that more sophisticated marginalists would depart from the textbook model in ways that injected more realism into their analysis, but remarkably the opposite seems to be the case. One influential group of financial economists advocates what is known as the "efficient markets hypothesis", which argues that the forces of demand and supply do lead the prices of securities to converge on their "intrinsic value" – the net present value of the associated revenue stream (Fama, 1965, 1970, 1991). They accept that different investors may have different views of the value of a security, but also believe that there is one correct intrinsic value of the security at any given time and that, subject to random short-term variations, markets rapidly arrive at prices that reflect all publicly available information about that intrinsic value (Fama, 1965, p. 4). This, in other words, is an objectivist theory of financial value. As Orléan puts it, "At the heart of this ... is a crucial and all but unspoken assumption... that the value of a financial security is wholly independent of the opinion of investors" (Orléan, 2014, p. 189) (for good critiques of the efficient markets hypothesis see Beckert, 2016, pp. 39–42, 144–147; Cassidy, 2010, pp. 86–96, 177–186; Orléan, 2014, pp. 181–189).

This theory of financial value, however, is deeply problematic. The first problem, widely known in the critical literature, is that the probabilistic postulate is false: many kinds of uncertainty cannot be calculated away by expressing them as a probability distribution. Frank Knight famously distinguished between risk, which is potentially calculable because we can know the probabilities of the different possible outcomes (e.g. when we throw a dice), and uncertainty, which is not calculable because we cannot know these probabilities (Beckert, 2016, pp. 43–45; Orléan, 2014, pp. 191–193). In the latter case, attempts to convert uncertainty about the future into a probability distribution just magnify the problem – instead of one uncertain outcome, a whole range of uncertain probabilities must now be predicted. The returns on most financial assets are subject to this kind of uncertainty rather than calculable risk, and "In a world characterized by radical uncertainty... it is impossible to determine the true value of a security" (Orléan, 2014, p. 195).

This brings us to the second major problem. Although revenue streams cannot be reliably predicted, even on a probabilistic basis, the value of a security still depends on the investor's expectations about those revenue streams. But once the illusion of predictability has been shattered, marginalist theory has nothing to say about how those expectations are formed. The extraordinary consequence is that the marginalist theory of financial value ends up leaving out the single most important set of factors that influence the price of financial assets.

A third problem is that the marginalist tradition assumes perfect information – it assumes that everyone is fully aware of all of the options available to them and understands the costs and benefits of every option. But in reality most economic actors are unaware of the very existence of the vast majority of financial assets, let alone their prices and the revenue streams they might provide access to.

Furthermore, net present value calculations are time-consuming and require a certain level of technical expertise, and many potential investors have neither the time nor the skills to perform them. Hence in practice "investors in financial markets do not necessarily seek to assess future earnings" (Beckert, 2016, p. 146). Many investment decisions are made on the basis of much cruder analyses of expected revenue streams. For example, investors may buy an asset because they think the price will go up or sell it because they think the price will go down. Although some professional investors may base such views on detailed knowledge and analysis, this is much less common amongst private investors. In practice, forming a view of the future direction of an asset's price requires little or no understanding of any other revenue stream or any analytical technique, but it may be all that investors need to guide their investment decisions. In practice different investors have varying levels of awareness of markets, varying levels of knowledge about the assets being traded, varying degrees of sophistication in understanding of the issues, and apply a broad range of theories of value. Furthermore, any given investor will have varying levels of knowledge about different financial assets. Rather than assuming away these complexities, a coherent theory of financial value must address the range of ways in which investors actually do assess the value of financial assets.

Economists have made some steps towards recognising this third problem in discussions of what they call "noise traders". The core argument is that many unsophisticated private investors act on limited and poor quality information, which then causes distortions in the market that cannot be ironed out by professional arbitrageurs because the noise traders may hold their positions long enough to impose losses on the professionals (De Long, Shleifer, Summers & Waldmann, 1990). In a nice example in early 2021, a group of private traders aligned with a Reddit discussion group drove up the price of stocks in the US retailer GameStop, imposing massive losses on hedge funds that had taken large short positions on the stock (Aliaj, Mackenzie & Fletcher, 2021). The "noise trader" concept remains problematic, though, because it treats speculative behaviour that conflicts with traditional notions of intrinsic value as driven by irrational private investors, whereas, as we shall see in the chapters on venture capital and structured securities below, professional investors at major financial institutions also drive such valuations.

Financial Valuation Conventions

For a more satisfactory discussion of financial value, we need to turn to the English economist John Maynard Keynes, and in particular his book *The General Theory of Employment, Interest and Money*, first published in 1936 (Keynes, 1973). Keynes recognises from the outset that when it comes to estimating the value of investments "[t]he outstanding fact is the extreme precariousness of the basis of know-ledge on which our estimates of prospective yield have to be made" (Keynes, 1973, p. 149). Given this precariousness, he says, "those who seriously attempt to make any such estimate are often so much in the minority that their behaviour does not govern the market" (Keynes, 1973, p. 150). Instead,

In practice we have tacitly agreed, as a rule, to fall back on what is, in truth, a *convention*. The essence of this convention – though it does not, of course, work out quite so simply – lies in assuming that the existing state of affairs will continue indefinitely, except in so far as we have specific reasons to expect a change (Keynes, 1973, p. 152 emphasis in original).

In other words, people tend to assume that things will continue much as they have in the recent past and base their estimates of a security's value on this. If, for example, a certain company has paid a dividend of 3 per cent of its stock price for the last few years, investors will tend to assume that it will continue to do so unless there has been some significant news that affects the company's prospects. Keynes explicitly calls this a convention, and in my terms this is a financial valuation convention or a lay theory of financial value: according to this conven-tion, the value of a stock is the net present value of the long-term income stream we would expect if things carry on as they have done in the recent past.

But Keynes is also conscious that not all investors value stocks in the same way. Many investors, and an increasing proportion of them, take little interest in the underlying long-term stream of revenue from a stock, and instead focus on much shorter-term price variations. Rather than valuing a stock in terms of future dividends, they value it on the basis of what price they think they may be able to sell it for in a relatively short period of time (Keynes, 1973, pp. 154–155). Here he introduces a metaphor that has come to be known as the *beauty contest*, comparing investment to:

those newspaper competitions in which the competitors have to pick out the six prettiest faces from a hundred photographs, the prize being awarded to the competitor whose choice most nearly corresponds to the average preferences of the competitors as a whole; so that each competitor has to pick, not those faces which he himself finds prettiest, but those which he thinks likeliest to catch the fancy of the other competitors, all of whom are looking at the problem from the same point of view (Keynes, 1973, p. 156).

In the context of investment, what this means is that investors try to anticipate how other investors will value a stock, and then buy those stocks that they expect to go up in price on this basis. Although Keynes himself does not use the term *convention* in this context, we can think of this as another financial valuation convention, or theory of value: the value of a stock depends on the price we expect other investors will be willing to pay for it in the short-term future.

This way of looking at valuation, incidentally, suggests a need to revisit my definition of value as the price that a thing *ought* to exchange at. So far I have stressed that this *ought* should be interpreted ethically: the value of a thing is a fair price for it, perhaps for example because the price reflects the benefits the product provides to a purchaser. In the case of financial assets, for example, we might say that the price of a security ought to reflect the benefits it is expected to deliver in terms of future revenues. But *ought* can also be used differently. If a convention is well established, we can expect buyers to value securities on the basis of it and therefore we can say that the price of a security *ought*, in a predictive rather than an ethical sense, to converge on the price implied by the convention. Once we start to value assets in terms of their expected future price movements, these two senses may coincide in quantitative but not semantic terms. Ethically, the price of a security *ought* to reflect the benefits it can bring to its purchaser and those benefits are determined by the price at which it can be sold, which buyers expect *ought* to converge upon the price predicted by the convention. Both *oughts* (in this case) produce the same quantitative estimates of the value of the security.

André Orléan links Keynes's work to the economics of conventions in his recent work on financial markets. He rejects objectivist theories of value – what he calls *substance* theories – and instead sees value as depending on personal judgement and *mimesis*, which refers to influence from others and a tendency to imitate others. In the context of value, one implication of mimesis is that people tend to think that something is valuable when they see that others think it is valuable, and therefore they pay careful attention to other people's valuations. There is a close parallel here to Keynes's beauty contest metaphor, but he generalises the argument further. People do not only pay careful attention to other people's valuations but also to the principles that other people use to make their valuations. This becomes "a powerfully and durably stabilizing force if one interpretation of events ends up receiving the general support of the market. In that case a model of valuation emerges that everyone recognizes as legitimate – what I will call a valuation convention" (Orléan, 2014, p. 228). One benefit of such conventions is that investors can use them to predict other investors' valuations, thus simplifying the process of anticipating market movements. If enough people accept the convention and make their buying and selling decisions on the basis of it, those predictions will tend to be accurate, which in turn sustains belief in the convention. But "Once the actual results of a certain investment depart too far from the prevailing picture of the world, however, the multiplication of anomalies eventually causes the market to renounce the convention in question and cast around for another" (Orléan, 2014, p. 228).

Orléan illustrates the argument using the internet bubble on the US stock exchanges, which burst in 2000. The bubble was based on the convention that internet companies could be valued on the basis of the number of visitors they attracted to their websites, in the belief that they would eventually be able to find a way to make money from those visitors, and this convention was used to value even companies that were making a substantial loss and had no clear plan for turning this into a profit. At a certain point in 2000, however, enough investors doubted this convention to cause the price of internet stocks to drop, and once others realised that the convention was no longer holding the bubble burst and prices tumbled dramatically (Orléan, 2014, p. 228) (also see Cassidy, 2002).

From a different strand of heterodox economics, Robert Shiller has argued that investors use an "ever-changing pool of popular theories and models" to make trading decisions, in a context where many such models can be in circulation at the same time, although they are unable to make "a proper decision-theoretic analysis of the evidence for all these competing models" (Shiller, 1990, p. 62). This leaves us in need of a more sociological explanation of *which* models they tend to use and why.

Jens Beckert has developed an overlapping argument in his important book *Imagined Futures* that helps to answer this question (Beckert, 2016). Beckert argues that "under conditions of uncertainty, expectations are contingent and should be understood as 'fictional expectations'" (Beckert, 2013, p. 323). These are views of the future that are fictional, not in the sense of being false, but in the sense of taking the form of speculative narratives, stories that we construct in the absence of a firm factual foundation (Beckert, 2013, p. 325). Although these fictions describe an inherently unknown future they are often treated as if they were reliable (Beckert, 2016, p. 62). They are held by individuals but influenced by the structural context:

under conditions of fundamental uncertainty, expectations cannot be understood as being determined through calculation of optimal choices taking into account all available information, but rather are based on contingent interpretations of the situation in the context of prevailing institutional structures, cultural templates, and social networks (Beckert, 2013, p. 325).

At least some of the narratives that underpin these expectations are valuation conventions or lay theories of value. Beckert goes beyond Keynes and Orléan, though, in examining the social causes and the politics that lie behind these narratives. "If expectations are contingent, if decisions depend on expectations, and if the decisions of others influence outcomes, then actors have an interest in influencing the expectations of other actors" (Beckert, 2016, p. 80). There is a politics of expectations and there are considerable rewards to be had by shaping the expectations of other actors: "Stories are told by all market participants in order to influence investors' confidence that markets will develop in a certain direction" (Beckert, 2016, p. 82). Charles Smith illustrates the point nicely with his account of the various narratives told by stockbrokers to persuade their clients to buy and sell stock, with the result that the broker earns a commission (C. W. Smith, 1999, Chapters 8–12).

Like Orléan, Beckert is looking more widely than just financial markets, but he does also apply his argument explicitly to the financial sector. "Financial markets", he says, "... are 'markets in stories'. Stories turn fundamental uncertainty into confidence, and thus function as placeholders that make it possible to act when outcomes cannot be known" (Beckert, 2016, p. 148). Financial markets depend completely on collective beliefs about financial value, and those beliefs themselves come from narratives "of how and why the prices of indexes, stocks, commodities, or bonds will develop" (Beckert, 2016, p. 150). These narratives in turn are produced (to serve their own interests) by a broad range of actors, including the companies and governments issuing the securities, investment banks, analysts, ratings agencies, stockbrokers, influential investors, the media, academics and governments. And the most successful of these stories become valuation conventions – a term that he adopts directly from Orléan (Beckert, 2016, p. 151).

The lessons from the conventions literature are clear: financial value depends on conventions, which are specific to particular markets and historical periods, rising when they secure the support of significant groups of market actors, and falling when they cease to predict prices reasonably accurately.

From Symbolic Value to Financial Value

Financial value, then, depends on symbolic narratives that claim certain qualities for the assets concerned and seek to associate them with particular theories of value. Hence, we can usefully draw on work on symbolic value more generally, notably that of Pierre Bourdieu. Although he is occasionally acknowledged (Lamont, 2012, p. 207), a great deal of work on conventions theory and the sociology of valuation seems to ignore Bourdieu. Orléan, for example, does not mention Bourdieu at all in *The Empire of Value*, and Lamont suggests that some of the work in the conventions tradition has even been framed in opposition to Bourdieu's legacy (Lamont, 2012, p. 207). Despite this, much of the work in valuation studies clearly replicates and develops themes from Bourdieu's work.

Bourdieu develops his account of symbolic value most completely in the papers collected in *The Field of Cultural Production* (Bourdieu, 1993). His focus here is on the art world (including not just fine art but also, for example, literature and theatre), and the ways in which cultural products are valued – not primarily in economic but rather in aesthetic terms, although Bourdieu is always aware of the relation between the two. Nevertheless, much of his argument can be transposed very straightforwardly to the financial sector. The most relevant parts of his argument are encapsulated in one passage:

Given that works of art exist as symbolic objects only if they are known and recognized, that is, socially instituted as works of art and received by spectators capable of knowing and recognizing them as such, the sociology of art and literature has to take as its object not only the material production but also the symbolic production of the work, i.e. the production of the value of the work or, which amounts to the same thing, of belief in the value of the work. It therefore has to consider as contributing to production not only the direct producers of the work in its materiality (artist, writer, etc.) but also the producers of the meaning and value of the work – critics, publishers, gallery directors and the whole set of agents whose combined efforts produce consumers capable of knowing and recognizing the work of art as such, in particular teachers (but also families, etc) (Bourdieu, 1993, p. 37).

For Bourdieu, the aesthetic value of a work of art is not determined by any objective quality of the work but by how it is positioned in a symbolic field of cultural appreciation, and this in turn depends on a whole infrastructure of participants in the field of cultural production.

The parallels with the financial sector are clear, as can be seen by substituting financial terms into Bourdieu's argument: financial assets exist as viable investments only if they are known and recognised as such by investors, and so the sociology of financial value must study not only the creation of financial assets but also the symbolic production of their value or, which amounts to the same thing, of belief in their value. It therefore has to consider as contributing to production not only the issuers of securities but also the producers of the meaning and value of the securities – analysts, ratings agencies, bankers and the whole set of agents whose combined efforts produce investors capable of knowing and recognising financial assets and their value.

This process is achieved primarily through discourse, by which I mean not simply narratives but narratives that come to be widely accepted as authoritative (Elder-Vass, 2011). As Bourdieu says about artistic work "one has to be blind not to see that discourse about a work is not a mere accompaniment, intended to assist its perception and appreciation, but a stage in the production of the work, of its meaning and value" (Bourdieu, 1993, p. 110), and the same argument applies just as strongly to financial assets and the invention of their value.

Perhaps one reason that the pragmatist tendency in valuation has disregarded Bourdieu is that, by comparison with most (though not all) pragmatists, he pays far more attention to the significance of social power and prestige in this process. Cultural entrepreneurs such as art dealers, theatre producers and publishers of literary fiction, but also critics, are constantly engaged in a struggle to establish and maintain a reputation that gives them the authority, framed as a kind of cultural wisdom, to consecrate works as having aesthetic value. Those critics and cultural entrepreneurs who achieve this symbolic authority then collaborate "in the effort of consecration which makes the reputation and, at least in the long term, the monetary value of works" (Bourdieu, 1993, p. 78). But Bourdieu also recognises that "among the makers of the work of art, we must finally include the public, which helps to make its value by appropriating it materially (collectors) or symbolically (audiences, readers)" (Bourdieu, 1993, p. 78). He thus recognises that symbolic value depends not only on the creators but also the consumers of discourses – there is no value without an audience, a public, a circle, that accepts these value claims – and indeed that the work of creating artistic value also operates by building these audiences.

Like much of Bourdieu's work, this formulation would benefit from more recognition of the autonomy of audiences, but with this qualification the argument again applies equally well to financial value. Investment banks, analysts, ratings agencies and the like are what I will call *value entrepreneurs* who strive constantly to establish and maintain a reputation that gives them the authority, framed as a kind of financial wisdom, to consecrate securities as having financial value (I use the term a little differently than Barman, for whom value entrepreneurs are those who innovate in the measurement of value: 2016, pp. 20, 22). Those actors who achieve this symbolic authority then collaborate in the effort of consecration that invents the monetary value of financial assets. But this value also depends on having an audience of investors that is capable of understanding their efforts and, to go beyond Bourdieu, a section of this audience that is willing to accept these value claims – and the work of creating financial value also operates by building this group.

It is not just a happy accident that Bourdieu's analysis of symbolic value in the cultural field parallels the processes that establish value in the financial field so closely. While the fields are different, the processes through which value is established in both are fundamentally homologous. In both cases this is a symbolic process in which actors embedded in positions of power in the field employ that power to construct discourses that attribute value to the objects that are the focus of the field.

How to Make Financial Instruments Valuable

Recent work in valuation studies allows us to go beyond these framings to look more closely at the processes through which financial value is established. Perhaps the starting point, once a product has been designed in the first place, is establishing it as something that is legitimately saleable. Financial products may seem like a perfectly respectable thing to purchase in contemporary society but it was not always so, and need not necessarily be so in the future. As Marieke de Goede has shown "less than two centuries ago [finance] stood condemned as irreputable gambling and fraud" (Goede, 2005, p. ix) and some futures trading was legally considered gambling in the United States as recently as the 1970s (MacKenzie, 2006, pp. 14–15, 144–145). Yet the outcome of centuries of discursive and political work by the finance sector is that today financial investments are perfectly acceptable morally and indeed regarded as a necessity in certain social groups (Goede, 2005).

Legitimacy, however, is only the first step in establishing a financial instrument as a worthwhile asset: potential buyers must also think of it as having value, and this means that the instrument must be linked to a theory of value that provides them with a reason to believe it may be valuable and a means to estimate that value. Often the most viable way of doing this is to position the asset as falling under an existing theory of value or a closely related variant (cf. Aspers & Beckert, 2010, p. 23). The product must come to be classified in a way that aligns it as part of, or at least similar to, an existing product category. This can be achieved by building and spreading narratives that make these connections, but this is easier when the instruments concerned already share some relevant characteristics with the target category, and this in turn is a factor in the design of instruments – they can deliberately be given features that will support the case for linking them to the desired category. The general process of qualification or classification of products has been a central focus of both the economics of convention and the sociological work that it has influenced. Callon and his colleagues, for example, point out that "economic agents devote a large share of their resources to positioning the products they design, produce, distribute or consume, in relation to others" (Callon et al., 2002, p. 196). Callon is primarily concerned here with how producing firms and other intermediaries try to position commodities as potential substitutes for others but also as sufficiently distinctive from others that they should not be substituted (Callon et al., 2002, p. 201). Nevertheless, this argument can be transposed to financial markets where it becomes relevant to the question of how financial instruments come to be seen as valuable.

The benefits of aligning a financial instrument with a particular category are nicely illustrated in Ezra Zuckerman's paper on the coverage of US stocks by securities analysts (E. W. Zuckerman, 1999). In a detailed quantitative study, Zuckerman found that "the stock price of an American firm was discounted to the extent that the firm was not covered by the securities analysts who specialized in its industries" (E. W. Zuckerman, 1999, p. 1398). Unlike most more recent discussions of valuation, Zuckerman places audiences centre stage. For a security to attract a strong valuation in a market, there must be an audience that values it and the security must attract the interest of that audience (E. W. Zuckerman, 1999, p. 1403). In many markets, including many financial markets, critics "replace consumers as the primary audience that determines the fate of products" (E. W. Zuckerman, 1999, p. 1400), and in the case of stock markets analysts who publish reports on the value of stocks in the sector that they cover are particularly crucial to the reputations of those stocks with investors and hence the value that they ascribe to them. A firm whose stocks are not classified by these analysts as belonging to the sector in which it primarily operates is therefore unlikely in principle to be as highly valued as one that is, and Zuckerman's study shows that this is indeed the case in practice (E. W. Zuckerman, 1999, p. 1424).

Disputes over the categorisation of firms can be of considerable importance to their value, particularly when this affects the theories of value that are taken to apply to their stock. This is very clear in Beunza and Garud's study of disputes between US stock market analysts on the value of the internet retailer Amazon.com during the period of the internet bubble (1998–2000) (Beunza & Garud, 2007). They compare three disputes, in which an analyst who classified Amazon as an internet company consistently valued the company's stock much higher than two other analysts who classified it as a retailer. As a consequence, he predicted higher revenue growth, higher future margins and therefore higher stock prices than the other analysts. Beunza and Garud explain this difference by saying that these analysts were applying different "calculative frames" to the company's stock, where a calculative frame includes "categorizations, analogies and key metrics" (Beunza & Garud, 2007, p. 14). Another way of looking at this is to say that these analysts were arguing about what theory of value should be used to value Amazon's stock, and we can break the argument down into two issues – an issue of categorisation, and an issue of espousing a particular theory of value for stock in a particular category. The more positive analyst was involved in developing ("frame-making") and applying the theory of value picked out by Orléan in his analysis of the internet bubble, while the others were applying a more conservative theory (Beunza & Garud, 2007, p. 27).

Analysts and similar intermediaries such as ratings agencies play a critical role in establishing the symbolic value of securities (Beckert, 2016, p. 122), but despite the importance of this audience of intermediaries, there must also be a secondary audience of actual investors at which the construction of this value is targeted. Ultimately the value of a security depends on there being investors willing to purchase it at the going price, and the process of constructing financial value therefore includes the creation of an audience at *both* of these levels. This is an issue that is largely ignored in marginalist theory, as the assumption of perfect information implies that all market actors are fully knowledgeable potential purchasers in all markets. But in practice most of us ignore many products, never knowing what they might be able to do for us and therefore never considering at all whether to buy them, and this is particularly true of financial assets. Making financial instruments into valuable assets therefore requires making people and/or institutions aware of them and of how to buy them – producing investors capable of knowing and recognising financial assets and their value, as I put it earlier. Just as the art market depends on an audience that possesses "the code into which it has been encoded" (Johnson, 1993, p. 23), the financial markets depend on an audience that possesses the expertise required to make judgements on the value of financial assets and to make deals on assets that they decide to purchase.

A number of privatisation initiatives provide particularly clear cases of the active construction of such audiences by value entrepreneurs: economic actors who deliberately seek to construct an asset as having value by promoting valuation narratives to relevant audiences. In the 1980s, for example, the UK government launched major advertising campaigns, notably the "Tell Sid" campaign related to the privatisation of British Gas, that encouraged hundreds of thousands of people, many of whom had never bought shares before, to subscribe to the issue of shares in the privatised company (BBC News, 2011). In the 1990s the German government pursued a similar strategy for the privatisation of Deutsche Telekom, "promoting its shares as 'Volksaktien' or 'people's shares', encouraging lots of small investors to get involved and helping to establish a stock investment culture in Germany" (Hornby, 2007). More recently the government of Kenya made heavy use of advertising "to stimulate share ownership among new, domestic investors in the frontier stock exchange in Kenya" (Yenkey, 2010, p. 247). This was linked to initial public offerings of shares in privatised companies from 2005 onwards, in a context where even the more prosperous sections of the general public didn't know much about the firms, their performance or how to value them. The state therefore used "mass advertising campaigns . . . to persuade inexperienced investors that share ownership represents an opportunity for upward social mobility" (Yenkey, 2010, p. 249). These campaigns broke down barriers to investing in financial assets in general by encouraging people to think that investing might be profitable for them personally and that it is something they would be able to do. But they also focused the attention of potential investors on particular investment opportunities that were made easily accessible to them, and encouraged them to see those investments as good value. These efforts brought these securities to the attention of a wider audience, but in a sense their objective was to construct what I will call an *asset circle*: a group of people and/or organisations who see these securities as worthwhile investments that they might realistically be prepared to purchase (asset circles are explained in more depth in the next chapter).

Similar processes are also used to build asset circles amongst professional investors. We can see this, for example, in Emily Barman's fascinating account of the growth of *impact investing*, "investment with the intentional expectation of social or environmental impact alongside financial return", since 2007 (Barman, 2015, p. 9). This is very much a political project – a neoliberal-style attempt to substitute market funding of social projects in place of the state and civil society, particularly in the context of developing countries (Barman, 2015, p. 10). But my interest here is in the way it has been driven, primarily by the Rockefeller Foundation, which observers see as "the 'architect' of this new financial market" (Barman, 2015, p. 19). This is a market where the investors are primarily large funds managed by investment professionals responding to demands for ethical investment, and the consequence is that these investors want to evaluate potential investments simultaneously on two different dimensions. On the one hand they want to make investments that will be profitable, while on the other they want some way of assessing the social or environmental impact that distinguishes this class of investments and provides it with its distinctive legitimacy, its unique selling point that attracts investors to this market. Barman traces the ways in which the Rockefeller Foundation built interest in the market by helping to develop new valuation standards for the non-financial benefits delivered by the companies whose shares were traded in this market – standards that were modelled on "existing market device[s] in traditional capital markets" such as the ratings systems operated by agencies like Moody's or Standard and Poor's (Barman, 2015, p. 33) and which enacted a complex new mixed theory of value for this set of securities. The consequence was that investors were able to assess the non-financial value of these securities more easily, which in turn helped to build an asset circle of investors prepared to invest in them. By 2014 investments in the market exceeded $10 billion (Barman, 2015, p. 15).

These examples already illustrate some of the ways in which power operates in the politics of value. We have seen how analysts, governments and private foundations shape the context of valuation in a variety of ways, including, but not restricted to, the formulation and advocacy of theories of financial value. These are among the key actors in what Beckert calls the *politics of expectations* (Beckert, 2016, p. 84). Certain actors benefit from the same kind of symbolic status in the financial markets that Bourdieu discussed in the art market. As Beckert puts it,

predictions from influential investors or analysts about future prices in commodity or currency markets are not more or less certain than from other analysts, but their authority and the investments they command in the respective markets mean that the stories they tell are more likely to shape investor expectations, and in this way to shape investment decisions (Beckert, 2016, p. 84).

Different actors back different stories, endorsing different theories of value, but some actors have more power than others to influence investors. As well as the direct participants in the financial sector, significant discursive power is exercised by the mass media, which influences public opinion about the state of the economy, for example, but also by the financial press, which is more likely to influence participants in the finance sector itself (Beckert, 2016, p. 123). Both companies that are valued and other market actors seek to influence the media and other intermediaries through, for example, roadshows, conferences and press releases (Beckert, 2016, p. 157). The politics of value is a complex web of competing interests and techniques used to advance them, and one focus of the later chapters of this book will be to disentangle some small parts of this web.

Performativity

Recent work in social studies of finance has emphasised another set of actors that may influence the politics of value: academics themselves, and in particular economists, whose contribution to the valuation of financial assets has been labelled *performative* by Donald MacKenzie (MacKenzie, 2006). MacKenzie takes the concept of performativity from the work of Michel Callon, but it comes originally from the philosopher J. L. Austin (Donald, MacKenzie, Muniesa & Siu, 2007, p. 3). Austin defined *performative utterances* as statements that do things simply by being uttered (Austin, 1962). A classic example is promises. By saying "I promise to ..." one does not describe a promise but actually makes it, as long as the words are uttered in an appropriate context. It is perhaps surprising that Callon, with his links to actor-network theory, adopts the language of performativity, which seems to entail a kind of collapse of causal complexity that clashes with the spirit of actor-network theory (and indeed with the kind of realism that I favour), and as we shall see, most doubts about performativity theory in the economic context spring from that collapse.

Callon uses the concept to make the point that "economics, in the broad sense of the term, performs, shapes and formats the economy, rather than observing how it functions" (Callon, 1998, p. 2). He gives a number of examples including Polanyi's argument that economic theory influenced the design of "free markets" in nineteenth-century England (Callon, 1998, p. 2) and the case of an official who designed a wholesale strawberry market in rural France under the influence of his economics textbooks (Callon, 1998, p. 22). His reference to the "broad" sense of economics means that he also includes other "disciplines and practices like accounting or marketing" (Callon, 1998, p. 28) in his definition. Thus accounting tools and practices, designed under the influence of economics, become a further example of the ways in which economics shapes the economy it purports to describe. The link to Austinian performativity is extremely loose – the textbook clearly does not bring about the strawberry market merely by being written – but a larger problem is that advocates of performativity sometimes express the argument in sweeping rhetorical terms, suggesting in particular that economics *creates* the phenomena it describes and so cannot be judged in terms of the quality of its attempt to represent and explain those phenomena (Curran, 2018, p. 497). These claims turn out to be rather overblown when they come to the details, at which point they tend to qualify the argument more carefully but without withdrawing the rhetoric. The development of the strawberry market, for example, also requires "material and metrological investments, property rights and money, but we should not forget the essential contribution of economics in the performing of the economy" (Callon, 1998, p. 23). This does not prevent other scholars from repeating the claim that economics "performs" the economy when a more plausible conclusion from Callon's argument would be to say that economists sometimes have some causal influence, amongst many other factors, over what happens in the economy (though they may also sometimes exaggerate it: Mirowski & Nik-Kah, 2007).

MacKenzie applies the idea that economics is performative to financial economics and financial markets. "Financial economics", he writes, "did more than analyse markets; it altered them. It was an 'engine' … transforming its environment, not a camera passively recording it" (MacKenzie, 2006, p. 12). MacKenzie discusses a variety of possible meanings of performativity, notably what he calls Barnesian performativity, which he illustrates with the idea that an economic model might alter "economic processes or their outcomes … so that they better correspond to the model" (MacKenzie, 2006, p. 19). The central case discussed by MacKenzie is the effects of the

Black–Scholes–Merton formula for pricing stock options on options and futures markets. The formula was developed by three economists (two of whom were subsequently awarded the Nobel memorial prize for their work on it) in the early 1970s when options trading was still rather undeveloped (MacKenzie, 2006, p. 31). Although the formula was based on assumptions that were unrealistic at the time, market conditions changed (partly under the influence of market actors who were persuaded by the model) to fit more closely with the assumptions (MacKenzie, 2006, p. 142; MacKenzie & Millo, 2003, p. 130). In these conditions the formula offered a rational way to price stock options that became widely accepted as good practice – it was a lay theory of value (though with academic origins) that became a valuation convention.

The impacts of the formula, according to MacKenzie, were multiple. First, in the 1970s, options trading was heavily restricted by the regulatory regime in the United States, because it was still widely seen as a kind of gambling. The formula helped advocates of options trading resist moral disapproval and helped their case for reductions in regulation by breaking down this idea: if options could be priced rationally this seemed to distinguish their purchase from gambling (MacKenzie, 2006, pp. 158–159). Second, although the formula itself was complex and difficult to use on trading floors in its pure form, one of its authors (Black) developed tables printed on sheets of paper that traders could use to assess options prices on the basis of the theory, and at least some traders started to use these to inform their buying and selling on the trading floors of options exchanges (MacKenzie, 2006, pp. 160–162). Third, the formula helped traders to design hedging strategies that reduced the risks of options trades (MacKenzie, 2006, p. 164). Fourth, between 1976 and 1987, actual pricing of options appears to have conformed quite well to the values predicted by the formula, although after the major stock market crash of 1987 the match broke down, never to be restored (MacKenzie, 2006, p. 202; MacKenzie & Millo, 2003, p. 130). Since 1987, variants of the formula continued to be used (and integrated into computer-based pricing systems) as one element in options price setting, but with significant and rather variable adjustments to cover traders for volatility risks that the formula radically understates (MacKenzie & Millo, 2003, pp. 130–132).

During the period of the formula's greatest influence the scale of trading in options and other derivatives (which could in principle be valued using variations of the Black–Scholes–Merton formula) exploded. The average number of options traded per day on the Chicago Board Options Exchange increased from 84,972 in 1976 to 719,813 in 1987, although even this seriously understates the scale of the explosion because this period also saw the rise of over-the-counter derivatives trading outside the more controlled environment of the formal exchanges (Chicago Board Options Exchange, 2000, p. 58; Das, 2012, pp. 31–32). Indeed, this may be connected to a further effect of the formula: "It provides a systematic way to calculate the value of an option *before it matures*. Then it can be sold" (I. Stewart, 2012, p. 305). This made them a more liquid and thus a less risky investment, but this kind of calculability is also part of a process that makes it possible to present financial instruments in a company's accounts as assets, and it also makes it more straightforward for trading staff to justify their purchasing decisions to senior managers – all factors that smooth the way to much larger scale investment in the asset. Charles Smith found that traders rarely used the formula to make actual pricing decisions but nevertheless argues that "the exponential growth in option markets since the 1980s has been due in large measure to the general acceptance of the Black-Scholes-Merton option-pricing model" (C. W. Smith, 2010, p. 274). Still, MacKenzie could be right that the formula did heavily influence prices if, as he suggests, some market actors were engaging in arbitrage based on the formula, which could create an environment where the rules of thumb employed by other traders were influenced by the formula.

Whether or not prices did fit the formula during the period picked out by MacKenzie, it is clear that the Black–Scholes–Merton model had a massive impact on the market for stock options and probably on the markets for other derivatives. But does this mean that the model was performative in a meaningful sense? Certainly not in Austin's sense: stating the formula does not in itself bring about any of the effects we have discussed above. This is nothing like the performativity of a promise. Nor do economic formulae in general have an effect on the economy – most of them moulder away in rarely read books and papers with no impact whatsoever. Some may even have the opposite effect to that predicted in the formula – what MacKenzie calls "counterperformativity" (MacKenzie, 2006, pp. 259–260). As Fourcade says, "the mere availability of certain economic technologies does not guarantee their performative effects for the simple reason that these technologies may not muster enough institutional and political support" (Fourcade, 2011, pp. 1724–1725).

In other words, models, theories and techniques produced by economists and their colleagues in accounting and marketing may well contribute to events (including the determination of prices) in the finance sector or the economy more generally, but they do so only as one element in a much larger causal complex. The performativity framework can be contrasted here with the concept of discourse, which in some ways plays an analogous role in social constructionism. Performativity theory appears to attribute causal influence to theoretical statements, and perhaps to their original authors, whereas discourse theory and in particular realist discourse theory looks at the causal role of statements in terms of the interests they serve and the deployment of power in pursuit of those interests to spread the influence of the ideas concerned (Elder-Vass, 2012). Theories are causally significant only when they are plausible and credible, when they fit with the interests of important market actors, when they can be employed for useful practical purposes, when they can be embedded effectively in a wider institutional context and when significant work is done to spread their impact. As MacKenzie, but not all of those who invoke performativity, recognises, theories and models do not change the world on their own (MacKenzie & Millo, 2003, pp. 138–139); on the contrary, they contribute to change only to the extent that they are adopted and endorsed. To make sense of their influence we must focus more on who is adopting and endorsing them, on why they are doing so and on how these actors are able to influence others. All those other elements are equally causally significant, and the rhetoric of performativity can sometimes blunt the critical edge of the analysis when it distracts our attention from the social power and institutions that co-determine these outcomes.

Reinterpreting MacKenzie's work in the terms developed in this book, we may say that the Black–Scholes–Merton formula is an academic theory of value (a local theory in the sense that it is specific to option pricing) which came to be used as a lay theory of value in actual options markets. Part of its credibility as a theory of value derives from the symbolic capital that attaches to professional economists from elite institutions (Chicago and MIT in this case). But the continuation of that credibility arose because like some other lay theories of financial value, it seems to have become self-fulfilling for a while. As we have

seen in other cases, when enough market actors make valuation decisions based on a theory, those valuation decisions can come to dominate actual market prices. That does not entail that the theory itself was
"right" in any meaningful sense – and so the success of the Black–
Scholes–Merton formula does not validate the neoclassical economic
assumptions built into it – but only that it came to be accepted as a
convention for setting prices for a while. All such theories, however,
are specific to particular historical conjunctures, and at risk of being
abandoned when circumstances change.

Conclusion

This chapter has combined a critical engagement with the literature on
financial value with concepts from the previous chapter to begin
assembling a theory of financial value. Marginalist accounts ignore
the most important factors that influence financial value, above all how
market actors form their expectations about the future payment
streams that could be obtained from an asset. As a range of thinkers
including Keynes, Orléan and Beckert have shown, the value of financial assets is entirely dependent on the expectations that potential
investors have about these revenue streams and particularly the potential resale price of the asset. Those expectations in turn are shaped by
financial valuation conventions (or, in my terms, lay theories of financial value) like those identified by these thinkers. The application of
those conventions to particular assets, however, is often strongly
shaped by value entrepreneurs, who craft narratives of value for assets
they wish to promote (usually because they will profit from their
promotion). These value entrepreneurs are the financial equivalent of
the producers of meaning and value of works of art described by
Bourdieu – the elite participants in the field who are invested with the
symbolic authority to consecrate certain items with aesthetic value.

Existing theories of financial value have paid relatively little attention to the audiences to which these value narratives are told, but the
entire success or failure of value entrepreneurs rests upon whether they
are able to use those narratives to develop *asset circles* for the assets
concerned: groups of investors who are prepared to actively consider
investing in the asset. The value of assets then depends, among other
things, on how many people or other social actors see them as a
potential purchase, that is, on the size of the asset circle for the type

of asset concerned. Whether or not an individual member of the asset circle does decide to buy the asset depends on further factors, such as how the price of the asset compares to the valuation the potential buyer places on it, and thus on the valuation conventions that she is employing, but to be motivated to make such assessments the actor must already be a potential buyer, a member of the asset circle for the asset concerned. Asset circles, in turn, are built by discursive processes in which interested actors advance value narratives designed to persuade individuals of the potential merits of the asset.

Their success or failure in establishing those circles depends on a wide range of factors including the plausibility of the narrative they are advancing, its coherence with the wider culture of valuation and accepted conventions for related types of assets, the extent to which it can be embedded in institutions and techniques and its relationship over time to actual outcomes. Different members of the potential audience may accept these arguments to different degrees, which affects when they are willing to enter or decide to leave a certain market, and the prices they are prepared to pay or accept. Actual price movements depend in turn on which valuation conventions/principles are currently able to command the support of the largest number of market actors.

This concept of *asset circles* is one of the distinctive innovations of the book, but it has only been introduced very briefly in this chapter and a fuller explanation is required. To avoid giving an unbalanced impression of their role and significance, however, it is necessary to locate them in a wider understanding of social ontology in general and the ontology of financial assets in particular. The next chapter picks up this task.

5 | *Valuation Structures*

This chapter develops an innovative explanation of a range of social structures that are deeply implicated in the construction of financial value. In particular, it explains the concept of asset circles, introduced in the previous chapter. An asset circle is a set of potential investors who see a particular security as investible in the sense that they are aware of its existence and would be prepared to purchase it in the right circumstances (where those circumstances include the price of the security but may also include other factors). The concept of an asset circle is the most distinctive original contribution of this book to the explanation of financial value, and as a novel idea it needs a little more explanation than some other parts of the argument. I will argue that asset circles are essential to the very existence of financial assets, and an important factor in determining their value, although many other causal factors also contribute. The point of introducing them is not to construct an "asset circles theory of financial value" but rather to add the influence of asset circles into explanations of financial value that also draw on many other factors that have been at least partially explained in the existing literature and in the preceding chapters.

The chapter begins by returning to the critical realist approach to social ontology that was introduced in Chapter 3, adding further elements that are essential to the argument that follows. The chapter is focused on arguments about the social ontology of financial assets. In particular, the critical realist approach to social structures is briefly explained, in order to make clear what sort of causal role asset circles can play even though they are not empirically obvious entities. The concept of an asset circle is quite complex, and so the chapter builds incrementally towards it by first discussing other, arguably simpler, structures that are also fundamental to understanding financial value. Readers who are familiar with critical realism and my earlier work on norm circles could skip the first two sections.

The first type of structure considered is *norm circles*: the social structures that underpin normativity and thus lay theories of value. I then move on to discuss the social ontology of money, and in particular the concepts of monetary complexes and monetary circles, which I argue underpin the capacity of money to be used in payment (and thus an aspect of the ontology of buying and selling that is fundamental to all discussions of value and price in monetary economies). These monetary structures are analogous in a number of ways to the structures that underpin financial assets, which I call *asset complexes* and *asset circles* and so this discussion positions us well to look more closely at the structure of financial assets themselves in the later parts of the chapter. These explain what an asset complex and an asset circle are, what sort of structure they have and what mechanisms and powers this leads to (where powers are understood as tendencies to exert a certain sort of influence on events, rather than in a more directly determinative sense). This is then related back to valuation and pricing events, in which these mechanisms interact with others to determine outcomes.

We can think of this chapter's argument about asset complexes and circles as an ontological hypothesis that complements the theoretical hypotheses of the previous chapters, obtained by reasoning from evidence but then subject to testing against further evidence. The chapter closes by discussing the implications of these ontological arguments for the empirical study of financial value and thus paves the way for the case studies that make up the following chapters.

Critical Realism and Social Structure

Social systems, including economic systems, are open systems in the sense that we can never fully explain any event that occurs within them in terms of one or a small number of causal influences because all social events are open to many interacting influences. Critical realism provides an account of how causation occurs in open systems – an account that was introduced briefly in Chapter 3. The core of the argument is that events are always the outcome of multiple interacting causal powers, that those causal powers are emergent properties of entities and depend on the structure and composition of the entities concerned, and that causal powers operate as tendencies rather than as directly and individually determinative of outcomes because they always interact with other causal powers and it is contingent which other causal powers will have a significant influence in any given case (Bhaskar, 1975; Elder-Vass, 2010b).

If this is so, then we must ask what entities exert causal powers in the social world, and how. As I and others have argued at length, there is a rich and varied range of such entities (Elder-Vass, 2010b, 2012). Loosely speaking, we can divide the most causally significant entities in the social world into three groups: human individuals, other material objects and social entities or structures, which are in turn composed of human individuals and often of other material objects as well (Elder-Vass, 2017a, 2017b). Few contemporary social scientists would dispute that human individuals influence social events, and in recent years it has become more or less universally accepted that material objects may also have an influence. The claim that social structures are causally influential is more contentious, however, and critical realists have already spent much ink on justifying it (e.g. Elder-Vass, 2010b; Lawson, 2019). The central principle is that when people (and often other objects as well) are organised into social entities the resulting larger entity develops capacities to influence social events that those same people (and objects) would not have, even collectively, if they were not organised into such an entity (Elder-Vass, 2010b, Chapters 2, 4, 2014). It is therefore not the people but the larger entity that has the capacity – the causal power – to have these influences, even though they are always exercised through the parts of the larger entity.

Such arguments are always clearer when illustrated, so let me offer the case of queues (this explanation draws on Elder-Vass, 2010b, pp. 146–9). Any given queue consists of a (changing) group of people who all wish to obtain access to some service or facility, but what distinguishes a queue from a disorganised scrum is that the people in it organise themselves in a specific order, usually corresponding to the order in which they joined the queue, and tacitly agree that they will access the resource concerned in that order. The queue, as a consequence, has a capacity to serialise access to the resource, a capacity that the same group of people would not have if they were not organised into a queue. Like all causal powers, this is a tendency, that may not always be realised – say, for example, if the service point (such as a supermarket checkout) closes and the members of the queue then have to redistribute themselves across other queues. Nevertheless, in many cultural contexts queues often work well.

Traditionally, queues worked through a very clear and immediate system of physical positioning: people stood in the order in which they arrived. But it is not only the relative spatial locations of its members that structure a queue; indeed, these locations are arguably secondary to what really structures the queue: a set of shared intentional commitments. Members of the queue are committed to waiting their turn, and their relative physical locations act as markers of turns. We can see the distinction, for example, when someone temporarily leaves a queue and is then allowed to return to their original place in it. Queues work not so much because people stand in order but rather because people implicitly agree to access the service in the order in which they joined the queue. This brings us to a characteristic feature of social entities more generally: their structures take the form of intentional relations between their members, typically in the form of shared commitments of some sort, by contrast with most ordinary material entities, whose structures typically take the form of spatial relations between their parts (Elder-Vass, 2010b, pp. 199–202, 2017a, pp. 97–98).

Norm Circles

These intentional relations and shared commitments are not necessarily empirically obvious. For example, when people join queues they do not usually need to discuss the principle of queuing with the other people who are already in the queue, or make an explicit commitment to follow the principle. Queues are social entities in their own right, but they only work because they are backed up by a set of norms about queuing that are widely accepted in some cultural contexts, and those norms themselves depend on a further type of social entity – the *norm circles* introduced in Chapter 3 (Elder-Vass, 2010b, Chapter 6, 2012, Chapter 2). A norm circle is a group of people who are committed to endorsing and enforcing a particular norm. Many of us, for example, are committed to the norm of queuing, both in the sense that we follow the norm but also in the sense that in some circumstances we are prepared to act in support of the norm, for example by expressing disapproval of those who break it or by advising people to follow it and how to follow it in a particular context. Both our commitment to following the norm and our willingness to support it are strongly conditioned by our knowledge that other people also have similar commitments. Thus, for example, we would be much less willing to express disapproval of someone who breaches the queuing norm if we did not believe that others would also share our disapproval. It is striking that people often hold and act on this belief (and similar ones) about other people that they have never discussed the issue with and whom they might never even have met before.

My argument is that we form the belief that other people back a norm by being exposed to previous cases of support of the norm. Let me call the particular individuals that I have previously seen supporting a norm my *proximate* norm circle for the norm concerned. We then tend to imagine that the set of people who support the norm extends beyond this group to others who we think of as normatively or culturally similar to them (and perhaps even to everyone) – what I call the individual's *imagined* norm circle for the norm concerned. Any individual's commitment to supporting a norm is influenced by the presence of members of their *imagined* norm circle. Whether or not those around them do enforce the norm depends in part on whether they are members of the *actual* norm circle for it. There is then a tendency for our estimates of the extent of the norm circle to be broadly accurate because we adjust it on the basis of continuing experience of the presence or absence of supporting action.

A queue, then, is a social structure in its own right but it also depends on the existence of a further set of social structures: the norm circles for queuing norms. Norm circles, however, are much more general than this case, providing the norms and thus the practices that form a substantial part of social reality. Perhaps the greatest advantage of thinking about normativity in terms of norm circles is that it helps us to make sense of the vast diversity of normative commitments. Early treatments of norms as products of "society" could not explain why different people in the same social space might be committed to different norms. Once we recognise that each norm has its own norm circle, however, it immediately becomes apparent that we can have many different norms competing for allegiance in the same social space, some of which may be in conflict with each other. We can portray this in a simple Venn diagram, as in Figure 5.1, which represents two people (X and Y) and their relationships to the norm circles for different norms (A–E). In this example, both X and Y are committed to norms B and E, neither is committed to norm D, X but not Y is committed to norm A and Y but not X is committed to norm C. A and C might be conflicting norms, say the norms for eating meat and for

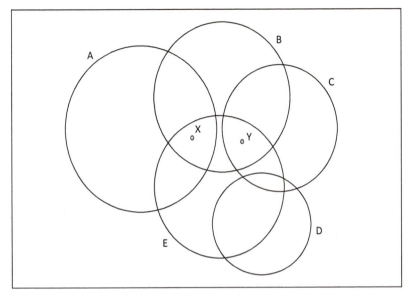

Figure 5.1 Intersecting norm circles, from Elder-Vass (2012, p. 161)

vegetarianism, for example, and so have entirely distinct norm circles because they are incompatible. Many norm circles overlap, however. E, for example, might be the norm that we should reduce our energy usage to reduce the risk of climate change, and in this case there are people committed to E who are also committed to one or more of all of the other norms represented here – but also people who are in those other norm circles but are not committed to E. The general model also still covers societies that are much more normatively homogeneous, which can be represented by drawing circles with much more overlap between them.

Norm Circles for Lay Theories of Value

As I argued in Chapter 3, lay theories of value and/or value conventions are themselves norms and thus, like other norms, depend on the existence of norm circles backing them. With the concept of norm circles in place, we can therefore say more about how lay theories of value work. Consider Figure 5.1 again, but now think of X and Y as the seller and a potential buyer of an item, discussing what would be a fair price for it, and A to E as a set of lay theories of value that could potentially be applied to the item. If X and Y can agree to apply some mix of theories B and E, they are more likely to come to an agreement about a fair price than if X insists on applying theory A, which Y does not accept, and Y insists on theory C, which X does not accept, while neither is likely to invoke theory D. The figure also casts some light on a possible difference between lay theories of value and conventions: Boltanski and Thévenot's work, for example, seems to assume that everyone involved accepts the same set of conventions and that negotiations are a matter of coming to an agreement on *which* conventions apply to the case (Boltanski & Thévenot, 2006).

For the purpose of examining the structure of value, it is also useful to recognise a further dimension of normativity, which is the distinction between *indexical* and *indexing* norms (Elder-Vass, 2012, pp. 70–73). The concept of *indexicality* comes from linguistics, where it refers to terms that have a fixed meaning in one sense but in another sense refer to different things depending on the context of use. The term "you", for example, has a clearly defined meaning, but it refers to different people depending on the context. This is important for normativity because many norms take an indexical form, often in multiple dimensions at the same time, and we also have other norms, which I call *indexing* norms, that are used to resolve some of this indexicality.

We can see how this distinction might apply to value by looking at the case of what Aspers calls "status markets" (Aspers, 2009). As I argued in Chapter 3, one widespread lay theory of value is that goods that enhance the apparent status of the purchaser should be valued more highly. We also saw that there are a variety of different markers of status goods, and that these are related to different cultural groups that validate them. We can see now that this is a case of indexical normativity. On the one hand, for example, we may have an indexical norm that fashionable goods should be valued more highly, and on the other a set of indexing norms defining what counts as fashionable for those in a given norm circle – these indexing norms are thus analogous to the concepts of qualification and classification that have been used in valuation studies, although the indexing norm concept also has further implications: notably that qualification is meaningless in the absence of wider normative (indexical) structures that confer significance on the categories that items are qualified into, and also that different groups may qualify or classify the same item in different ways depending on which indexing norms they are committed to. One part of the stratification of culture documented by Bourdieu (Bourdieu, 1984) is that different social groups adopt different indexing norms of what is fashionable. One group, for example, may identify fashionable clothing as garments by designers who exhibit at the leading fashion shows, while another may identify it as garments endorsed by sports stars, and another may identify it as garments endorsed by social media influencers. One can get a flavour of the complexity of these normative structures when one recognises that some members of these groups define their identities, at least in part, in terms of which of these status-indexing norms they endorse and obtain a sense of their own status by following them.

Norm circles themselves, like all social structures, are subject to a continuous process of reproduction and transformation, through the kinds of processes described in Archer's model of the morphogenetic cycle (M. S. Archer, 1995, pp. 65–79, 192–194). Each step in such processes is itself a multiply-determined social event, hence many different influences can contribute to the evolution of social structures like norm circles. Some of these may be unintended, but others are quite deliberate, such as the various forms of advertising and other marketing strategies employed by producers to have their products indexed as high-status goods, including the development of new strategies of distinction. One fascinating example is the relatively recent narration of "craft" alcoholic drinks by their producers as more "authentic" or traditional than mainstream competitors (despite the fact that the mainstream drinks have been produced for much longer), which is tied in with appealing to a variety of status indexing that has come to be associated with hipster culture (Thurnell-Read, 2019).

This dynamic is illustrated nicely in Delmestri and Greenwood's paper on how the Italian spirit grappa came to be recategorised from a low-status product to one that spanned a range of statuses, with premium brands selling in Italy for as much as, or even more than, premium cognacs and whiskies (Delmestri & Greenwood, 2016). At the beginning of their story, in the late 1960s, grappa was almost universally seen as "a coarse spirit consumed 'at the margin of society' by peasants and alpine soldiers" and produced by primitive artisans (Delmestri & Greenwood, 2016, p. 508) (internal quote from Solari, 2007, p. 337). Higher status spirits drinkers ignored it in favour of imported spirits like cognac and whisky. However, a small group of grappa producers, in particular Giannola Nonino, and a handful of

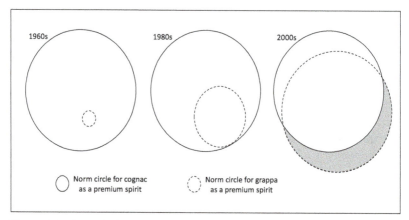

Figure 5.2 Norm circles for grappa status, based on Delmestri and Greenwood (2016)

food critics who valued artisanal production, believed that grappa had the potential to be seen as a premium spirit. Nonino and some other producers made a series of attempts to produce and market a higher-priced premium quality grappa, and in 1978 she eventually launched a product that succeeded commercially. To achieve this, she not only designed a premium product based on a single high status grape, but also enlisted the help of food and wine critics who shared the artisanal vision, she dressed in high fashion to clothe herself in high cultural status, she visited sommeliers in elite restaurants to persuade them of the quality of the product and she gave free samples to prominent citizens: a conscious strategy of breaking the links to the traditional vision of grappa and establishing new connections to high status across a variety of dimensions. By the 1980s this strategy had succeeded in establishing a rapidly growing market for premium brands of grappa, assisted by the emergence of the pro-artisanal Slow Food movement, and by the 2000s almost all remaining artisanal producers had switched to premium production (while factory produced mass market grappa remained at a lower status).

Figure 5.2 represents this story in terms of changes in the norm circle for the idea that some varieties of grappa should be treated, and thus valued, as a premium spirit (an indexing norm linked to the indexical norm that premium or high-status brands or styles should be valued more highly than low-status styles). At stage one of our story, only a very small group of producers and critics accepted and advocated this belief, but their carefully focused work on growing the norm circle created a viable market by the 1980s. By the end of the story, grappa was "lauded in the media as an exemplary Italian cultural product and 'lo spirito nazionale' (national spirit)", "its consumption became socially acceptable for women, younger adults, and the higher social classes" and its producers were "proclaimed as proudly upholding the traditions and innovations of Italian culture" (Delmestri & Greenwood, 2016, p. 530) (internal quote from Finzi, 2007). The shaded area in Figure 5.2 represents what we might call the "spirit nationalism" implicit in these last quotes – the idea that grappa *rather than* foreign spirits like cognac should be seen as a premium, high-status drink.

The story illustrates a number of points about norm circles and their implication for lay theories of value. The first is that theories do not become normative and thus influential until there is a group of people backing them. They may sometimes start off as a single person's idea or project, but progress depends on enlisting others. The second is that producers have a particular interest in promoting theories of value favourable to their products and inventing connections between them, although they may need the help of other influencers to gain traction. These are the critics and gatekeepers, such as sommeliers in elite restaurants, that Bourdieu calls the consecrators of value – and there is little hope of success until they can also enrol consumers into the norm circles for the theory concerned. But having said that, it need not always be producers that drive the growth in influence of theories of value. At around the same time that grappa was being recategorised in Italy, for example, the consumer-led Campaign for Real Ale was pushing (very successfully) for a similar revaluation of traditionally artisan-produced forms of beer in the United Kingdom and in this case it was the producers who had to be persuaded to follow suit (Thurnell-Read, 2018). Nevertheless, such campaigns appear to be much less common in practice than producer-led attempts to influence status categorisation and theories of value.

Money as a Standard of Value

We can take two further steps towards understanding value, and in particular the value of financial assets, by first considering the case of money. The first step is perhaps obvious: when we are assessing the monetary value of a thing we can only do so by using a monetary scale that we take to be a measure of value. This is the concept of a *unit of account*, widely considered to be one of the core functions of money, and a function that is inherent in processes of valuation. The second is that monetary instruments have some important similarities to financial assets, and we can prepare the way for a deeper understanding of the ontology of financial assets by first looking at the ontology of monetary instruments.

   It is common to think of money as having four key functions: "It is a *medium of exchange, store of value, means of unilateral payment (settlement)*, and *measure of value (unit of account)*" (Ingham, 2004, p. 3). Here I will focus on only two, unit of account and means of payment: I take it that anything that can function as a means of payment can also act as a medium of exchange and store of value, hence these functions do not imply any further ontological differentiation (cf. Ingham, 2004, p. 70). A unit of account is a standard by which we measure quantities of monetary value, for example in prices, in bank accounts and in business accounting (typically it is the currency unit of the country or monetary region concerned). A means of payment is something that will be accepted in payment for a commodity or in payment of a debt. Most accounts of the nature of money assume that these functions are both performed by the same thing, but I follow the eighteenth-century political economist James Steuart in believing that this is an error (Steuart, 1767 Book 3, Chapter 1). On the one hand, I suggest, the function of unit of account is performed by a complex of normative institutions. Most significantly, for each unit of account, there is a norm that in certain circumstances this unit should be used for the measurement of monetary value, and this norm (like any other) is produced by a norm circle, though it may also be supported by other social institutions such as laws about legal tender or accounting. In modern society, this function is typically performed by an abstract conception of the value of the official currency. An item can be priced at one US dollar, for example, without any concrete dollars being present. On the other hand, the function of means of payment is performed by specific concrete *monetary instruments*, such as notes, coins and credit cards, which indicate that their carriers are the bearers of a quantified power to pay.

One empirical phenomenon that lends support to this division is the many cases in which these two functions have been dissociated from each other. Davies tells us, for example, that "for around half the long monetary history of the £ sterling in Britain... there was no such *thing* as a pound; it existed only as a unit of account. There are numerous similar examples" (Davies, 1994, p. 29). Similarly, the Euro existed as a unit of account for two years before corresponding notes and coins were introduced (Ingham, 2004, p. 227 n9). It is hard to justify the belief that the unit of account and means of payment functions are both functions of the same thing when they are patently not performed by the same thing. This distinction is less obvious when the means of payment is a form of claim (such as modern paper currencies) that has no value independent of its status as an instantiation of the unit of account. Yet, I will argue, even in these cases these two functions are the product of two distinct types of social structure requiring two distinct ontological analyses.

Early units of account were linked to commodities, such as barley or silver (Ingham, 2004, pp. 94–95). In such cases, the establishment of a unit of account depends on the prior establishment of norms of counting and quantification, but also on the establishment of a norm that the commodity concerned should be used as the measure of value. Things are complicated further when commodity money is replaced by paper money and then by inconvertible paper money. Once paper money becomes inconvertible the unit of account can float free of any physical measure and becomes doubly a matter of convention. First, in the sense that was already true of commodity units of account: that it is only by agreement that this unit rather than some other is used as the unit of account. Second, however, the use of a unit as a measure of value also implies that we understand how much value the unit itself is equivalent to. In the case of commodity-based units of account, value equivalence is straightforwardly rooted in the exchange value of the corresponding physical quantity of the reference commodity. This is no longer the case for modern forms of money, whose value equivalence is entirely socially constructed, implicit in our monetary practices. In a sense the value-equivalent of such a unit of account is the obverse face of the normative valuations of other goods that are made in its terms. Once we have a normatively backed unit of account, we have a scale against which to measure the value of other things, and the existence of such a scale has been implicit in this book's argument so far.

Monetary Instruments

A unit of account provides us with a collective scale against which we can make an assessment of value and agree a price, but to actually make a payment we need something else: we must have money in the form of *monetary instruments*, transferable entitlements to a certain amount of money. Notes and coins, for example, are monetary instruments, as are bank balances that can be sent by digital transfer, or credit cards that allow their holders to spend by building up a debit balance that must be repaid later. A further reason to think of monetary instruments as ontologically distinct from units of account, incidentally, is that as this list already shows there may be multiple different forms of money, different monetary instruments, denominated in the same unit of account.

Money in the form of monetary instruments provides us with the capacity to pay for commodities and to pay off our debts, and part of the purpose of this section is to examine the mechanism behind this capacity (employing the approach to retroduction outlined in Elder-Vass, 2007). I will conclude that the capacity of any given monetary instrument to be used as payment is produced by a social structure that I will call a *monetary complex*, where all monetary complexes have (at least) two groups of parts: a *monetary circle* and a *payment infrastructure*. We may be tempted to think that this capacity to be used in payment is a causal power of the monetary instruments themselves, but this would be an error from an ontological perspective: these instruments are merely tokens that depend for their effectiveness on the social structures behind them. They *show* which social actors possess the capacity to pay, and in what quantity, but do not *confer* that capacity themselves. Rather, the power to pay using a monetary instrument is a causal power of the monetary complex for that instrument that is delegated to the holders of monetary instruments in proportion to the face value (in terms of the unit of account) of the instruments that they hold.

Let us look more closely at the structure to which I am attributing this power: its parts, the relations between them and the mechanisms that depend on these parts and relations and produce the power of payment. Although it is essential, I will say relatively little about the payment infrastructure on the assumption that this part of the argument is well known: we cannot have a monetary instrument without there being some sort of token that indicates possession of a monetary balance, such as a cowrie shell, a bank note or a credit card. In the very simplest possible cases such as some possible versions of cowrie shell money, the token is all the infrastructure required, as long as it is supported by a monetary circle: a group of people who are committed to accepting it in payment (a community that positions it as money, as Lawson would put it: 2019, pp. 155–165). But most modern money is more complex than this: credit cards, for example, will not function as money without a technological infrastructure including card readers, communication networks and computer servers that validate payment requests and an institutional infrastructure including card issuers (usually banks) and payment networks (the companies, this time, rather than the hardware) like Visa and Mastercard (Evans & Schmalensee, 2005). Any payment infrastructure must include what Searle calls a *status indicator* that indicates how much money any given individual has available to spend (Searle, 1995, p. 85). A bank note is a status indicator, for example, as is the remaining unspent balance on a credit card account, or its representation within a computer system (although Searle himself treats money differently: 1995, p. 119).

The second part of any monetary complex is a *monetary circle*: a group of people and organisational structures such as corporations that are willing to accept the monetary instruments concerned in payment (there are some similarities between monetary circles and what Dodd calls monetary networks in Dodd, 1994, pp. xxiii–xxiv). Just as there is one norm circle for each norm, there is one monetary circle for each type of monetary instrument (this follows from the definition of a monetary circle). And just as norm circles are diverse and may overlap profusely, so may monetary circles. Some merchants may accept multiple currencies in payment and so are parts of multiple monetary circles, while even merchants who will accept only one currency may vary in which instruments they will accept: until the COVID-19 pandemic reduced the acceptability of cash, for example, many small vendors in the United Kingdom, for example, would accept cash payments but not card payments.

Although this concept thus has some similarity to the concept of a norm circle, it also differs in important ways. Norm circles operate through actions in which their members express approval or disapproval of other actions. Monetary circles operate through actions in which their members accept, or indicate that they are willing to accept, specific monetary instruments in payment. And although it also bears some similarity to the concept of a *community*, it also differs from this in important ways: the concept of community implies a group of people who are linked by multiple types of interaction, whereas I adopt the concept of a circle (cf. Simmel, 1955) precisely because it does *not* assume this. The members of a monetary circle need not form a community in any other sense than that they are willing to accept the corresponding monetary instrument in payment. Of course, other links between them may help to sustain this willingness, but this is a contingent empirical question and by no means a necessary feature of a monetary circle.

The acceptability of monetary instruments in payment is sometimes attributed to legal tender laws, which specify that certain monetary instruments, usually state issued bank notes, may be used in certain types of payment (Lawson, 2019, p. 158). Some, at least, of these laws were linked to the ending of the gold standard and the perceived need to ensure that paper currency would continue to be accepted once it was no longer convertible to gold. They may have had some effect in influencing the monetary circles for state bank notes at the time, and it is interesting that they are currently being used by the Chinese state to support the launch of their own digital currency (Yu & Kynge, 2021). On the whole, however, they are irrelevant to most payments today since they say nothing about the bank and credit card balances that dominate payments in most contemporary economies. These are accepted because people believe they will be reusable in further payments, not because of any legal requirement. Still, states may play other important roles in establishing the acceptability of monetary instruments. As the chartalists have argued (although they overstate the case), when states are willing to accept a monetary instrument as payment for tax liabilities this provides substantial support for confidence in its value – here, in effect, the state bolsters the credibility of an instrument by becoming part of its monetary circle (Ingham, 2004, pp. 47–48). But states may also play other sorts of roles in establishing monetary circles, most obviously when they lead currency innovations. The most striking example in recent times is the introduction of the Euro, which was backed by enormous state support for new institutions such as the European Central Bank and extensive work to establish the acceptability of the new currency in payment (Kaelberer, 2007). We may think of the entire Euro project as the state-driven construction of a set of new monetary circles (and at the same time the destruction of a set of older ones).

The power we exercise when we use a monetary instrument is the power to pay (a power that may *contingently* give us the ability to command other resources). This is not a power of the physical token that acts as a monetary instrument, because the physical properties of the token – the ink and paper that makes up a bank note, for example – are not capable of generating such a power. Rather, it is a power of the larger monetary complex, a power that only exists when a group committed to accepting the instrument in payment exists, although it also depends on the existence of a functioning payment infrastructure. But it is a power that is delegated, in quantified amounts, to the holders of the monetary instruments concerned. In ontological terms, this is similar to the way in which the powers of an organisation (e.g. to hire and fire staff) may be delegated to particular employees (Elder-Vass, 2010b, pp. 158–159, 162). We must strip the word *delegated* here of any connotation of intentionality: the monetary complex as such does not have a consciousness, let alone the capacity to intentionally transfer its powers. But in other respects the word delegation is entirely appropriate: this is a power of the whole social entity, the monetary complex, that is *exercised* by one of its parts, the user of the monetary instrument concerned, and there is also a sense in which the delegation is *performed* by another of its parts: the acceptor of the instrument in the same transaction. The power of money, or rather of a monetary instrument, is a socially authorised quantified entitlement to pay, a causal power of a monetary complex that is delegated to payers by payees who tacitly act on behalf of the complex, and in particular on behalf of the monetary circle that is part of it, in accepting a monetary instrument in payment, knowing that they themselves may reuse the instrument on the same basis.

The mechanism that produces this power rests on a set of intentional relations between the members of the monetary circle (note that I use *intentional* here in the philosophical sense of a belief or attitude about something rather than in the narrower everyday sense of intending to perform a particular act). First, they are committed (an intentional relation) to accepting the monetary instrument concerned (through the payment infrastructure) in payment from others for commodities or to discharge debts. Second, this commitment rests on their belief that they themselves will also be able to use the monetary instrument in payment, and this belief in turn depends indirectly on the fact that other members of the monetary circle are *also* committed to accepting the instrument in payment (Carruthers & Babb, 1996, p. 1557; M. Weber, 1978, p. 75). The belief, in other words, is sustained by the experience of others accepting the instrument, and thus rests on the iterative nature of practices like these. This is a doubly intentional relation. First, it is a belief about other members of the monetary circle, and second, it is an intention to accept the monetary instrument in payment. These intentional relations are the structure that make the monetary circle something more than an unrelated group of people.

The mechanism itself – the process of interaction between the parts that produces the power we are interested in – is simply the repeated iteration of the practice of accepting the monetary instrument in payment, which both realises the causal power of the monetary complex and provides support for the belief that the instrument will be accepted in payment in future and thus supports the continuing power of the complex. The experience of an instrument being accepted in payment by other transaction partners generates a kind of trust in the instrument concerned. As Ingham points out, this is not trust in the traditional sense, since it is not trust of one individual by another, not "*personal* trust" but rather "*assignable* trust" (Ingham, 2004, p. 74) – with money in our hand we may trust that it will be redeemable in transactions with other members of the monetary circle.

Although I have focused here on the structural source of the power of a monetary instrument to be used in payment, I hope it is clear that in explaining this we are also, partly, explaining the value of the monetary instrument. The value of a monetary instrument is a quantified assessment of its capacity to be used in payment – the obverse, as I said above, of the values of other commodities expressed in it – hence to understand how that capacity is produced is implicitly also to understand how its value is produced.

The Structure of Financial Assets

One reason I have devoted so much attention to the ontological structure of monetary instruments is that there are strong parallels with the ontological structure of financial instruments. As we have seen, the value of financial instruments depends on the potential purchaser's expectation that it will entitle them to a revenue stream. Whenever resale of the asset is a significant element of these anticipated returns, this expectation depends on the potential purchaser believing that there will be other investors willing to buy the instrument at any time when they might wish to resell it. Thus, the value of a financial instrument depends on the buyer's expectation that they will be able to use it in exchange at a later date, just as the value of a monetary instrument depends on the recipient's expectation that they will be able to use it in exchange at a later date. Even in the case of financial assets that are held to maturity by their original purchaser, the *possibility* of selling the asset prior to maturity may contribute to assessments of its value. In other words, the value of a financial asset to any given purchaser (and therefore, to an extent, the price that can be realised for it) typically depends, among other things, on the existence of an *asset circle* for the asset, which I will argue forms part of a larger *asset complex*, just as the value of a monetary instrument depends on the existence of a monetary circle for it, which forms part of a larger monetary complex. Given these similarities, the argument below follows a similar plan to that of the previous section.

To put the argument in more causal terms, the value of a financial instrument depends on the fact that such instruments have a capacity to be sold, and I argue that this capacity is an emergent property of an *asset complex* for the type of asset concerned. To continue the parallel with the case of money, an asset complex is composed of both an *asset infrastructure* that provides the technical and institutional underpinnings of the asset and an *asset circle*: a group of people and institutional structures such as corporations who are willing to purchase the financial instruments in certain conditions (which may relate to the price but also to other circumstances such as their particular financial situation at the time). Although much of the asset infrastructure may be shared with other assets, each asset has its own asset circle and thus its own asset complex, composed of the conjunction of its specific asset circle with the relevant asset infrastructure. As in the case of money, it would be an error to think that the capacity to be sold is a power of the assets themselves, since in physical terms they typically exist as nothing more than traces recorded in some sort of ledger, whether in digital form or on paper. On the contrary, that capacity is an emergent causal power of the larger asset complex, which is delegated to those investors who are positioned as holders of the related financial instruments. The traces that record this positioning are status indicators: they have no powers in their own right. We are accustomed to reifying financial assets – thinking of them as things in their own right – but it would be more accurate to think of them as relational properties produced within a larger system. If they were not, it would be quite extraordinary for anyone to believe that these distal traces of paper or digital recording could be sold on to anyone else.

The infrastructure element of an asset complex includes both a property infrastructure and an exchange infrastructure. The former records and legitimates entitlements to payment streams in the form of financial instruments. It includes both technological elements such as computer systems that maintain registers of asset holdings and institutional elements such as organisations that act as keepers and managers of assets for others (e.g. stockbrokers and mutual funds) and legal provisions around ownership of financial assets. As Katharina Pistor has argued, assets are legal constructions – they not only depend on a general framework of contract and property law and the coercive power of the state to enforce them, but may also depend on specific legal developments supporting specific asset types, such as the possibility of demanding collateral in support of debt instruments (Pistor, 2019). The exchange infrastructure again includes both technological elements and institutional elements: a stock exchange, for example, is both an organisation and a set of computer systems that enacts stock transfers. Again, this infrastructure is already quite familiar and so I will focus more on the other element of asset complexes: asset circles.

It is a condition of possibility of the saleability of any financial asset whose value depends in part on the possibility of reselling it that the purchaser should believe that there are likely to be potential repurchasers of the asset at any time when the purchaser might expect to resell them (an imagined asset circle). Although some investors may be duped by fraudsters into believing that there is such an asset circle when there is not, most investors are sufficiently cautious that they will only buy assets when they have good evidence to support this belief. This usually requires evidence that the asset concerned, or a closely equivalent asset class, is already being traded and thus that there are already enough potential purchasers to sustain a market in them (there are partial exceptions, such as highly customised over-the-counter derivatives). In other words, there must generally be an asset circle for an asset or a very good reason to believe that there will be one in the future before investors will buy it, although they are likely to think of it in different terms than this: in terms, perhaps, of the existence of a market, or the existence of buyers, or the degree of liquidity of the asset. We cannot have a functioning financial asset without *both* the asset circle and the institutionalised asset technology, which between them create the power of an asset to be sold.

Like all social mechanisms, the mechanism that produces this power rests on a set of intentional relations between the members of the corresponding social structure, in this case the asset circle component of the asset complex. First, the members of the asset circle are willing (an intentional relation) to purchase the instrument as an investment from others in certain circumstances. Second, this intention rests in part on their belief that they themselves will also be able to sell on the financial instrument when required, and this belief in turn depends indirectly on the fact that other members of the asset circle are also willing to purchase the instrument in certain circumstances. Thus their commitment to membership of the asset circle, which they experience as an intention to consider the asset for purchase, depends on the matching intention (or at least their belief in the matching intention) of others (cf. Gilbert, 1990). Their belief in this matching intention is sustained by the experience of others purchasing the instrument, and thus rests on the iterative nature of practices like these. This is a doubly intentional relation. First, it is a belief about other members of the asset circle, and second, it is a conditional intention to purchase the financial instrument in certain circumstances. These intentional relations are the structure that give the asset circle an influence that the constituent people and firms would not otherwise have.

The mechanism itself – the process of interaction between the parts that produces the power we are interested in – is simply the repeated iteration of the practice of purchasing the financial instrument, which both realises the causal power of the asset circle and provides support for the belief that the instrument will be saleable in future and thus supports the continuing power of the circle. This is the sort of process that Archer has called a morphogenetic cycle (M. S. Archer, 1995). At time one, there is an asset circle, a set of potential purchasers of the asset. This generates a kind of trust in the instrument concerned. At time two, a prospective purchaser, aware of and influenced by the existence of these other potential purchasers, decides to go ahead and buy the asset. At time three, if enough prospective purchasers do so, they collectively reproduce the asset circle and produce at time four (which is also time one of the next cycle) the awareness of it amongst other potential purchasers, leading us into the next iteration of the cycle.

So far, this argument has paralleled my explanation of the ontology of money quite closely. However, the relation of asset complexes and asset circles to the value and price of financial assets is arguably more complex than the relation of monetary complexes and monetary circles to the value of money, and the next section moves on to address this issue.

Asset Circles and the Price of Financial Assets

Although they depend on a structural context, values and prices are not themselves structures but rather events: each moment at which a person assesses or negotiates the value of a thing, or agrees or pays a price for it, is an event. As the previous chapter argued, then, values and prices, like all other events, are multiply-determined by many interacting factors. Any given valuation of a financial asset will depend, at least, on the lay theories of value held by the valuer, the characteristics of the asset itself such as what future payment streams it confers an entitlement to, and expectations about those payment streams which may in turn depend on the valuer's beliefs about the many factors that could affect them in the future. Actual prices achieved for assets will depend on these valuations but also on the supply of assets available and on the number of investors considering an investment in the asset: the size of its asset circle.

We may contrast this last point with a view implicit in neoclassical accounts of markets, which simply takes for granted that there is a group of economic actors willing to buy any given product, although at varying prices. In a purist marginalist model all actors are assumed to be participants in all markets because they have complete and accurate information about all commodities and prices and respond rationally to them all. In that model there is no need for the concept of an asset circle because every economic actor is automatically a member of every asset circle. But in the real world, people do not have such information and in these circumstances "the range of choices available in the stock market is so large as to utterly swamp and defy rational analysis" (Harrington, 2008, p. 38). In an example of what Simon called bounded rationality, they can only function by narrowing down the range of options under consideration (Simon, 1972).

Different types of investors narrow the range in different ways. At one end of the scale, index funds are committed to investing in the stocks in the relevant index, usually in proportion to their weighting in the index. Their rules automatically make them part of the asset circle for the stocks in the index and exclude them from the asset circles for other assets (perhaps with a little ambiguity at times when stocks move in and out of indexes). Many other investment funds are more flexible but still publicly committed to investing in a certain sector or according to certain rules, which imply that they will monitor and consider investing in any stocks that fit within their rules, and again these are clear members of the asset circles for those stocks (and not for others), even though they do not invest in all of them. More speculative investors such as private day traders and professional traders using algorithmic methods are often also committed to monitoring specific assets with a clear intention to trade when prices meet their criteria. More generally, most investors specialise in particular types of assets and seek to understand possible investments before deciding whether to invest in them – such as the hedge fund partner observed by MacKenzie and Hardie who was carefully assessing arbitrage opportunities in the Brazilian government bond market at the time (MacKenzie, 2009, pp. 90–91) or the investors who shorted mortgage-backed securities by buying credit default swaps in the run up to the 2008 financial crisis (Lewis, 2011).

Although asset circles are different from norm circles, we can represent them in a similar way – as circles on a diagram, in which the space inside the circle represents the investors who are members of the corresponding asset circle. This helps us to explore the relationships between different asset circles, and indeed some of the relationships between asset circles and other types of groups, such as norm circles and monetary circles. As with norm circles, a key feature of asset circles is that they are not all the same – different asset circles include different groups of investors, who may all have different reasons for their interest in the security concerned. Also, asset circles overlap diversely with each other and indeed with norm circles and monetary circles – in other words, the same investor may be a member of many different asset circles and also other types of circle. At its simplest, we can represent this as in Figure 5.3.

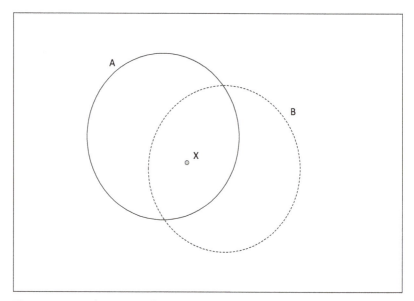

Figure 5.3 Overlapping circles

Figure 5.3 is deliberately abstract, so that it can be used to represent a variety of different cases. For example, if X is an investor, A might be the asset circle for one particular security, say shares in Tesla, and B might be the asset circle for an entirely different security, say a mutual fund or unit trust investing in Asian stocks. The diagram now tells us that X is willing to invest in either (or both) of these securities but also that the larger groups willing to invest in them are different, although they overlap. Or let us imagine that A is still the asset circle for shares in Tesla but now B is the monetary circle for monetary instruments denominated in US dollars. Now the diagram expresses a necessary condition for X to be willing to sell Tesla shares for US dollars – they must be (or at least very recently have been) a member of the asset circle for Tesla to hold its stock in the first place, and must be a member of the monetary circle for US dollars to be willing to accept them in exchange for their stock.

We may also use a slightly more complex diagram to clarify the relationship between asset circles and the norm circles for lay theories of value. Consider Figure 5.4 (which is identical to Figure 5.1). Here X and Y are two investors, who are both members of B, the asset circle for an asset B*, while A, C, D and E represent the norm circles for

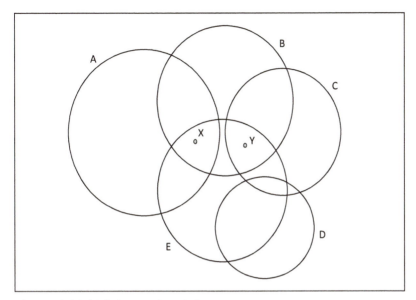

Figure 5.4 Multiple intersecting circles

various lay theories of asset value. X and Y will each form their own views of the value of B*, with X employing theories A* and E* to value B*, and Y employing theories C* and E*. These valuations will then determine what prices X and Y are willing to trade the asset at.

In this world of limited time and information, the price of an asset with a given supply can be increased by growing the asset circle for it. The concept of an asset circle thus gives us a means to ask questions that are generally ignored in neoclassical theory: which economic actors are not only aware of but also willing to consider purchasing any given financial asset, and how are they drawn into this group in the first place? One symptom of this deficiency in mainstream theory is that it finds the phenomenon of home bias amongst equity investors puzzling. Home bias is "the empirical finding that people overinvest in domestic stocks relative to the optimal investment portfolio implied by the modern portfolio theory" (Ardalan, 2019, p. 949). This is puzzling if you start from the assumption that investors are perfectly informed about all possible assets, but not at all if you consider that they only join the asset circles for stocks of which they are aware, and that they are more likely to become aware of companies that they interact with in daily life and stocks that are discussed in their local financial media.

The concept of an asset circle also allows us to go a step further, and consider the causal role that such groups and their creation may play in the valuation and prices of assets. This brings us back to questions of demand and supply and the role that they play in commodity exchange and the determination of price. As I have argued previously (Elder-Vass, 2016, pp. 75–78), the marginalist reduction of the explanation of price determination to the balancing of supply and demand obscures many of the most important features of how buying and selling works. I am now going to reintroduce demand and supply considerations into the argument, but this should not be seen as an acceptance of the marginalist model. When we relocate discussions of demand and supply into the context of a multiple determination model of open systems causality they function merely to describe a subset of the mechanisms at work. The marginalist tradition may have some useful things to say about these mechanisms but it fails to recognise that they form only one part of a larger, more complex causal picture.

In general, we can say that when the size of an asset circle increases, the demand for the asset will have a tendency to increase: more investors will want to buy it. Conversely, when the size of an asset circle shrinks, demand for the asset will tend to reduce. Indeed, in the more extreme cases, such as when mortgage-backed securities were downrated by the ratings agencies in the 2008 financial crisis (discussed in more detail in Chapter 8), the asset circle may shrink so precipitously that demand for the asset will dry up altogether: a crisis of liquidity. One way of putting this would be to say that the demand for an asset is an emergent property of the asset circle for it, although it is not only affected by the size of the asset circle, but also by the beliefs of its members about the classification of the asset and about what lay theories of value should be applied in what way to value it. Unlike in the marginalist model, however, this does not imply that we can postulate an implicit schedule of how much people want at any particular price – a demand curve. Every buying decision is a unique event that is sensitive to other things as well as price. The "demand" implicit in this model is far more conditional than the marginalist version, because it is not only conditional on price but also on other circumstances. Also, as was noted in the previous chapter, demand and supply are not independent of each other in financial markets. Unlike many material commodities, financial assets are constantly recycled from one buyer to another, and when we are looking at assets which recirculate like this, the same group of investors (or at least overlapping subsets of the group) is the source of both demand and supply. Hence the size of the asset circle and the valuation decisions made by asset circle members affect both.

In the previous chapter I defined an asset circle as a group of people and/or organisations who see the asset concerned as a worthwhile investment that they might realistically be prepared to purchase. One potential challenge to the concept is that the boundaries of such a group seem rather vague: the intention that defines membership of the asset circle is so conditional that the distinction between someone who is willing to purchase an asset under the right circumstances and someone who is aware of it but not currently seriously considering purchasing it is quite tenuous. Is there no circumstance in which the outsider might be willing to buy? Is someone who is following the stock but wouldn't buy it at anything like its current price really willing to purchase? Where is the line between the two? And how can we tell when an investor has moved into or out of an asset circle, unless they do actually buy the asset? What about investors who only rarely consider investment decisions and may identify an asset as a potential investment at one point and then not return to consider buying it for months afterwards?

These are fair challenges, but things with vague boundaries can still be real and causally effective. Even if there are investors whose membership in asset circles is ambiguous, there are others that clearly are members, and others again that clearly are not. It helps to remember that there are many different types of investors, and many of them are committed to actively considering a particular range of assets as potential investments, as we saw earlier – index funds, sector-specific mutual funds, day traders and hedge funds, for example, each have their own specific range of candidate investments. Hence, we can say that for most assets most of the time there are potential investors who clearly are part of its asset circle and others who are not, even if there is also a more ambiguous group on the boundary. This is enough to carry the ontological burden required by the concept of an asset circle: as long as there are enough investors actively considering purchasing an asset and going on to trade for the market to be liquid, there is an asset circle and it will tend to generate confidence in the future saleability of the asset.

Another challenge is how to define the size of an asset circle. The obvious answer would be to define it in terms of the number of investors open to investing in the asset concerned, but this misses the crucial issue of *how much* the investors might be open to investing. If a single large institutional investor joins or leaves an asset circle, this may have a much larger impact than hundreds or even thousands of small investors doing the same because they have far greater funds to invest. It may therefore make more sense to define the size in terms of investible funds at the disposal of the members of the circle. This still abstracts from other issues. For example, investors rarely invest all of their funds in a single security, so the scale of their potential commitment to an asset is rarely equal to the total funds at their disposal. We can talk in broad terms about the impact of the changing size of an asset circle without confronting some of these issues, but they would need to be addressed before asset circle sizes could be quantified more precisely.

Assetisation

Perhaps the section of the contemporary valuation literature that approaches most closely to the issues raised here is the innovative recent work on the concept of assetisation (Birch, 2017; Birch & Muniesa, 2020a; Muniesa et al., 2017). This literature asks a similar question to that examined above: how are assets constructed *as* assets (Birch & Muniesa, 2020b, p. 2)? It tends to approach it through the empirical study of specific cases, often at the micro-interactionist level, whereas I have argued from a broad range of existing evidence to an ontological hypothesis about the conditions of possibility of financial assets. The assetisation literature has made important advances in both recognising the increasing contemporary importance of financial assets and examining how they come into existence. The ontological arguments do not supplant but rather complement these findings and build on them by adding concepts that are empirically relevant even though they may not be empirically obvious.

While audiences are not generally treated as central to assetisation in this literature, neither are they entirely ignored. Birch's paper on assetisation in the biotech sector, for example, provides some interesting interview material with a venture capital investor who tells us how important it is for them to manage investor sentiment (Birch, 2017, pp. 480–481). Ouma has investigated how farmland asset managers have sought to persuade institutional investors to take farmland seriously as an investment (Ouma, 2018). Williams examines the challenges faced by social impact bond practitioners in engaging and recruiting investors (Williams, 2020). Birch and Muniesa's introduction to their collection on assetisation tells us that "the urge to attract investors becomes a crucial political imperative" (Birch & Muniesa, 2020b, p. 20) but doesn't say much more about the issue. Beyond these examples, the slightly distant relation of most of the assetisation literature to what I have called the construction of asset circles is captured nicely in Muniesa and his co-authors' collective work on capitalisation (a word that they use as a synonym of assetisation):

> Capitalization, considered as a transitive process of valuation, requires some sort of a focal point–a gaze–from which to make sense of the answer to the "for whom" question. This is the investor, a free investor that we have characterized as a persona, a figure, rather than as an actual somebody, a virtual investor whose gaze needs to be adopted by actual people (Muniesa et al., 2017, l. 1957).

There is a recognition of the significance of the investor in principle here, but a relative neglect in practice. Other strands of the valuation literature have also engaged occasionally with the issues raised by the asset circles hypothesis. Harrington's work on investment clubs, in particular, provides a rare but substantial engagement with private investors, examining how they select stocks and how this is influenced by the various "signals and symbolic communication that firms are directing toward the market" (Harrington, 2008, p. 45). Thrift also takes private investors seriously, although his work is oriented more to how they were persuaded to take a whole new class of stocks seriously, rather than any one stock in particular (Thrift, 2001).

Studying Asset Circles

Like norm circles and monetary circles, asset circles as such are unobservable. We can only observe the behaviour of their members, those affected by their members and the work that is done to build them. The existence of an asset circle as an organising structure over and above these actors and actions is an ontological hypothesis, an inference from the evidence to the best explanation of the conditions of possibility of the phenomena that we observe. As such, it is an application of the critical realist method of retroduction, employed to hypothesise structures, mechanisms and powers that contribute, in interaction with others, to the causation of events (Elder-Vass, 2007).

Because they are unobservable, we cannot measure or count asset circles using standard quantitative methods, nor can we prove their existence by examining the meanings available to interpretivist researchers. Instead, like other hypotheses about unobservables, we can only assess the validity of the argument by considering how well it coheres with the evidence available. Because we cannot observe the structures and mechanisms themselves, we have to ask what we *would* observe if they existed and acted as hypothesised (a method widely practised in the natural sciences). If we find evidence that fits, the hypothesis is supported – though not proven – while if we find none, or if we find countervailing evidence, it is not.

If asset circles are real and causally significant, we should be able to find evidence about how they are constructed. On the argument that investors do not *automatically* become open to investing in any new putative financial asset, we would expect to find efforts being made by financial value entrepreneurs to recruit investors into the corresponding asset circles. Every asset circle, in other words, must have a causal history, unlike the perfectly informed investors of marginalist theory, and by studying those causal histories we should find evidence that coheres with the hypothesis of their existence. Identifying such causal histories is a key element of the three case study chapters that follow, although this can only be one part of the argument, given that the construction of financial value is multiply-determined, and so many other forces will also appear in these accounts.

This sort of approach need not rest on new primary research. When we are developing new theoretical ideas and investigating their coherence with the evidence, we do not necessarily need *new* evidence in order to assess that coherence. When there are many existing empirical studies of a topic, and large amounts of primary material available in the public domain, then coherence with this evidence is often more important than coherence with one new set of empirical evidence. I have therefore focused my efforts in this book on using existing empirical material rather than uncovering new evidence.

Conclusion

This chapter expands the theoretical hypothesis developed in the earlier chapters with an ontological hypothesis: that financial assets only exist within asset complexes composed of both asset infrastructures and asset circles, and that the capacity of an asset to be sold is an emergent causal power of the corresponding asset complex. We cannot make sense of the value of financial assets without locating it in a clear understanding of this ontology of financial instruments themselves.

Asset circles are enormously important to the determination of the value and thus the prices of financial assets. This does not mean that we can quantify the relative causal contributions of asset circles and other factors: causal contributions are rarely additive or multiplicative in a way that makes this a coherent objective. We can, however, say that asset circles are vitally important in the sense that they are a *condition of possibility* of financial assets: without asset circles, assets simply cannot exist as assets. They are not, however, the only conditions of possibility. Others I have touched on include the existence of a unit of account and practices of quantification that make it possible to express value and prices in quantitative terms, and the existence of a legal framework of contract and property law. Because there are multiple such conditions of possibility, this does not make any one of them *the* master concept for explaining assets. It is always complexes of causal factors that bring things about, not one master factor, and there are strong limits to what can be said about the relative weight of different factors. What we can do, and what I have started to do in this chapter, is to examine the mechanisms that asset circles are involved in and the tendencies that result, in particular the tendency for increases in the size of asset circles to increase the price of the associated asset.

Asset complexes and in particular asset circles are the products of a non-stop politics of value, in which a range of interested actors – value entrepreneurs – strive to persuade audiences of the value of financial assets. On the one hand, they strive to create asset infrastructures and asset circles – groups of economic actors who recognise the type of asset concerned as a potential investment for them. On the other, they strive to establish norm circles for particular conventions or theories of value – groups of economic actors who consider it appropriate to value a certain type of asset on the basis of the convention or theory concerned – and/or to persuade investors to apply these conventions to the particular assets they are promoting. These structures exert a causal influence on the valuation decisions made by investors and through that on the prices achieved for financial assets, but always in conjunction with a broad range of other causal factors that influence valuation and prices. The work that value entrepreneurs do to manipulate these structures attempts to *invent* value for the assets concerned, although like any other form of invention, it can only ever operate by recombining existing elements in ways that are constrained by the wider context.

Given this theory, there are at least two kinds of process that any study of financial value must attend to: the processes in which valuation and pricing decisions are made, and those in which asset credibility and theories of value are established, buttressed with institutional and technological support and marketed to the relevant audiences. The latter processes are most visible in the case of financial innovations, where we can trace the invention of socially constructed institutions that later come to be taken for granted. This may involve a range of processes, for example: a new type of asset is designed; a discourse or narrative develops that links the asset to established principles of value, construing it as valuable in terms like those that are already recognised for other assets; the asset is given characteristics that support the case for linking it to these principles; it is embedded in an institutional context, including organisations, discursive standards and sometimes state support or laws that support the narrative; and a wider community is persuaded that claims for the value of the new asset are justified. The process culminates when the community concerned starts investing in the asset and buys into the supporting discourse because they now have a direct interest in sustaining it.

The following chapters will challenge the theory and the social ontology developed above by putting it to work to trace these processes in a selection of significant contemporary financial innovations.

6 | *Venture Capital and Unicorns*

On 2 March 2017 the shares of Snap Inc., the maker of the Snapchat social media app, were launched on the New York Stock Exchange. In 2016, the last year for which results were available at the time, Snap had total revenues of $404.5 million and incurred a net loss overall of $514.6 million (Snap Inc., 2017, p. 4). Its costs, in other words, were over twice its income, and its own prospectus listed a series of major risks to its future, including

> We face significant competition that we anticipate will continue to intensify ... We have incurred operating losses in the past, expect to incur operating losses in the future, and may never achieve or maintain profitability ... We have a short operating history and a new business model, which makes it difficult to evaluate our prospects and future financial results and increases the risk that we will not be successful (Snap Inc., 2017, p. 6).

The shares (which were unusual in offering no voting rights to their holders, leaving control of the company in the hands of its founders) were offered at $17 each and rose 44 per cent over the first day to close at $24.48, valuing the company at $28.3 billion (Kuchler & Bullock, 2017).

Such extraordinary valuations of digital businesses are not entirely a new phenomenon. Most strikingly, they were a central feature of the internet bubble on the US stock exchanges at the beginning of the twenty-first century, which saw "a capital market intoxicated by the prospects of digital technologies" (Feng, Froud, Johal, Haslam & Williams, 2001, p. 468). As Thrift argued, this bubble was driven in part by "new stories" that established the digital economy as an attractive investment category (Thrift, 2001, p. 425), and venture capitalists were among the most important forces who drove the boom (Feng et al., 2001, p. 494). What is perhaps most surprising is that these extraordinary valuations have returned so soon after the resulting crash and its impact on investors. These valuations have contributed to huge profits for venture capital companies, who have a direct interest in driving them up. Yet in contributing to a series of bubbles in technology stocks they also pose substantial risks for subsequent investors, the larger financial system and thus for society more widely when these bubbles burst. As Kenney and Zysman have argued, they also lead to massive misallocations of capital, when unicorns – private companies valued at over a billion dollars – with access to vast amounts of private capital use it to run businesses at a loss, undercutting previously successful businesses and thus "destroying economic value". This is perhaps most striking in its latest iteration, with venture capital driving the growth of platform businesses like Uber that are arguably also "destroying social value while also devaluing labor and work in the enterprise" (Kenney & Zysman, 2019, p. 39). The processes by which venture capitalists create the valuations that support these activities are thus central to the contemporary phenomenon of platform capitalism (Langley & Leyshon, 2017; Srnicek, 2016).

Why would anyone pay so much for shares in a company like Snap, with no history of delivering profits and with extraordinarily uncertain prospects of delivering future revenues that might justify this valuation? This chapter investigates how such companies come to be valued so highly, paying particular attention to the role of venture capitalists in constructing the value of unicorns and similar companies. In doing so it provides the first of the three case studies that apply this book's arguments on the construction of financial value to contemporary financial assets. It shows, in particular, how integral a focus on building asset circles has been to the process of constructing the value of the companies invested in by venture capitalists and thus how we need to extend established explanations of venture capital and company valuation to encompass this factor.

The chapter begins with an introductory overview of the venture capital process (which can be skipped by those familiar with venture capital). Venture capitalists generally operate by buying stakes in young companies, helping to build up the value of those companies, launching the shares of the most successful companies in their portfolios onto the stock exchange (although the majority of their investments produce low or negative returns) and then exiting their successful investments by selling off their stake. The chapter then looks at how each of these four stages contributes to inventing the value of companies like Snap, focusing on venture capital in the United States, where it has been most influential.

The Venture Capital Process

Venture capital (VC) funds in the United States are typically organised in the legal form of limited liability partnerships. They raise funds from outside investors (known as the *limited partners*), invest those funds in private companies (i.e. companies whose shares cannot be purchased on a public stock exchange) and aim to grow the companies in their portfolio so that they can sell on their stake at a large profit. Much of the funding is provided by pension funds (44 per cent in the United States since 1980) followed by financial institutions like banks and insurance companies (18 per cent) and endowments and foundations (17 per cent) (Metrick & Yasuda, 2010, pp. 27–28). The investment process is controlled by the *general partners* – the people we normally think of as venture capitalists – who manage the fund, identify suitable companies to invest in, work with those companies and look for profitable exit opportunities (for more detail on the structure of VC partnerships see Sahlman, 1990). Venture capital funds are time-limited, typically lasting ten years from initial funding to closing the fund, and because investments are spread over the first few years of this period, general partners usually aim to exit investments in individual companies in their portfolio in significantly less than ten years. They therefore tend to invest only in companies with prospects for rapid growth, with the result that they have been particularly focused on technology companies. Indeed two-thirds of the top US venture capital firms are based in Silicon Valley in California (Metrick & Yasuda, 2010, pp. 87–88), where they have been deeply involved in the explosion of internet-related technology companies over the last few decades. Silicon Valley attracted as much VC funding as the next four US regions combined all the way through from 1981 to 2017 (Kenney & Zysman, 2019, p. 37).

Venture capital began as a US phenomenon and although venture capital is becoming increasingly important elsewhere, notably in China, this chapter focuses on US cases as it is in the United States where venture capital remains most prominent and as a result the US cases are the most thoroughly documented in the literature so far (Nicholas, 2019). Tom Nicholas traces its roots back to the funding of New England whaling trips in the early nineteenth century (Nicholas, 2019, pp. 3–4). The first venture capital funds in their contemporary form date back to the 1940s and 1950s but they were relatively small until the end of the 1970s. At this point regulatory changes made it possible for US pension funds to invest in venture capital – one of a number of ways in which the venture capital business was made more viable by government action (Gompers & Lerner, 2006, p. 8; Nicholas, 2019, pp. 5, 315–316). The amount of capital committed to VC funds in the United States then grew steadily from $4.1 billion in 1980 to $40.6 billion in 1995 and much more rapidly to $253 billion in 2001, then stabilised at roughly this level for several years after the collapse of the internet stock bubble (Metrick & Yasuda, 2010, p. 24).

There is enormous variation in the success of venture capital investments (Langley & Leyshon, 2017, p. 24). Many fail – around 49 per cent of VC portfolio companies are defunct within ten years (Metrick & Yasuda, 2010, p. 125). The rest are sold. Some are acquired by larger businesses, at a range of prices reflecting the potential of the firm's product. At the bottom end of this range, companies may be bought solely in order to acquire their staff to deploy in other projects. The target outcome for the venture capitalist, however, has traditionally been to sell their stake in the portfolio company at a huge profit, either in a lucrative acquisition or by launching its shares onto a public stock exchange in an initial public offering (IPO), like the Snap IPO with which this chapter was introduced (Gompers & Lerner, 2006, pp. 7–8; Metrick & Yasuda, 2010, pp. 124–134). Recently some unicorns, notably Uber, have remained private for considerably longer, seeking to build a monopolistic position in a platform business by drawing on larger amounts of private capital, although it remains to be seen how this will play out over the longer term. Because of this range of possible outcomes, venture capital funds are rather risky investments, and VC firms can only attract investment in later funds by delivering high returns to their limited partners in earlier ones. This means that they need to make exceptional profits on their most successful investments to recover the costs of the failures and the run-of-the-mill cases where portfolio firms survive but deliver only ordinary levels of profit. In the most extreme cases, returns can be spectacular. The most successful venture capital investment in history is generally believed to be Benchmark Capital's investment in eBay. According to

Metrick and Yasuda (estimates vary), this generated a profit of $2.5 billion for the fund on an investment of $5 million (Metrick & Yasuda, 2010, pp. 89, 126) (for another estimate see Stross, 2000, p. xv).

Venture capitalists do not, however, simply supply cash to portfolio firms and wait for growth to happen. They take ownership of a portion of the company concerned in exchange for their investment then usually take an active role in supporting and directing the company's growth. Often they will take a seat on the board, supply ongoing strategy advice to the firm's founders, connect the firm up with reliable service suppliers and recruit new executives with the experience to manage the growth process (Metrick & Yasuda, 2010, pp. 95–97; there are many examples in Stross, 2000).

Enthusiasts for venture capital stress that it provides a mechanism to reallocate capital to dynamic and promising new companies, that it supports the development of those companies and that the high rates of return it claims are a reward for the high risks it takes in order to deliver successful new businesses. My purpose, however, is to cast light on a different aspect of the venture capital process – how it invents narratives of value that sometimes sustain quite extraordinary valuations when the venture capital fund disposes of its stake.

Buying into the Business

Whether the process begins with proactive research by venture capital firms, or through an approach to the venture capitalist by a company seeking investment, a potential investment is unlikely to be taken seriously without a business plan prepared by the owners of the firm concerned. These proposals are the first value narratives constructed in the venture capital process. Metrick and Yasuda estimate that for every investment VCs make they see of the order of 1,000 business ideas. Perhaps 100 of those receive some formal attention and only a handful enter the negotiation process (Metrick & Yasuda, 2010, pp. 135–136). Few make much progress without a business model – a speculative narrative about the future earning potential of the firm given a gloss of legitimacy by the employment of quantification and calculation. As Doganova and Muniesa put it, the purpose of such models is to "enrol allies" (Doganova & Muniesa, 2015, p. 113). To be more specific, the purpose is to create an asset circle for shares in the company by persuading venture capitalists to take the company seriously as a potential investment.

From the beginning, the interest of the venture capitalist is in selling their potential stake at a large profit within their time horizon, often through an IPO. For an IPO to be viable a company will usually need to be worth at least $150 million, and so the VC begins by asking how likely it is that this company could achieve this and how long it will take (Freeman, 2005, p. 148). Typically, the first questions for the venture capitalist will be what Metrick and Yasuda call "the market test and the management test" – is the market that it proposes to sell into big enough to offer this level of potential, and does the company's management have the capacity to deliver it (Metrick & Yasuda, 2010, p. 137)?

The firm's own business model will rarely be taken at face value by the venture capitalist, who is more likely to see a persuasive business plan as an indicator of business competence than a reliable forecast (Muniesa et al., 2017, ll. 1043–1088). Instead, it will be reworked by the venture capitalist in order to arrive at her own valuation of the firm, though again this inevitably remains a speculative narrative, with the figures providing an estimation of possibilities rather than anything more certain. There are two broad methods employed – two valuation conventions – known as *absolute valuation* and *relative valuation* (Metrick & Yasuda, 2010, pp. 179–180). In absolute valuation, the future cash flows of the business are forecast and discounted to produce an estimate of its net present value. This method is advocated by purists like Damodaran (2018) but it arguably fails to capture what matters to the venture capitalist. Take Snap, for example, with its history of loss making and its uncertain prospects of future profit. One might doubt whether any venture capitalist would have funded it based on an absolute valuation of Snap's cash flows, though perhaps their forecasts at the time might have been more optimistic than the outcomes so far. But for the venture capitalist, cash flows only matter to the extent that they affect the price that can be realised for the company's stock, and as numerous internet companies have shown, heavy losses are not necessarily an obstacle to a lucrative flotation. Indeed, for private platform companies seeking market dominance, heavy losses have become part of the standard growth model (Kenney & Zysman, 2019). Relative valuation, by contrast, involves valuing a company by comparing it with other similar companies – by aligning it with an existing category. Snap, for example, could be valued by comparing it with Facebook, another social media company that makes its money from advertising, currently (March 2021) valued by the stock market at over $700 billion. Snap's current valuation reflects the market's belief, or hope, that it may someday be able to raise advertising revenue that reflects the relative size of its user population and Facebook's. For a venture capitalist, what matters is the exit price, and in the case of Snap, it is clear that the exit price would have been more accurately reflected by using relative rather than absolute valuation methods. That exit price in turn, however, rested on persuading potential investors at the time of the IPO to adopt the relative valuation convention, and so the prospects of establishing such valuation narratives for their potential investments are also an important consideration.

If they lead to a funding decision, however, valuations also shape negotiations over the venture capitalist's stake in the business. If a venture capitalist values an existing business at $4 million, for example, and makes an investment of $1 million (giving a *post-money* valuation of $5 million), they will demand a 20 per cent share in the ownership of the business in return. There is thus a strategic element to such valuations, which need to be high enough to persuade the company to take the offer (particularly if there is competition from other venture capitalists) and low enough to extract maximum profit for the venture capitalist from future growth.

It is unusual for a portfolio company to need only one round of venture capital funding, indeed venture capitalists prefer to release funding in a series of rounds, enabling them to make their commitment contingent on progress in growing the company (Freeman, 2005, p. 152). At each stage, that progress should lead to a higher valuation for the company, but at each stage the venture capitalist will also expect to take a further stake in the company in return for the new investment, and it is common for the original owners to progressively lose control of their companies as a result (Freeman, 2005, pp. 161–163).

It is also common for the lead venture capitalist to involve other venture capitalists in later rounds (known as *syndication*), where they share the investment and thus both the risk and the potential reward. One benefit of this is that "other venture firms [provide] a second opinion on the investment opportunity" (Gompers & Lerner, 2006, p. 167). Indeed, for syndication to occur, the different venture capitalists involved must agree on a valuation for the firm, and thus also on the applicability of the conventions used to value it. This is therefore a step towards establishing both a larger asset circle and a more public valuation of the firm, and indeed it is striking that later funding round valuations are often made fully public, in sharp contrast to the secrecy with which the rest of venture capital performance is surrounded (Hook, 2016; Metrick & Yasuda, 2010, p. 46). Thus, for example, Xiaomi announced in December 2014 that it had raised $1.1 billion in a new funding round, valuing the company at $45 billion (BBC News, 2014), and Airbnb announced in March 2016 that it had raised $1 billion, valuing it at $30 billion (Hook, 2017).

It is hard to avoid the conclusion that these valuation announcements are part of a deliberate strategy to build expectations about the value of the firm in the public market, in preparation for a future IPO, thus starting to build a broader circle that is open to valuing the company in line with the venture capitalists' chosen valuation conventions. As one commentator has put it, "Financial experts refer to these headline valuations as 'marketing numbers', highlighting that they are a function of image as much as anything else" (Hook, 2015). Leading venture capitalists themselves have suggested that some of these valuations are "built on the flimsiest of edifices" or outright "fake" (Michael Moritz, chairman of the venture capital fund Sequoia, and Bill Gurley of Benchmark Capital, quoted in *Financial Times*, 2015). One of the most remarkable recent cases relates to an investment by SoftBank into Uber in 2017. The deal was structured so that SoftBank bought new shares at the same valuation as the previous funding round, nominally maintaining Uber's headline value of $68 billion, but at the same time (and as a condition of the deal), SoftBank also bought shares from existing investors at a substantially lower price, so that the average price they were paying for a share implied a significantly lower overall value for Uber (Waters, 2017). Investors in Uber thus sought to maintain the apparent public value of their shares at a higher level than they accepted in a private sale.

The case also illustrates the point that different members of an asset circle may come to different conclusions about the value of an asset. In this case, the investors selling shares to SoftBank appear to have had a lower valuation of the company than SoftBank did (since the average price SoftBank paid for shares was higher than the price that the sellers accepted). There are multiple possible reasons for this. The different investors might have all applied the same lay theories of value but evaluated the prospects of Uber differently in terms of those theories, or they might have applied different mixes of theories of value: perhaps some started to think of Uber as more of a taxi firm than a digital platform, for example, and thus to apply a different theory of what it would be considered worth in the market. Even within the same asset circle there can be disagreement, and negotiation between conflicting views, over the value of the asset concerned. One of the potential sources of such disagreement, as argued in Chapter 5, is that any given asset circle may intersect with the norm circles for multiple different theories of value, and hence different members of the asset circle may be members of different combinations of those norm circles.

Building the Business

Having acquired a stake in a portfolio firm, venture capitalists typically provide practical support to help the firm grow, primarily in the form of advice and in the form of introductions to a range of important business connections. According to Metrick and Yasuda, "Many VCs argue that these activities provide the best opportunity to add value and are the main source of comparative advantage for a successful VC" (Metrick & Yasuda, 2010, pp. 9–10). Ironically, they are often neglected in the economics literature because they are difficult to quantify (Metrick & Yasuda, 2010, p. 10). Conventionally the value of these contributions is seen as internal, as helping the company to become more capable of building its revenues and controlling its costs. However, there is a second aspect that is equally important: these activities contribute not just to building the business but also to building the *reputation* of the business.

The most striking way in which this is done is by association. Successful venture capitalists themselves have a reputation for launching successful companies, and having such a venture capitalist as an investor is already a mark of approval from a symbolic authority of financial value, a "consecration" of its potential value, to use Bourdieu's term (Bourdieu, 1993, p. 78). But venture capitalists also build networks of other symbolic actors in the field, and deploy them in the task of consecration. Thus, for example, not only do venture capitalists take seats on the board of their portfolio companies, but they may also bring in other board members, typically highly successful people whose very presence adds to the reputation of the firm.

Objectively small firms with little or no history of making profits can be rapidly elevated in the hierarchy of evaluations by the simple step of appointing a billionaire or a former government minister to the board of directors.

Similarly, venture capitalists often bring in new executives, including CEOs, to drive forward a portfolio company (Hellmann & Puri, 2002; Metrick & Yasuda, 2010, p. 97). Again, these may have stellar reputations out of all proportion to the current standing of the company (a process that is assisted by giving them substantial stock options, with the potential to dwarf their current compensation packages in the event of a successful IPO). Benchmark Capital, for example, recruited Meg Whitman from a job running a $600 million a year division of the world's largest toy company to take over as CEO of eBay in 1997 when its revenues were still a tiny fraction of that (Stross, 2000, pp. 55–60) (not many stock option packages work out quite this well: by 1999 the options she received were worth over $1 billion. Stross, 2000, p. 216). Press releases follow, and other investors start to notice companies that would otherwise have stayed below their radar and/or raise their expectations of the company's future performance. Venture capitalists may also introduce their portfolio companies to highly regarded potential customers and suppliers, such as "bankers, law firms, accountants, and executive search firms" (Freeman, 2005, p. 153). These may sometimes provide better services than less well-known competitors, but more importantly, they consistently help to raise the reputation – by association with their symbolic capital – of the portfolio firm.

The general public and smaller investors may be unaffected by these moves, but reputations are specific to audiences, and for a venture capitalist tending a company destined for an IPO, the audience that matters is the set of large institutional investors who might be persuaded to buy substantial blocks of the company's shares when they come to the market. This is exactly the audience that is likely to be impressed by big name directors, executives and suppliers, many of whom they may interact with in other contexts. As we shall see, the same effect operates when it comes to appointing financial institutions to handle a company's initial public offering.

As well as embedding the company in a high-status network, venture capitalists often also address the governance structures of the companies they invest in. Institutional investors are often wary of companies, for example, where the board is controlled by the founders of the company and their appointees, or where they are not confident that the incentives provided to managers align their interests with those of shareholders. These are both aspects of what is known as the *agency problem* in corporate governance: the problem that the interests of the managers and shareholders in a company might diverge, and therefore that shareholders need ways to ensure that managers do not pursue their own interests at the expense of the shareholders. As outside investors themselves, venture capitalists often take action to address these issues in portfolio firms, for example, by introducing outsiders (including themselves) onto the board and by separating the role of chairman and CEO (Hochberg, 2012). They also usually introduce stock options schemes for key managers and employees, which gives those staff a direct personal interest in helping to raise the stock price following an IPO (Freeman, 2005, p. 150).

While these measures reflect the needs of venture capitalists to protect their own interests, there is also a second motivation, which is that other potential investors also value such structures. Firms that adopt currently popular corporate governance mechanisms (or at least signal their adoption of them) have higher stock prices, implying that these mechanisms have symbolic value for investors (Zajac & Westphal, 2004). The presence of such mechanisms also leads US investors to attach greater legitimacy to foreign firms launching initial public offerings in the United States and to value their stocks more highly as a result (Bell Filatotchev & Aguilera, 2014).

Like all causal factors, however, this is only one mechanism amongst others, as we can see from some of the largest and most successful tech firms, such as Facebook and Google. In these cases, the founders have succeeded in retaining a substantial degree of control despite selling the majority of the business, through the practice of issuing different classes of stock to outside investors with heavily diluted voting rights (Neate, 2019; E. Stewart, 2018). Here the preference of venture capitalists and outside investors for removing control from the founders was overridden by other causal factors: notably, that these companies were so attractive to competing investors that their founders were in a stronger negotiating position and so were able to secure more advantageous terms.

Both the networks and the governance mechanisms that venture capitalists put in place, then, contribute to building the reputation of their portfolio firms among potential future purchasers of their stock.

They are implicitly responding to two lay theories of value that are prevalent in this population: first, that companies with familiar and respected executives, board members, investors and suppliers are good investments because they are worth more than those without them; and second, that companies with corporate governance mechanisms that are believed to protect the interests of shareholders are also worth more.

Approaching the IPO

The pay-off to venture capitalists depends on selling their stakes in their most successful portfolio firms at a large profit, and one of the best prospects of doing so is usually by launching the shares of the firm on the stock market in an *initial public offering* and then subsequently selling their own shares into the public market that this creates. Usually venture capitalists are not allowed to sell their own stake during the initial offering, but rather must hold it for a *lock-up* period of perhaps four or six months after the IPO before they can sell. Hence the IPO itself is not usually an exit event for the venture capitalist, but it creates the conditions in which they will exit their investment, and makes a crucial contribution to determining the price at which they will eventually be able to sell. This section will consider how venture capitalists approach the IPO process, and the next two will look at IPO outcomes and VC exits.

The IPO process is heavily regulated, particularly in the United States, again because of the agency problem – regulators are concerned about existing owners misleading potential shareholders about the business. There are therefore strict rules about what must be divulged during the period running up to the IPO, including properly audited accounts, sales history and full disclosure of the risks facing the business. This material, along with a description of the business and its plans, must be included in a document known as a *prospectus*, which in the United States must be submitted to the Securities Exchange Commission, approved by them and published to potential purchasers. The material on Snap with which this chapter began, for example, is taken from Snap's IPO prospectus (Snap Inc., 2017). Other written communications from and about the issuing firm are heavily restricted during this period to avoid the spread of misleading information. The merits of the business, however, can be marketed to potential institutional investors at events known as *roadshows* run by the investment bank that is handling the IPO, where attendees must be provided with the prospectus and no other written material. As the venture capitalist Gus Fuldner of Benchmark Capital puts it, "The roadshow is an opportunity for management to tell the story behind the numbers in the prospectus and to answer questions to improve investors' understanding of the business and the information contained in the prospectus" (Fuldner, 2012).

Telling "the story behind the numbers" takes on a new significance when the numbers are as unfavourable as those reported by Snap. Snap, however, is only one of many information technology firms that have been brought to market over the last two decades with negative earnings and radically uncertain prospects (Morgan, 2008, pp. 57–60). In such cases those behind the IPO need to construct a value narrative to justify the proposed valuation of the business – although usually they will have been working on this narrative long before the official IPO process. Biotech companies have often followed a similar pattern (Birch, 2017, pp. 461–462). Here, the narrative is generally that they are developing a new medical treatment and thus have heavy research and development costs until they can begin licensing the treatment to a manufacturer. Many biotech firms never succeed in making a profit, but a few make very large profits (Birch, 2017, pp. 471–472), and the narrative for new firms must be constructed in such a way as to align the public view of the business with those favourable comparators.

Indeed, this is also the hope for digital technology firms – investors in firms like Snap are betting that it will be the next major financial success story like Facebook, and the narratives built around Snap encourage this belief. Evan Spiegel, for example, the co-founder and chief executive of Snap, argued in August 2017 (in this case after Snap's IPO – public communications in the pre-IPO period are very limited so direct evidence of the narratives advanced in this period is hard to come by) that investors should pay more attention to the average revenue per user earned by the company. For Snap this was $1.05, and for Facebook $4.73, and the clear implication was that Snap could be expected to drive up its revenues per user to a comparable level (Lex, 2017b).

Prospectuses, roadshows and the value narratives constructed to support IPOs have two broad objectives. The first is to build the asset circle for the stock: a set of investors who are persuaded that the firm is a legitimate investment with promising prospects and are therefore prepared to consider investing in it. There is a sense in which these asset circles are segmented: there is an "insider" segment of financial institutions that disposes of the most capital and at which pre-IPO communications are directed. Meanwhile the media and particularly the financial press provide communication to the "outsider" segment of private investors, who may also develop some enthusiasm for the stock, particularly if it is a consumer-oriented company with high public visibility. The second objective is to establish belief amongst the asset circle on the applicability of particular categorisations and lay theories of value to justify a target price for the stock (e.g. in the case of Snap, comparability to Facebook). It is not only the narrative itself that counts, but also who delivers it: in another case of exploiting symbolic or reputational capital, venture capitalists tend to appoint high status investment bankers to act as advisors and underwriters for their IPOs, exploiting the networks of contacts and previous interactions these bankers have with large institutional investors.

While prospectuses are public, much of this process is carried through behind the scenes by the bookbuilders for the IPO – underwriters, usually employed by the investment banks, who consult institutional investors to establish what prices they might be willing to pay for the new shares and construct an order book for them (Ritter, 2011, pp. 8–9). While investors' decisions are based on how profitable they believe the purchase will be, their expectations of profits are influenced by the credibility of the various actors involved in the IPO process. In addition to the firm's executives and directors, these include the venture capitalists themselves. Gompers and Lerner, for example, argue that established venture capitalists build up reputational capital by bringing firms to market at fair value, and so their presence acts to certify the quality of the firm to investors (Gompers & Lerner, 2006, pp. 347–348). They also include the investment banks advising the firm on its offering and the underwriters themselves, whose reputations also function as certifying mechanisms (Chemmanur & Krishnan, 2012, p. 770). Snap's IPO, for example, was led by Morgan Stanley, named by the *Financial Times* as "the top US tech IPO bank in five of the last seven years" (Kuchler, 2017). Megginson and Weiss found that "VC backed firms have higher quality underwriters and auditors as well as a larger institutional following than do non-VC backed offers" (Megginson & Weiss, 1991, p. 892).

The underwriters will test a range of possible prices with investors, then before the public market opens set the official *offer price* at which the stock will be sold to subscribing investors (Chemmanur & Krishnan, 2012, p. 770). Investors may then apply to the underwriters to buy blocks of stock, so that the new stock can be placed in an orderly fashion with subscribers at a fixed price rather than waiting for the market to open. Often, the offer is oversubscribed, meaning that investors want to buy more shares than the issuing company is ready to offer. In such cases institutional investors receive only a part of the allocation they have bid for, and typically the share price will rise once the market opens.

These outcomes, however, are never guaranteed, and the IPO acts as a sort of reality test for the narratives constructed by venture capitalists and investment bankers, as demonstrated by the spectacular failure of the proposed $47 billion IPO of WeWork in 2019 (Edgecliffe-Johnson & Badkar, 2019). WeWork had constructed a narrative that positioned it as a new technology company that was going to transform the world of work, but the vast majority of its actual (heavily loss making) business consisted of renting and then re-letting office space. While the collapse of the IPO was also blamed to some extent on governance issues, the failure to convince potential investors of the valuation narrative meant that the underwriters were unable to build an asset circle for the stock amongst institutional investors (Platt & Fontanella-Khan, 2019).

The IPO

From the theoretical perspective of the previous chapter, one part of the purpose of the IPO is to insert the portfolio firm's stock into a pre-existing asset infrastructure: to make its shares recordable in an existing property infrastructure and purchasable in an existing exchange infrastructure. This is why the present chapter focuses on the construction of the asset circle element of the asset complex for these shares: the infrastructure element does not need to be created afresh because the process revolves around existing infrastructure. The IPO is on the one hand the insertion of the stock into an existing infrastructure and on the other a spectacular reality test – a test of the reality of the asset circle that the venture capitalists and their bankers have been attempting to construct.

Having set an offer price for those institutional investors that have made firm orders in advance of the market opening, the underwriters also act as market makers – that is, they agree to buy and sell stock on the open market, keeping a supply of the stock to enable them to bridge buy and sell orders and adjusting the price as orders come in. On the opening day they will assess demand for the share before setting an opening price, which is often higher than the offer price. The price will then move in response to supply and demand, and initial public offerings are generally judged on the closing price at the end of the first day of trading – commentators will say that an IPO was *underpriced* if the first day closing price is higher than the offer price (Ritter, 2011, p. 4). For example, Snap's shares were offered to advance investors at $17, but the market opened at $24 and closed on the first day at $24.48, an increase of 44 per cent over the offer price (Kuchler & Bullock, 2017). Annual average first day returns for US IPOs have rarely dropped below 10 per cent since 1990 and have occasionally been much higher, peaking at 70 per cent in 1999 (although not all IPOs are underpriced) (Ritter, 2011, p. 5). At least part of the explanation for this is that individual private investors are unable to obtain allocations of shares in advance of the IPO, and so if they have been drawn into the asset circle for the stock on the basis of the pre-IPO publicity this is their first opportunity to buy shares.

First day underpricing is a curious phenomenon. As VC backed offerings tend to be underpriced, it would appear that the issuing firms are effectively giving away part of the capital they could raise in the market to the institutional investors who are buying in at the offer price, since they could have sold the same shares at a higher price on the open market instead (this is known as "leaving money on the table"). It is entirely viable to reduce the gap between offer and market prices – a small proportion of US IPOs are conducted using an auction method to set the offer price and these show much less underpricing (Lowry, Officer & Schwert, 2010, pp. 427–428, 455–456).

Why, then, does underpricing occur? There are at least two plausible explanations, both of which may be valid. The first relates to the interests of the various parties. Let us begin with the underwriters. Although underwriting is a little more competitive in other countries (Ritter, 2011, p. 6), in the United States there appears to be an oligopoly, in which high status underwriters do not compete on price and all receive a more or less standard 7 per cent commission on the shares placed at the offer price (Liu & Ritter, 2011, pp. 585–586). While a lower offer price means lower commission on the IPO itself, under-writers have various techniques for taking advantage of underpricing that may more than compensate (Ritter, 2011, pp. 14–16). One is to exploit their capacity to allocate oversubscribed stock "by giving pref-erence in allocations to rent-seeking investors who repay part of their trading profits by paying commissions in excess of direct execution costs, known as soft dollars, on other trades" – in other words, underwriters can capture "part of the money left on the table" – as much as 45 per cent of it according to one estimate (Ritter, 2011, p. 14). Underwriters, in other words, benefit from underpricing.

But why would the firm issuing stock and the venture capitalists with investments in it accept this? Here the lock-up restrictions mentioned earlier play a role. Because neither the venture capital investors nor the staff of the issuing firm who hold stock options can dispose of their shares until several months after the IPO, they lose nothing from an underpriced IPO – it is not *their* money that is being left on the table. On the contrary, when a company's shares perform well after an IPO, this contributes to building its reputation as an attractive investment, both attracting new investors to the asset circle and increasing the valuation that existing members are willing to place on it. This improves the chances that when the VC and staff are eventually able to sell their shares they will get a good price for them. Venture capitalists also have a longer term incentive to underprice IPOs because the resulting publicity will improve their prospects of attracting capital for future VC funds (Gompers & Lerner, 2006, p. 349). Arguably, it is the longer-term shareholders in the business that lose out from underpricing, as the firm has less capital to fund future growth than it would otherwise have.

The concept of "underpricing", however, depends on the rather dubious assumption that there is a correct price for the stock on the day of the IPO, and that the correct price is the one that the market arrives at by the end of the day. It is only if we assume that this price reflects the intrinsic value of the company concerned that we will see a lower offer price as leaving money on the table. But cases like Snap should make us suspicious of this way of thinking about share prices. It is quite clear that there was no rational objective way of assessing the intrinsic value of Snap on the day of the IPO. In practice, and not only in the more extreme cases like this one, the price of a stock depends on who is willing to consider buying it – the size of the asset circle – the lay theories of value they are persuaded to apply in valuing the company and the beliefs they have about how other potential investors are likely to value it (Keynes's beauty contest – 1973, p. 156). All of these can in principle be influenced by the underwriters themselves. As Chemmanur and Krishnan put it,

high-reputation underwriters are able to obtain higher IPO valuations by generating greater participation by higher quality market players such as high-reputation co-managing underwriters and institutional investors, and by obtaining greater analyst coverage for IPOs backed by them. This, in turn, induces retail investors to become more optimistic about the future prospects of these IPO firms, thus ... resulting in higher firm valuations (Chemmanur & Krishnan, 2012, p. 775).

The paradoxical result is that it is possible (though difficult to prove, as it rests on a counterfactual comparison) that employing a high reputation underwriter as a bookbuilder might lead to a higher offer price *as well as* greater underpricing in the sense of a larger first day price increase – both the offer price and the closing price on the day of the IPO may be higher than they would be with a less well-connected underwriter or if an auction process was used to set the offer price. This does not conflict with the first set of explanations for underpricing, but it does put a different spin on it: in these circumstances, the use of high-status underwriters would no longer reduce the amount of capital raised at the IPO but rather increase it. Chemmanur and Krishnan link this to the market power of under-writers – rather than the underwriter's reputation certifying that the offer price is a fair reflection of the intrinsic value of the firm's shares, the underwriter's reputation and connections actually contribute to creating the value of the firm's shares in the first place, thus affecting both the viability of a given offer price and the subsequent performance of the shares on the open market (Chemmanur & Krishnan, 2012). To put it differently, there is no such thing as the intrinsic value of a firm's shares: the notion of intrinsic value is merely part of the ideology of share valuation, and the actual value of a share depends in part on the value invention work that underwriters do to grow the asset circle for it and influence the lay theories of value applied to it.

After the IPO

The venture capitalist's interest in a firm is by no means over when the IPO is complete, because lock-up provisions in the contract with the underwriters usually prevent them (and the portfolio firm's founders and staff) from disposing of their own shares until some time after the IPO, typically 180 days later (Gompers & Lerner, 2006, pp. 425–426). Lock-ups, however, are not universal – on average venture capitalists sell 8 per cent of their holdings at IPO time (Megginson & Weiss, 1991, p. 900), and even when lock-up agreements are in place underwriters often do allow some sales during the restricted period (Gompers & Lerner, 2006, p. 424).

While their stock is locked up (and indeed after the lock-up period if they retain shares beyond it), the venture capitalist and the firm's managers have a continuing interest in the maintenance of the firm's share price, which can vary enormously over the course of the period, particularly where the basis of the firm's valuation is highly uncertain and thus the share price is particularly vulnerable to changing sentiment amongst potential investors. Snap's share price, for example, varied between 73 per cent over its offer price and 30 per cent below it over the course of the first year of trading (and its three lock-up periods) (Singer, 2018). Venture capitalists remain actively involved in discursive work to sustain the value of their investment. Birch, for example, quotes one venture capitalist investor in biosciences companies as saying that "you've got to spend a huge amount of time managing sentiment and, you know, maintaining investor interest" once a firm has launched on the stock market (Birch, 2017, pp. 480–481). The portfolio firm's managers will also be involved – Evan Spiegel's comments on Snap's valuation noted earlier, for example, were made during the lock-up period on its shares.

Insiders, however, do not have a monopoly on value narratives, particularly once a company has gone public. Among the other groups of actors who shape beliefs on the valuation of a company, the most prominent are the stock analysts, many of them employed by investment banks, who research companies and issue reports assessing their valuation for the benefit of potential investors. They may adopt and further legitimise the narratives generated by the venture capitalists and the firm itself, or they may dispute them, and it is common for different analysts to take different stances.

One well-known case is the dispute between analysts over the valuation of Amazon in December 1998, mentioned in Chapter 3. On one side, Henry Blodget, an analyst at the Canadian bank CIBC Oppenheimer, gave a "buy" recommendation for the stock, raising his target price for it from $150 to $400; on the other Jonathan Cohen at Merrill Lynch issued a "sell" recommendation, valuing the stock at $50 (Beunza & Garud, 2007, p. 24). The difference between the two was largely due to the way they categorised the company. Cohen compared it with other booksellers, and forecast its revenue growth and margins on this basis, whereas Blodget categorised it as an internet company (a new category at the time) and as a result forecast both higher margins and a radically higher growth in sales than Cohen (Beunza & Garud, 2007, pp. 25–26). Arguably both analysts were applying the same theory of value, that a company's value could be established by comparing it with other companies in the same sector, but using a different sector to make the comparison. In April 1999, Amazon's annual results showed unexpectedly large losses, which led to a further dispute. On this occasion Abel Abelson, a journalist at *Barron's*, wrote an article claiming that Amazon was overvalued, and Blodget once again entered the fray to defend his high valuation for the stock, arguing that Amazon's losses should be seen as investments in gaining market share (Beunza & Garud, 2007, pp. 27–28). Blodget's arguments not only helped to sustain substantial growth in Amazon's share price, but also came to be used to justify extraordinarily high valuations for a whole range of internet stocks, and thus contributed to the dot.com share price bubble – and subsequent collapse – in the years leading up to 2001.

Investors, of course, have discretion about which analysts' reports they choose to take seriously, but when the balance of recommendations tips strongly to one side or another they do shape the discursive environment and influence decisions. For a more recent example, we can look again at the case of Snap. The initial response of the analysts to Snap's IPO was overwhelmingly negative: "The first 10 research notes rated the messaging app 'sell' or 'neutral', according to Bloomberg data" (Lex, 2017a). Indeed the first analyst to issue a sell rating gave a target price of just $10, versus the offer price of $17 and the opening price of $24, describing the company as "promising" (Bullock & Kuchler, 2017) but "significantly overvalued" (Kuchler & Bullock, 2017). Within three days of the IPO, Snap's stock price had dropped below the initial opening price and it stayed there for the following three years.

Analysts, however, are not necessarily objective sources of opinion. In particular, the analysts employed by the underwriters involved in an

IPO are known for giving upbeat recommendations on the stocks launched by their employers, typically publicising favourable value narratives and linking the stock to favourable theories of value while ignoring or downplaying narratives of overvaluation (Ritter, 2011, p. 15). The US Securities Exchange Commission prohibits analysts affiliated to IPO underwriters from publishing research for forty days after the launch, but when this quiet period is over, the underwriters' analysts are free to publish (Bradley, Jordan, Ritter & Wolf, 2004). In the case of Snap, for example, as the *Financial Times* put it:

Then on Monday came a flurry of "buy" ratings. Who were these gallant heroes, riding to the rescue of the besmirched Snap and boosting its worth by 5 per cent to almost $28bn? It was the underwriters, who had waited for a quiet period to elapse before publishing (Lex, 2017a).

Indeed it has been argued that one of the key motivations for venture capitalists to choose specific underwriters is precisely that they have influential analysts who can issue positive research on the company being floated (Liu & Ritter, 2011). In particular, each year the magazine *Institutional Investor* publishes a list of the three top analysts for each industrial sector, who are known as "all-star" analysts, and the underwriters who employ those analysts are particularly sought after when IPOs for firms in that sector are being planned (Liu & Ritter, 2011, p. 582). The prospect of securing favourable coverage from multiple influential analysts also appears to be one reason why many VCs engage multiple underwriters for an IPO (Liu & Ritter, 2011, p. 586). For smaller firms, getting analyst coverage at all is an important step towards establishing an asset circle for the firm's stock, and venture capitalists can sometimes use their network and their reputation to secure analyst coverage for their portfolio firms at the time of an IPO (Gompers & Lerner, 2006, pp. 484–485). There is also considerable evidence that increased analyst coverage has a positive impact on a firm's share price (Liu & Ritter, 2011, p. 582).

The quiet period restriction prevents underwriters' analysts from influencing the stock price at the time of an IPO and immediately after it, but as we have seen, the lock-up provision means that venture capitalists and the issuing firm's staff have no direct interest in the IPO price. Instead, they are interested in the price at the end of the lock-up period, and there is evidence that underwriters' analysts "are especially likely to release a positive recommendation shortly before the

lockup period expires" (Ritter, 2011, p. 15). This is particularly useful
to the inside investors as the share price often falls at the expiration of
the lock-up period due to the release of more stock onto the market
(Gompers & Lerner, 2006, p. 424). It is difficult to estimate the effect
for a single stock, as stock prices are always subject to multiple
interacting influences, but press reports suggest that Snap shares fell
in anticipation of the expiry of its lock-up periods (S. Archer, 2017).

The venture capitalist's final task is to manage the price that they
receive when they dispose of their own shares. They may, for example,
manage the impact of the release of more shares by employing underwriters to make a "secondary offering", in which large blocks of shares
are placed directly with institutional investors rather than being
released onto the open market without a buyer lined up in advance
(Freeman, 2005, p. 163).

Conclusion

According to the orthodox explanations of valuing corporate stocks,
each company has an intrinsic value that can be obtained by discounting reliable estimates of future cash flows. But as Jens Beckert has
pointed out, all estimates of future cash flows are fictions (Beckert,
2016). For most of the unicorns that have been launched onto the
stock market in the twenty-first century, these estimates have clearly
and openly been highly uncertain. Potential investors are not persuaded by such cash flow figures but rather by speculative valuation
stories. The central feature of these valuation stories is that they
associate the firms concerned with valuation conventions and with
categories or qualities that allow the firm to be positioned in relation
to the convention – the claim, for example, that Snap should be valued
by comparing its user population to Facebook's. These are familiar
tropes from the recent literature on valuation studies, but this book
goes beyond them by asking where these narratives come from, who
they are aimed at and why their originators are able to persuade their
target audience. This introduces considerations that are less common,
and in some cases rather neglected, in the valuation literature.

On one hand, we must recognise the interests and the power of the
value entrepreneurs that generate and propagate these narratives. For
unicorns, it is primarily venture capitalists and investment banks that
play this role, and their discursive power arises from their accumulated

social and symbolic capital – the networks of connection and obliga-
tion that they have built up with other financial institutions, and their
reputations with the wider investment community. Potential investors
may or may not be convinced by valuation stories, and this depends
not only on the cogency of the argument but also on how much trust
they place in the people telling the stories. Institutional investors in
particular tend to place their trust in the representatives of other
financial institutions, and so tend to be persuaded by the stories they
hear from respected investment banks, their underwriters and analysts,
by venture capitalists with reputations for launching successful shares
in the past and by companies whose representatives have already
acquired a reputation as effective business people.

On the other hand, narratives can have no effect whatsoever unless
they have audiences and those audiences are persuaded by them. In the
case of these financial valuation narratives, to be persuaded is, first, to
join the asset circle for the stocks of the unicorn concerned, or in other
words to become open to investing in it. Second, it is to assess the price
at which one is willing to buy in terms of the valuation narratives being
advocated. While authors like Beckert have started to introduce considerations of the power of institutions into the financial valuation
literature, there has been very little attention to the role of audiences,
and the concept of asset circles introduced in this book is the first
systematic attempt to theorise the crucial role of audiences in the
valuation process. This goes significantly beyond the existing literature
by showing that the venture capital process is heavily oriented to
building an asset circle for the stock of the portfolio company, and
tracing some of the different ways in which this process typically works
at different stages.

In weaving their stories and deploying their symbolic capital to
gather asset circles and invent value for their products, venture capitalists have played the central role in a process of diverting huge
amounts of capital into funding the so-called new economy (Kenney
& Zysman, 2019; Thrift, 2001). Some of the firms that venture capitalists launch onto the stock market become major global companies;
some succeed more modestly; some collapse or shrivel away, reflecting
how speculative all of their valuations were at IPO time: valuations
achieved by spinning stories and building audiences for them, rather
than by discounting reliable estimates of future cash flows to determine
the intrinsic value of the business. At the systemic level, this process has

created massive risks – risks of losses for ordinary investors in the stocks that venture capitalists have promoted, and risks of the destruction of businesses and jobs in the collapse that will presumably follow when the bubble bursts. Indeed, with the recent focus on sinking capital into platform economy businesses running at a loss to disrupt established business sectors, they are now destroying businesses and jobs even before such a collapse. By recognising that this process depends utterly on building an asset circle, we can see how fundamentally these harms depend on the complicity of investors in the stories woven by venture capital and their bankers.

While venture capitalists constantly create new financial assets in the form of the shares of new companies, these are new instances of a familiar *type* of financial asset, and they are therefore able to tap into an existing set of discourses about the valuation of this type of asset. By contrast, the next two chapters will be looking at more radical financial innovations: the creation and marketing of new *kinds* of financial asset, and the techniques that are used to establish legitimacy and valuation conventions for them.

7 | Bitcoin

The spectacular, if erratic, growth in the price of Bitcoin since its first implementation in 2009 has attracted substantial public interest. Unlike the stocks promoted by venture capitalists, it is not simply another instance of a well-established asset class, but rather a completely new asset class. Unlike those stocks, it is not promoted by well-connected finance industry insiders, but has been established by outsiders whose agenda was in part to escape the influence of established institutions. Unlike those stocks, it was conceived of and introduced, not as a financial asset in the usual sense but as a new form of money. And yet, as this chapter will argue, there are some striking similarities in how its value has been constructed. Above all, the process has depended upon the development of a series of narratives about the value of Bitcoin, which have sought to connect it to lay theories of value or valuation conventions, and those narratives have been marketed to specific groups of potential buyers leading to the construction of an asset circle. As an entirely new asset class, the creation of Bitcoin has required the invention of a complete asset complex, including both an asset circle and an infrastructure with both property and exchange elements. This chapter traces some of the narratives that have been told about Bitcoin and how they have contributed to (or, in some cases, undermined) the growth of an asset circle for Bitcoin and thus to its spectacular growth in price, but also discusses the growth of these infrastructures.

In doing so, it develops an alternative view to the most common mainstream explanation of Bitcoin's rising price, which is simply that it is a consequence of the irrationality of its unsophisticated buyers, who have been caught up in a kind of crowd madness that will all come crashing down when they realise that the bubble is unsustainable. This perspective is radically unsatisfactory. In many respects, the dynamic behind Bitcoin's price is rather similar to that behind the prices of mainstream assets – it is no less rational, for example, to invest in

Bitcoin than it was to invest in Amazon when it was losing money hand over fist. Both require(d) a leap of faith in speculative stories about the future, and dismissing this as irrational simply fails to provide an explanation of how valuation is established in such circumstances. This chapter assumes a model of asset value that is influenced by the factors discussed in the earlier chapters, in interaction with current events. Contributory factors include (a) the size of the asset circle for the asset and what contributes to increases and decreases in it; (b) the theories of value held by members of the asset circle and how these develop over time; (c) the development of the asset infrastructure – it has, for example, become much easier to buy and sell Bitcoin over time – including the legal context; and (d) news and events that affect valuations framed in terms of the current theories of value held by members of the asset circle. What should be striking about this model is that we can apply much the same model to explain changing prices of *any* type of financial asset, and indeed this is one of the consequences of the theoretical argument developed in earlier chapters.

The chapter begins by introducing Bitcoin and explaining both how it works and why valuing it is problematic. The rest of the chapter is divided into three empirical sections, discussing three dominant themes from the discourses on Bitcoin's value. It is loosely chronological, tracing the development of the asset circle for Bitcoin and how it has been extended through a series of transformations of the narratives of Bitcoin's value. We begin with the early narratives seeking to establish the case for valuing Bitcoin on the grounds that it is a viable form of money, and the groups of financial outsiders at which these narratives were directed. These early discourses were directed, not at the creation of an asset circle but at the creation of a *monetary circle*: a group of social actors prepared to accept Bitcoin in payment. The infrastructure constructed during this stage was also primarily oriented to the monetary function. The next section is devoted to the counter narratives that have sought to undermine the argument that Bitcoin is a viable form of money. Arguably these served to limit the growth of Bitcoin's appeal as a form of money, but in parallel Bitcoin has attracted increasing interest as an investment and thus developed an asset circle as well as its monetary circle. Finally, we consider more recent narratives positioning Bitcoin as a respectable financial investment, which have begun to extend its asset circle into new territory. Alongside this development, there has been substantial growth of the infrastructure around Bitcoin, making ownership and exchange more accessible and thus making it possible for more investors to join the asset circle.

The chapter draws on a mixture of sources, including conventional academic sources, but also extensively on material published between 2014 and 2018 on technology news sites, in the financial press and to a lesser extent on various online forums for the Bitcoin community (148 sources loaded into NVivo, of which 60 were sufficiently relevant to be included in the detailed analysis). These include material from a broad mix of sources and influencers, making it possible to trace the development of a set of discourses that has repeatedly shifted over the short life of Bitcoin as the character of the influencers and their audiences has changed.

What Is Bitcoin?

Bitcoin is an electronic currency. It was first proposed in October 2008 on an online forum for cryptographers in a paper attributed to Satoshi Nakamoto (a pseudonym) (Nakamoto, 2008a; Pagliery, 2014, p. 5) and first implemented by Nakamoto in January 2009 (Pagliery, 2014, p. 16). Even its name reflects the central thesis of this book: it includes the word "coin" in order to link it discursively with existing forms of currency and thus to help establish the belief that this too can operate and have value as a form of money. But bitcoins are utterly unlike ordinary coins. Nakamoto's paper defined "an electronic coin as a chain of digital signatures" (Nakamoto, 2008a, p. 2) but even this understates the difference between bitcoins and conventional coins. As Swartz and Maurer put it, "A Bitcoin is inseparable from the database of its agents' transactions since its creation" (Swartz & Maurer, 2014). There is no such material thing as a Bitcoin, and there is not even a distinct chain of signatures corresponding to a specific Bitcoin. At the material level the core property infrastructure of Bitcoin consists of a cryptographically secured distributed database of previous transactions, in each of which a quantity of bitcoin was assigned to a specific address, and sometimes these are subsequently split and transferred to other addresses. An individual only "owns" a quantity of bitcoin in the sense that they control further transfers of the bitcoins currently assigned to one or more of these addresses, which requires that they know the cryptographic *private key* required to make transfers from the address concerned. "*A* bitcoin" in the singular is just a quantity of bitcoin recorded in this way that happens to be numerically equal to the unit of account.

While this may sound confusing, in some ways it is not very different to holding our money in bank accounts. Contemporary bank accounts are equally virtual and depend in a similar way on individuals having the access required to control further assignments of the notional balances in their electronic accounts, which are themselves the result of previous chains of transactions. There are, however, important differences. First, bank accounts are associated with named owners, while Bitcoin addresses are in principle anonymous. Second, bank accounts are under the private control of the bank concerned and the account records or ledgers are kept on computers operated by the bank. By contrast, the database of Bitcoin transactions, known as a *blockchain*, is a distributed ledger in the sense that equally valid copies of it are held on thousands of personal computers and servers (which can be owned and operated by anyone) each running a piece of software known as a *full Bitcoin node*. Third, the bank takes responsibility for maintaining the security and accuracy of bank account records, whereas the accuracy of the Bitcoin blockchain is sustained by a complex process of chaining cryptographic proofs together into blocks of data, which are kept in sync across the many different distributed nodes. Fourth, the entire process depends on this being a *public* ledger, so that balances and transaction records are in principle available for anyone to inspect. The result is that Bitcoin can in principle operate as an electronic monetary system without the need for banks controlling account and transaction records.

Bitcoin was at first used only by a small group of enthusiasts, but both interest in Bitcoin and its price have exploded in recent years. Most spectacularly, in 2017 the total value of Bitcoin in circulation rose from US $15 billion to $216 billion, dropped back to $65 billion by the end of 2018 and rose again to over $1 trillion in February 2021 (Coinmarketcap.com, 2019a; Statista, 2021). Nevertheless, it might at first seem to be an odd case with which to illustrate issues in the valuation of financial assets. The value of money, after all, is often thought to raise rather different issues than the value of financial assets such as stocks and derivatives. In general, the value of money depends on whether you can buy things with it, what things you can buy and how much of them you get for a given quantity of money, whereas the value of a financial asset is generally thought to depend on the size and timing of the monetary income stream you believe it will provide in the future. But Bitcoin has also come to be seen as a financial asset, and the majority of Bitcoin transactions are now believed to be investment transactions (Yermack, 2014, p. 10).

Bitcoin therefore raises precisely the questions raised in the earlier chapters of this book. How has the value of this new type of asset been invented? What kinds of discourses have been deployed to support its construction? What valuation conventions have been invoked or developed within these discourses? Which audiences have these discourses been addressed to, what forums have been used to address them and how have they been persuaded to join an asset circle for Bitcoin? The chapter thus traces the growth of Bitcoin's asset circle and how it has been extended through a series of transformations of five key narratives of Bitcoin's value. Until recently both the audiences for these narratives and the actors involved in establishing them have been largely outside the mainstream financial system and yet they have succeeded (at least for the time being) in constructing a purely virtual asset as valuable. This provides a fascinating opportunity to consider some of the generic processes involved in creating value for financial assets in isolation from its connections with established political, economic and discursive power in mainstream finance.

The Problem of Valuing Bitcoin

Bitcoin has come to be treated as a financial asset in the sense that investors buy it in the hope of making a profit, rather than in order to "spend" it as a currency. Unlike many financial assets, however, a quantity of bitcoin does not entitle its holder to any stream of income at all, except the (rather uncertain) proceeds from selling it on at a later date. Bitcoin's critics, including the prominent economist Joseph Stiglitz, are fond of saying that this means it has no intrinsic value (Bloomberg.com, 2017; Lehdonvirta, 2017). In the monetary context this might seem to echo criticisms of paper currency by the advocates of the gold standard after the American Civil War, who saw precious metals as having an intrinsic value that paper lacks (Carruthers & Babb, 1996). Stiglitz, however, is drawing on a different sense of "intrinsic value", which arises from mainstream understandings of financial assets rather than money. In this context, the intrinsic value of an asset is understood to be the net present value of the income stream it confers control over. Stiglitz's message is that the lack of an income stream means that Bitcoin is not a respectable investment, yet the lack of an income stream is by no means unusual for financial assets, and it is common for shares, for example, to be bought primarily in the expectation of capital gains. Indeed the overwhelming proportion of the trade in conventional currencies is also speculative, with buyers hoping to make gains from movements in exchange rates (Andreou, 2013). Still, conventional currencies do have a value that derives from the possibility of using them to buy things, and in most cases that value is relatively stable, rarely changing by more than a few per cent per annum even if exchange rates vary rather more. By contrast, there are relatively few things that can be bought with Bitcoin and in the vast majority of cases the prices of those things are set in terms of another currency, so their bitcoin prices are as unstable as the exchange rate of the currency itself. The consequence is that the value of a Bitcoin is much less firmly anchored in the price of goods than the value of a conventional currency, which means it cannot be valued on the same basis, and makes it more difficult to justify placing any particular value on bitcoins.

This in turn lies behind widespread claims that the recent price rises of bitcoin and other cryptocurrencies (e.g. Litecoin, Ether, Ripple and over a thousand others which have followed in the footsteps of Bitcoin) are nothing more than a speculative bubble that might burst at any moment leaving purchasers massively out of pocket. Indeed, Bitcoin's price dropped by around 65 per cent from its peak on 18 December 2017 to 7 February 2018, and by 16 December 2018 had fallen by 83 per cent from its 2017 peak (Coinmarketcap.com, 2019b). This is by no means the first time that similar or even larger reverses have occurred – yet even at its trough in December 2018, the market capitalisation of Bitcoin remained almost four times its level at the beginning of 2017, and as I write in early 2021, the price of Bitcoin has recently hit a new peak of over 2.5 times the peak of 2017. Although the future is even more unpredictable for Bitcoin than it is for more mainstream financial assets, the pattern so far has been that bubbles in the price of Bitcoin have been followed by crashes that eventually plateau out at a much higher level than was normal before the bubble.

Even Bitcoin enthusiasts tend to accept that there are bubble phases in the price movements, but they also tend to see the successively rising plateaus as evidence of increasing intrinsic value. For much of Bitcoin's life, this claim has been organised around a central discursive theme: that Bitcoin is a form of money with major advantages over previous forms and therefore there will be a high future demand for it in this role. Thus, for example, on the FAQ page of bitcoin.org (perhaps the closest thing there is to an official Bitcoin web presence), we are told that "bitcoins have value because they are useful as a form of money" (Bitcoin.org, 2018). This is therefore a very different concept of intrinsic value than that adopted by advocates of the gold standard (Carruthers & Babb, 1996). We may see this as a rather loosely specified lay theory of value: Bitcoin's value should be assessed on the basis of its potential as a form of money. Asserting that potential is central to the value discourse of Bitcoin, although it is also the focus of robust disputes. The next two sections will examine the arguments commonly made for both sides.

Selling Bitcoin as Money

From the very beginning, the intention of Bitcoin's creators was to make it superior to existing forms of money for online payments because it would remove the need for "a trusted third party" – a financial institution that handled the payment process and took a fee for doing so – and thus the "cost of mediation" (Nakamoto, 2008a, p. 1). Nakamoto was particularly concerned about what he called "the inherent weaknesses of the trust based model", arguing that "merchants must be wary of their customers, hassling them for more information than they would otherwise need" because they were concerned about the dangers of customers demanding reversal of payments via the third party, and thus chargebacks to the merchant (Nakamoto, 2008a, p. 1). Because financial institutions carry the cost of this mediation process, they must charge higher transaction fees than would otherwise be necessary. The claim that Bitcoin is superior to existing forms of money is the first key narrative used to build support for it, and has remained central to claims for its value. It was not initially intended as an argument that would build an asset circle, however, but rather as an argument that would build a monetary circle: a set of social actors that would be willing to accept Bitcoin in payment and thus as a form of money.

Bitcoin was by no means the first attempt to develop a digital currency that would fulfil this role, but earlier attempts had failed to overcome a number of obstacles. One of the central obstacles to electronic cash is the double spending problem: because digital files are so easy to copy perfectly, how do you prevent someone copying their "money" and spending it in multiple different places? If people could spend the same electronic money repeatedly, it would rapidly become worthless. The problem is easily solved by financial institutions, using a secure central ledger to record how much everyone has in their accounts, but the cryptographers wanted a solution that was more like physical cash: private, untraceable and independent of third parties like the banks. Other cryptographers had been working for some time on alternative forms of money, but had not succeeded in creating a system that could eliminate this trusted third party (Popper, 2015, pp. 17–19). As an alternative, Nakamoto proposed a decentralised network that used chains of cryptographic proofs to eliminate the double spending problem. From the merchant's point of view, Nakamoto's proposal also solved the problem of chargebacks – customers could never reclaim the money they had paid for goods that had already been despatched to them. Nakamoto, on the other hand, took little interest in the problem of how customers could protect themselves against failures by suppliers, such as the non-delivery of goods that had been paid for. He handled this with a throwaway comment about "routine escrow mechanisms" while ignoring the question of how to operate escrow without the third parties that the system was designed to remove (Nakamoto, 2008a, p. 1).

With the need for trust in third parties supposedly eliminated, Nakamoto argued that his proposed system would have several advantages over conventional payment systems (I follow the usual practice of referring to Nakamoto with singular male pronouns, though neither his singularity nor his gender is known). In particular, he expected his solution to eliminate or radically reduce transaction costs. As well as being an advantage for existing types of payments, he expected that this would also make possible micropayments for "small casual transactions" that are currently not viable because the transaction fees would often be larger than the original transaction (Nakamoto, 2008a, p. 1; for an enthusiastic explanation of the case for micropayments, see Pagliery, 2014, pp. 106–115). Another important benefit, he believed, would be increased privacy – customers would no longer need to share as much personal information with vendors, indeed the payment itself could be anonymous and there was no data collection by the financial institutions who had previously acted as intermediaries (Nakamoto, 2008a, p. 7).

As we shall see in the next section, trust is certainly not eliminated in this system and we may also doubt some of Nakamoto's other claims. Nevertheless, the technology *does* eliminate the need for financial institutions to process payments, and in the early months of Bitcoin's existence this was enough to enthuse a very committed but initially very small community of cryptographers interested in the electronic money problem, who gradually began to download the Bitcoin software and run it on their machines (for a flavour of this period, see Popper, 2015, Chapters 2–4). Bitcoin had found the first audience for its narratives of value, who became the first members of its asset circle: the first people to believe that acquiring and holding Bitcoin was a reasonable thing to do. Most of them, however, were not buying but mining Bitcoin and monetary transactions using it were vanishingly rare. Hence, no one really knew how to value it, so this was rather different to the typical asset circle – and not yet a functioning monetary circle.

The asset circle was also quickly expanded to a second overlapping audience. The crypto-money enthusiasts had roots in the libertarian cypherpunk movement, which had earlier defeated US government attempts to snoop on all electronic conversations by introducing the PGP protocol (Karlstrøm, 2014, p. 29). Nakamoto soon developed a second set of narratives in order to market the Bitcoin idea to this audience. As Popper puts it, "Back when Satoshi had first launched the software, his writings were drily focused on the technical specifications of the programming. But after the first few weeks, Satoshi began emphasizing the broader ideological motivations for the software to help win over a broader audience" (Popper, 2015, p. 30). This was quite a deliberate strategy: in an email to early collaborator Hal Finney, Nakamoto said: "It's very attractive to the libertarian viewpoint if we can explain it properly" (Nakamoto, 2008b). At least some of the crypto-money enthusiasts, perhaps including Nakamoto, had also been influenced by the anti-state monetary theory of the Austrian economist Friedrich Hayek (Lawrence & Mudge, 2019).

Many elements of the more technical discourse in the initial white paper already appealed to this audience: disintermediation of monolithic financial institutions, privacy from surveillance by both the state and the banks and a decentralised architecture with no central authority. These were complemented with a further, explicitly anti-state argument: existing money was denounced as *fiat currency* – "a term for money generated by government decree" (Popper, 2015, p. 30), and as unreliable in value because "[t]he central bank must be trusted not to debase the currency, but the history of fiat currencies is full of breaches of that trust" (Nakamoto, cited in Popper, 2015, p. 30). At a relatively late stage before releasing the software and launching Bitcoin in January 2009, Nakamoto built in a feature that was designed to prevent the possibility of similar debasement of Bitcoin: although new coins would be issued every 10 minutes or so through the process of mining, the amount mined would gradually decline until the total in circulation stabilised at the arbitrary figure of 21 million bitcoins (Popper, 2015, p. 25).

As a number of studies have shown, this second, libertarian narrative positioning Bitcoin as a challenging alternative to the system dominated by the state and large corporations has played a significant role in the growth of the Bitcoin community. Karlstrøm argues, for example, that "the currency is viewed as much as an ideological instrument as it is a practical mode of exchange" (Karlstrøm, 2014, p. 26), and Lustig and Nardi found that "for many, using Bitcoin was an act of resistance against institutions they felt had failed them" (Lustig & Nardi, 2015, p. 747). One prominent proponent, Roger Ver, has said that "at first, almost everyone who got involved did so for philosophical reasons. We saw bitcoin as a great idea, as a way to separate money from the state" (Feuer, 2013). Neither lay theories of value nor the possibility of using bitcoin in exchange was as important to these early adopters as it was to use their money to make a political statement, or simply to align themselves with a cultural innovation.

Golumbia goes so far as to say that "Bitcoin is politics masquerading as technology" and to describe that politics is a mix of "right-wing, libertarian anti-government politics" and "conspiratorial anti-Central Bank rhetoric propagated by the extremist right in the US" (Golumbia, 2015, p. 119) (also see Gerard, 2017, Chapter 2). Weber sees the politics more in terms of market populism, in which "markets represent the will of the people, grant democratic legitimacy and represent an anti-elitist challenge to power" but the inegalitarian nature of markets is ignored (B. Weber, 2016, p. 20). More generally, there are different varieties of libertarianism and degrees of attachment to it

(Talmud & Darr, 2014, p. 30; B. Weber, 2016, p. 19) but adherents of many of them have been attracted to Bitcoin.

Bitcoin became known further afield in July 2010, when an article about Bitcoin was published on the popular technology website Slashdot.org, which bills itself as "News for nerds". After the article appeared interest in running the Bitcoin software leapt dramatically (Popper, 2015, pp. 47–49). The audience for Bitcoin's narrative had widened out beyond crypto geeks and committed libertarians to technology nerds who often did not understand the complex cryptography behind Bitcoin and were by no means specifically libertarian but who still liked the idea of clever technology being used to undermine authority. The openness of this wider community to libertarian arguments was in part a product of the wider discursive regime (to use Foucault's term) of market populism (Frank, 2000), and more particularly the Californian ideology so brilliantly analysed in the very early days of the Internet by Barbrook and Cameron (1995). This represents a coming together of hippie ideas of personal autonomy with glorification of entrepreneurs, faith in the technology being developed in Silicon Valley and an injection of libertarian philosophy (Gerard, 2017, p. 18). In the dominant version

Information technologies … empower the individual, enhance personal freedom, and radically reduce the power of the nation-state. Existing social, political and legal power structures will wither away to be replaced by unfettered interactions between autonomous individuals and their software. These restyled McLuhanites vigorously argue that big government should stay off the backs of resourceful entrepreneurs who are the only people cool and courageous enough to take risks (Barbrook & Cameron, 1995).

This blend of ideas remains prominent not only in online communities but also in influential technology publications like the magazine *Wired*. It gained some of its traction from still wider discursive trends, and in particular the growing influence in the 1980s and 1990s of neoliberal discourses lionising the market and demonising the state. Neoliberalism, despite its anti-statist rhetoric, remained a discourse aimed at changing the functioning of the state rather than replacing it: an "art of government" (Sotirakopoulos, 2017, p. 191). Yet it enlarged the space for superficially more rebellious discourses that accepted the new anti-statist common sense but carried it through to a more logical and even more individualist conclusion. Under the influence of the insidious neoliberal redefinition of common sense, and without necessarily being dogmatic libertarians, many technologists were comfortable with the libertarian cast of the Bitcoin community's sense of its own identity (Sotirakopoulos, 2017).

This was a crucial stage in the development of Bitcoin's value narrative, because it provided access to a much larger audience than the cryptographers alone by aligning Bitcoin's discourse to existing narratives. In this case these were political narratives rather than narratives of monetary value but they still had the effect of attracting a growing group of people who were interested in buying bitcoins.

Conflicting Narratives

As Bitcoin came to wider attention challenges to its monetary narrative started to appear, questioning the core claims from Nakamoto's white paper and thus the first key narrative of Bitcoin's value as a superior form of money. At the theoretical level it is important to recognise that the discursive environment is rarely homogeneous: different people accept and endorse different statements and it is not uncommon for different groups to become attached to ideas that are in conflict with each other (Elder-Vass, 2010b, pp. 131–137). Larger scale and longer-term social outcomes depend on which ideas end up securing widespread acceptance, and the discursive battles over Bitcoin's viability as a monetary system have had an effect on how it has come to be positioned. This section is more concerned with the practical level, and in particular with the ways in which Bitcoin's position has evolved under the influence of some of the issues raised in these debates. I do not propose to provide a comprehensive account of the challenges to Bitcoin's viability here but focus instead on a subset that seems most relevant to its status as a financial asset.

First, Nakamoto's insistence on the need for irreversible transactions invites two challenges: is irreversibility actually a good thing? And are Bitcoin transactions really irreversible? While vendors may not like the risk of a payment being reversed, customers generally value the possibility in cases where the vendor has failed to live up to their responsibilities, for example, by not providing the goods promised. No system that lacks a mechanism for resolving payment disputes is likely to replace payment solutions like credit cards and PayPal (Ciaian Rajcaniova & Kancs, 2016, p. 893; Gerard, 2017, p. 27). Pagliery quotes a gloriously ironic interview with a bitcoin miner who lost money when the company TerraHash.com ceased trading and failed to deliver mining kit that the miner had ordered and paid for in bitcoin: "It was poetic, ironic, ridiculous ... I said 'I'll never try to order mining hardware with bitcoin again'" (quoted in Pagliery, 2014, p. 55). Irreversibility also means that there are no mechanisms for resolving payment mistakes. For example, "If you send bitcoins to a non-existent address, they're lost forever" because the transaction cannot be reversed and the blockchain will forever show those bitcoins as belonging to an address that no one will ever be able to control (Gerard, 2017, p. 12). It would be possible to introduce partial solutions into the infrastructure, like the escrow system briefly alluded to in Nakamoto's paper, but they involve the insertion of trusted third parties into the payment process prior to registering a transaction on the blockchain, and thus reproduce the kind of structure that Nakamoto was trying to dispense with (B. Weber, 2016, pp. 29–30).

Another issue is that transactions on the blockchain actually *can* be reversed, using what is known as a 51 per cent attack, where a majority of Bitcoin miners co-operate to rewrite the most recent blocks on the chain. This is usually thought of as a problem for Bitcoin, but it has actually been openly organised on at least two occasions to address discrepancies on the blockchain that threatened the viability of the Bitcoin system (Bitcoin Wiki, 2016; Milne, 2017, p. 56; Popper, 2015, pp. 192–193). While this undermines claims that bitcoin transactions are irreversible in principle, it is clearly not a viable solution to everyday payment disputes.

Second, Nakamoto claimed that making payment transactions in bitcoin would incur low or zero costs, to the extent that micropayments would be possible using bitcoin payments. In the early days of Bitcoin, when each Bitcoin was worth a fraction of a cent and transaction fees were minimal, this might have seemed like a plausible claim, but as Bitcoin's value and usage has grown, so have transaction fees payable to the miners of new blocks. These grew to the point where between 7 December 2017 and 26 January 2018 daily average transaction fees were consistently over 10 US dollars, peaking at $55 on 22 December (BitInfoCharts, 2018). Although they have since dropped back, they remain highly variable, with even daily averages varying between 30c and $6.50 in the first half of 2020 (BitInfoCharts, 2020). Even at a few cents, transaction fees destroy the viability of micropayments and it is clear that bitcoin will not be a viable transactional currency unless this problem can be overcome. In practice, only investment-level transactions are viable at this kind of fee level – but if bitcoin is unusable as money, then the central thrust of its original value discourse melts away.

Third, Nakamoto argued for privacy for transactors and it is often claimed that Bitcoin can provide it, although Nakamoto's paper itself was rightly cautious over this claim. Again, there are two main challenges – to the desirability and to the achievability of full privacy. Let me begin this time with achievability. Strictly speaking Bitcoin is pseudonymous rather than anonymous, because each account is identified with a public key that is published on the blockchain for anyone to see, and indeed every transaction using that public key is also freely viewable on the blockchain. While users can reduce traceability by using a different public key for every transaction (as Nakamoto already recommended in the original white paper: 2008a, p. 6), there is always a link between any transaction in which bitcoin is spent and the previous transaction in which that bitcoin is received. The consequence is that it is straightforward to follow chains of transactions through the blockchain, and if you know, for example, the delivery address or bank account associated with one transaction, as you might if you were a bitcoin exchange or the other party to the transaction, these can be connected to specific individuals (Ciaian et al., 2016, p. 891). It has been argued that up to 40 per cent of the users of Bitcoin could be identified in this way (Karlstrøm, 2014, p. 33).

Question marks have also been raised against the desirability of complete transaction privacy, most obviously because it allows criminal activities to be concealed, as in the case of the Silk Road dark market where Bitcoin was used, primarily for the purchase of illegal drugs (Sotirakopoulos, 2017). This is why governments generally require authorised payment processors and deposit holders to follow "know your customer" and "anti money laundering" rules that require them to check the identity of account holders. Despite the libertarian ambitions of Bitcoin's founders, it is unlikely that it will ever establish itself as a mainstream monetary system without coming under the jurisdiction of such rules, and resistance to that merely encourages state crackdowns on alternative currencies (Milne, 2017, p. 52). Having said that, usage for illegal purposes did for a while drive increased non-speculative adoption of Bitcoin and acted as a test case for its viability as a form of money (Bradbury, 2014). There is a variety of use cases for money – different types of case where it may be used – and it is possible that a currency like Bitcoin could be successful in some niche use cases even if it is never used as widely as conventional currencies.

Still, if it *is* to achieve more widespread acceptance, it will have to address the issue raised by Nakamoto's fourth argument: the need for trust in institutions. The Bitcoin network that processes transactions does not in itself require trust in conventional financial institutions. Instead, users must trust the software that runs Bitcoin nodes (Dodd, 2014, p. 362; Popper, 2015, p. 55), they must trust the network of nodes on which it runs and they must trust the community of *miners* that process the transactions (in return for newly minted bitcoins) (Lustig & Nardi, 2015, pp. 750–751). Because these are decentralised, the user is not dependent on any single node or miner, but they must nevertheless trust the developers not to introduce accidentally or maliciously harmful changes to the software (as of 2018, new releases were controlled by a group of three people: see Bitcoin Core, 2018). They must also trust the miners not to collude in a malicious 51 per cent attack, which would allow them to rewrite the blockchain as they please (Hern, 2014; Spaven, 2015). In practice they must also trust a range of other software and/or service providers that have developed to fill the initial gaps in the property and exchange infrastructure of Bitcoin. To transact in bitcoins, for example, you will need either a wallet (a piece of software you download from the web and run on your own computer) or an account at an exchange (a service that holds Bitcoin on your behalf). Bitcoin wallets have generally been reliable, although there have been cases of fraudulent wallet software for other cryptocurrencies, but running your own wallet requires non-trivial technical knowledge and guarding against a range of security risks. Exchanges provide a more accessible way of holding Bitcoin, but Bitcoin exchanges have been notoriously unreliable. One study of forty exchanges found that eighteen had closed within three years, "with customer account balances often wiped out" (Moore & Christin, 2013). In the best known case, the MtGox exchange collapsed in February 2014, as a result of the operator's failure to detect or prevent the activities of a hacker who fraudulently withdrew huge amounts of Bitcoin from the exchange (for a full account, see Popper, 2015,

Chapter 29). Customers lost $400 million worth of Bitcoin in the collapse (Popper, 2015, p. 315).

Bitcoin, in other words, needs the very trust, institutional support and government regulation that its original designers set out to eliminate. At the practical level, the Bitcoin ecosystem has developed in response to these challenges, slowly building the kind of institutional and technical infrastructure that is required to build trust in it, often under the influence of established businesses. Wallet apps, for example, are appearing in app stores controlled by Apple and Google; price updates are published in business media outlets (e.g. CNBC, 2018); futures contracts are now traded on the two big Chicago futures exchanges (BBC News, 2017); and Visa debit cards have been introduced that allow purchasers to pay the merchant in conventional currencies but draw on a Bitcoin balance to fund the purchase (Smart, 2016). Failures like MtGox, according to the critics, do not mean that institutions are a problem, but rather that institutions need to be trustworthy, and this will generally mean that they need to be professionally run with oversight from regulatory agencies to ensure, for example, that they are not run by known criminals, that they take adequate measures to protect their users' funds and that they have adequate reserves or insurance to compensate users if problems do occur. Indeed, a number of governments are starting to introduce such regulation of cryptocurrency exchanges, notably Japan (M. J. Zuckerman, 2018). Even many existing Bitcoin users recognise that it needs institutional oversight (Lustig & Nardi, 2015, pp. 746–748). Bitcoin is living proof that the libertarian vision of market populism is internally contradictory: not only do markets depend on regulatory oversight from the state to work effectively, but lightly regulated markets also tend to generate corporate institutions that come to dominate the space.

At the discursive level, these challenges have tended to undermine the case for Bitcoin's viability as a major monetary system, and they have played a significant role in inhibiting the development of the asset circle for Bitcoin. Until relatively recently most more conventional investors were exposed to Bitcoin primarily through these narratives questioning its viability, and this tended to prevent those outside the technology community from taking it seriously as a viable monetary system and thus as an asset to consider purchasing. Ironically, this may also have helped to sustain Bitcoin's early community by bolstering its identity as an outsider group – a subculture – that is bound together by sharing what it sees as superior knowledge to the mainstream.

Selling Bitcoin as an Investment

Although the core rationale for valuing Bitcoin was originally its potential as a form of money, assets can be sustained by multiple distinct, possibly overlapping and perhaps even contradictory, narratives. While some members of Bitcoin's asset circle are persuaded by the political agenda, some by its potential as an alternative currency and some by a mixture of these arguments, there is an increasingly important group that is persuaded by a different but overlapping set of narratives: the speculative and growth cases for investing in Bitcoin. Alongside the monetary circle for Bitcoin, in other words, a non-monetary asset circle has developed: a set of social actors that see Bitcoin not as something to be accepted in payment for goods and services but as a potential financial investment. The total asset circle for Bitcoin is obtained by adding these two groups together.

Since its founding a little over a decade ago, the price of Bitcoin has grown spectacularly. Although it has seen spectacular peaks and troughs, the long-term trend has been one of underlying growth, with short-term spikes each moving the price up from one plateau to another higher one (price history charts are widely available on the web). This growth, originally driven by the increasing population of Bitcoin enthusiasts who were motivated at least as much by the idea of an alternative digital currency as by the prospects of profit, has attracted the attention of more financially oriented investors and this, combined with the inflexible supply of bitcoin, has contributed to further increasing the price. This cycle, however, is not built only by the price itself, but also by a range of other factors, including institutional and technical developments that make Bitcoin easier to buy, sell and hold, changes in regulatory environments (notably when governments indicated that bitcoin holdings would not be treated as illegal) and in particular discourses that build expectations of sustained and increasing price levels. There are several different groups of more financially oriented investors, motivated by different considerations, and different narratives that appeal to each group.

The third key set of narratives supporting Bitcoin is closely associated with the most distinctive group of investors, which marks the

Bitcoin investment community out from others: the *hodlers*. The term comes from a mis-spelling of *hold*, in what has become an iconic message on the Bitcointalk forum posted by an apparently inebriated user who was determined to hold his/her bitcoins despite constant messages from day traders advocating selling (GameKyuubi, 2013). The hodl meme has been supplemented with several others, notably the phrase "To the moon!" that expresses the hodlers' belief in the future price trajectory of Bitcoin (as at 2018 the phrase had 178,000 hits on the Bitcointalk forums), and the lambo meme, a tongue in cheek reference to buying Lamborghini cars with the proceeds of their investments. The spirit of these memes places the hodlers as technically savvy young people who typically picked up some Bitcoin relatively early because they were attracted to the project. At least some members of this group are sitting on a substantial profit, which contributes to a spirit of celebration of Bitcoin's growth so far. As Ilan Talmud has put it, this group "view themselves as both idealists and speculators" (Talmud & Darr, 2014, p. 30). There is a sense in which they joined the monetary circle as idealists and stayed on in the asset circle as speculators. This third set of narratives is distinguished by a kind of countercultural levity that is quite alien to more conventional investors, but helps to generate a sense of virtual community among the hodlers and a commitment to holding on to Bitcoin through thick and thin. This group has for some time provided the stable bedrock of Bitcoin's asset circle.

Alongside the hodlers, there are arguably three less committed and more explicitly financially oriented groups of investors: day traders, short-term speculators drawn in by Bitcoin's price spikes and an emerging group of longer-term investors who have rational arguments for seeing fundamental value in Bitcoin as an investment. Here we find the fourth and fifth key narratives of Bitcoin's value: as a speculative investment, and as a rational investment for professional investors.

The day traders are attracted by the volatility of Bitcoin – because the price often moves so far in such a short time compared to more conventional investments, there are lots of opportunities to make a quick profit (or a quick loss). Like day traders in other types of assets, they generally have no real interest in the underlying asset or its long-term prospects, and their discourses are typically focused on technical analysis of short-term price movements, speculation on the effect of the latest news on the price and often rather thinly veiled attempts to influence the price, through a mixture of planting posts in the more widely read forums and linked buying or selling on the exchanges – a practice, by no means confined to cryptocurrency, known as *pump and dump*. The larger the market capitalisation of Bitcoin has grown, the more difficult it is for these operators to move the price, and with the appearance of hundreds of new cryptocurrencies with much smaller market capitalisation it may be that this activity has shifted towards those other currencies. The degree of influence of day trading on both the price and the discussions on related forums is probably an indicator of the immaturity of Bitcoin as a financial asset and one might expect it to reduce if Bitcoin continues its long-term growth.

Day traders are a more or less constant presence regardless of the price level, but may not systematically influence the overall price, other than encouraging volatility. But other kinds of speculators are drawn in when Bitcoin seems to be rising over a sustained period of several months. Such episodes tend to be accompanied by press articles, both online and offline, that label the increase as a *bubble* – a period when an asset's price has risen substantially beyond the norm but without any apparent corresponding improvement in the "fundamentals", which in conventional asset markets is usually the expected income stream to which the asset holder is entitled. Ironically, the bubble discourse of over-valuation can actually attract investors, of two kinds. On the one hand there are relatively naïve investors who hear about price rises and are tempted to believe the price is bound to continue rising, often investors who were not really aware of this asset class before but learn about it through the publicity generated by the bubble. On the other, it can also attract more sophisticated investors (again including some who had not previously thought of Bitcoin as invest-ible) who fully expect the bubble to burst, but hope and intend to sell before this happens. These are the believers in the "Greater Fool" theory of investing, "the hope that another buyer down the line will pay even more money for the coins" (Lehdonvirta, 2017). Some market commentators are quite open about this situation, including this investment manager:

the current market regime is not fundamentally driven whatsoever, but is instead driven by narrative and investor sentiment. The market is a Keynesian beauty contest. It's crucial to practice second-level thinking – the question isn't just why a protocol is interesting, but why and when the market will find it interesting (Bernstein, 2018).

Both classes form part of a feedback mechanism that Robert Shiller makes the focus of his definition of a bubble: "[A] situation in which news of price increases spurs investor enthusiasm, which spreads by psychological contagion from person to person" (Shiller, 2015, p. xiii). Not all price increases lead to bubbles, however, and in the case of Bitcoin, with its absence of a linked revenue stream, the monetary discourse of its fundamental value remains important to persuading potential investors. As the commentator Ajit Tripathi has put it, "Bubbles are driven by sentiment and stories, and Bitcoin has a great story with a lot of mystery and spectacle to it" (quoted in Partington, 2017).

Bubbles, however, usually burst at some point. The risk in holding Bitcoin is that in the absence of a revenue stream, there is no obvious stopping point for a price crash. Ironically, the more ideological hodlers may help to provide a floor for the market that mitigates risk for more speculative investors (Song, 2017). But there is also another group starting to enter the market. One Bitcoin entrepreneur who has been running Bitcoin meet-ups in London since 2014 told Tom Redshaw that the make-up of the group has been changing: "I've had people who run hedge funds ... the whole City, the whole financial sector has been starting to research it. So now, you've still got the early adopters who are still very libertarian. You've got that group, but they're kind of starting to be eclipsed" (Redshaw, 2017, p. 64). Some of the more professional investors are investing in companies building businesses within the institutional ecology of Bitcoin, but there is also a growing discourse suggesting that Bitcoin itself has long-term value, and thus a further expansion of the asset circle, this time to long-term investors and institutional investors motivated by the growth prospects for Bitcoin and/or related cryptoassets. This development has brought an element of conflict into the discourses around Bitcoin, between those committed to its earlier political drivers and those who see it as a financial opportunity (Lawrence & Mudge, 2019).

This fifth narrative of long-term fundamental value as a rational professional investment is expressed particularly clearly in Burniske and Tatar's book *Cryptoassets: The Innovative Investor's Guide to Bitcoin and Beyond* (2017). They frame their approach by citing Benjamin Graham's well-known advice "to focus on the inherent value of an investment without getting caught up in the irrational behavior of the markets" (Burniske & Tatar, 2017, p. xxvi). There are two main threads to the narrative of investment value that they construct for Bitcoin. The first is simply that although Bitcoin's price is volatile, its movements are uncorrelated with other major financial assets, which according to modern portfolio theory makes it a useful investment for reducing the overall risk in a portfolio (Burniske & Tatar, 2017, Chapters 6–7). The second is more fundamental. They argue that Bitcoin's price is composed of two elements, which they call *utility value* and *speculative value* (Burniske & Tatar, 2017, pp. 117–119). While the speculative element is responsible for bubbles it also includes a more rational element: anticipation of future utility value. The utility value of a currency is simply the value that it needs in order to serve the purposes for which people actively use it: its use cases, which are what create sustainable demand for it (Burniske & Tatar, 2017, p. 35). As they put it, "bitcoin's utility value can be determined by assessing how much bitcoin is necessary for it to serve the internet economy it supports" (Burniske & Tatar, 2017, p. 176). Given that the maximum supply of Bitcoin is fixed at 21 million, the utility value of a single bitcoin can be calculated by dividing the total Bitcoin value required for it to fulfil its use cases by 21 million.

They select two use cases for Bitcoin (out of a much larger set of possible use cases) to estimate more precisely. First, there is a substantial international market for sending money between countries – remittances – and they speculate that Bitcoin might come to be used for 20 per cent of the current level of remittances. Given a reasonable assumption about velocity – the frequency, on average, with which money changes hands – they estimate that bitcoin would need to be valued at $952 to service 20 per cent of global remittances. Second, they see it as an alternative to gold for those who want to hold a store of value independent of any particular country's economy. If it were to take 10 per cent of this role from gold, this would account for a further $11,430 utility value per bitcoin, and because these utility values are additive, this produces a forecast utility value of $12,382 arising from these two use cases (Burniske & Tatar, 2017, pp. 178–179).

This is a fascinating argument. On the plus side, it provides a reasoned argument for a long-term fundamental value for Bitcoin, in contrast to the many critics who insist that it has no intrinsic value at all (e.g. Webb, 2018). Furthermore, in many ways the argument is quite conservative. It completely ignores the possibility that people will use Bitcoin to buy things, which is the use case originally anticipated by its founders, and if this use case did take off it would add further to Bitcoin's predicted value – potentially increasing it by orders of magnitude. On the other side, however, Bitcoin will have to overcome some of the difficulties discussed earlier if it is to be a viable vehicle for remittances on a large scale (and even more so if it is to be viable for a large volume of purchase transactions). Furthermore, the "gold" use case, which dominates the calculated value, depends on investors developing rather more confidence in its potential as a store of value than its price volatility currently warrants.

It is also an innovative argument, but one that rests on the same principle I have emphasised earlier in this book: that valuation conventions for new assets are consistently developed by drawing parallels with assets that are already established as having value and seeking to transpose to the new assets suitably amended versions of the conventions that have been used to construct value for the existing assets.

A related discursive move employed by Burniske and Tatar (but also other commentators) is to compare the cryptocurrency bubble with the internet bubble of 1997–2001. As we saw in Chapter 3, one of the striking features of this period was the vast amounts of money invested into immature businesses with very dubious business plans and prospects. While, predictably, the bubble burst and many people lost a great deal of money, investing in internet businesses was by no means as irrational as this might suggest. Those investors, it turned out, were quite right to believe that the new business models built on internet technology had massive transformative potential, and two decades later half of the top ten companies in the world by market capitalisation are internet companies (Alphabet, Amazon, Facebook, Tencent and Alibaba) (Wikipedia, 2020). Burniske and Tatar, and indeed some (but not all) technology commentators, see blockchain technology as equally transformative (2017, p. 27; Pagliery, 2014, p. 225). In the early stages of a major transformation, however, it is impossible to be sure which implementations of the technology will succeed, so there is some logic in investing across the most promising candidates, in the hope of catching this cycle's Google or Amazon. As they put it, "Whether specific cryptoassets will survive … remains to be seen. What's clear, however, is that some will be big winners" (2017, p. xxv).

Amongst the cryptocurrencies, Bitcoin is not only the most highly valued but also the most firmly embedded in the kind of institutional infrastructure that will be needed to succeed. As a result, it is the easiest to understand, buy, own and sell, thus currently providing the safest exposure to the cryptocurrency phenomenon for investors. It also attracts significant complementary investment in its institutional eco-system – its asset infrastructure – for similar reasons, and this in turn increases the likelihood that it will continue to be a leading cryptocur-rency. On this logic, it is worth investing even if the value proposition is still highly uncertain because the investment that converges on the sector leader gives it a first mover advantage. Technology is path dependent, and the more that is invested in cryptocurrencies in general and Bitcoin in particular the higher the chances are that they will end up justifying those investments. This too is part of the discourse that is encouraging new investors to take it seriously as a potential invest-ment, but it remains to be seen how much influence this will have in building the asset circle for Bitcoin out into the audience of professional investors.

In late 2020 and early 2021 some significant further steps seem to have been taken in this direction. Most notably, in December 2020 the software company Microstrategy announced that it had purchased over $1 billion worth of bitcoin, and in February, following a series of pro-Bitcoin tweets by its founder and main shareholder Elon Musk, the electric vehicle manufacturer Tesla announced that its treasury department had purchased $1.5 billion worth of bitcoin "to further diversify and maximize returns on our cash" (Kovach, 2021; MicroStrategy, 2020; Salzman, 2021). Even this short statement seems to confirm that one of the world's most highly valued corporations (and, at the time concerned, the world's richest man) has accepted the Burniske and Tatar argument that diversifying into Bitcoin is a useful strategy for a large investment portfolio, while also expressing a belief in the likelihood of further increases in Bitcoin's price. These purchases represent a significant extension in Bitcoin's asset circle, particularly if we measure asset circle size in terms of the funds controlled by the investors concerned, and not just the number of investors, as suggested in Chapter 5, although it seems likely that they will also encourage other investors to take Bitcoin more seriously. They appear to have been a major factor behind a further peak in Bitcoin's price, which hit $58,000 in February 2021, taking the total value of Bitcoin in circula-tion (briefly) over $1 trillion. No doubt there will be further troughs, but if these major corporations remain members of its asset circle, and particularly if their moves encourage others to follow suit, it would be reasonable to expect a new plateau at a considerably higher level than before.

Conclusion

As the peak of 2018 and the subsequent crash demonstrated, the value of Bitcoin is a fragile accomplishment, which depends not only on Bitcoin's infrastructure, but just as significantly on the narratives of monetary and investment value that have been constructed around it and the audiences that have accepted those narratives and thus become part of Bitcoin's asset circle. This asset circle and the corresponding value narratives are more diverse than those of more conventional financial assets. Yet, as we have seen in earlier chapters, at least some of the discourses of Bitcoin's value have been borrowed and adapted from those already used to justify the value of other assets.

Although the early narratives sought to establish Bitcoin as a form of money, they have had limited success in this respect, partly as a consequence of the growing influence of counter narratives disputing these claims. Ironically, Bitcoin has been much more successful as a financial asset, and the changing balance of its valuation narratives reflects this progression. Its price volatility is in part a product of shifting allegiances between these narratives, as sometimes external events appear to justify the doubts in the negative narratives and at other times to justify the optimism of the positive ones, and without clearly established valuation conventions there is little basis yet for stabilising prices.

The framework developed in this book gives us a way to see these price movements, not merely as symptoms of the foolishness of Bitcoin enthusiasts, as many mainstream commentators have suggested, but as the product of the same sorts of factors that influence the prices of all financial assets. These factors interact and play out in different ways for different assets. Bitcoin's price history so far seems to be the product of two interacting dynamics. On the one hand, the long-term increase can be seen as the product of a series of expansions of the asset circle and the application of a widening set of theories of value, driven by the discursive developments documented in this chapter. On the other, the short-term volatility appears to arise from the combination of doubts about the sustainability of Bitcoin's position with a constant stream of news affecting investors' beliefs about that sustainability. One day a government will take regulatory action against Bitcoin – or unveil a more favourable treatment. Another day, a major investment or a new piece of infrastructure provided by a mainstream financial institution will be announced – or an established exchange will collapse in a flurry of recriminations. Because beliefs in Bitcoin's value lack the anchoring factor of an expected income stream, the theories of value applied to it are particularly sensitive to expectations about its future price and so news items like these create greater volatility than we might otherwise expect.

One reason why Bitcoin's early story is particularly interesting is that because the entire monetary complex was invented from scratch in an inherently public process, both the work required to construct the infrastructure and that required to build the monetary circle are apparent. It is fascinating that this work could proceed so far in the absence of support from major institutional power, but we are starting to see the creeping arrival of such power. On the one hand, the Bitcoin ecosystem has gradually generated its own sources of power in the shape, for example, of mining pools, major exchanges and enormously wealthy "whales" – owners of large quantities of bitcoin. On the other, the old financial institutions have gradually become involved, such as hedge funds and the Chicago options exchanges.

Whatever path Bitcoin takes in the future, it has already become a significant financial asset, with a market capitalisation that peaked at over one trillion dollars in early 2021, a mere twelve years after its first implementation. This extraordinary growth in value has depended on the creation of a community of individuals who are prepared to take it seriously as an asset worth purchasing: the growth in Bitcoin's value has been driven, at least in part, by the growth in Bitcoin's asset circle, and this in turn has been driven by the dissemination of narratives of Bitcoin's value. While mainstream commentators are often dismissive of Bitcoin as lacking inherent value, all asset market values depend on narrative processes like these, and they are all vulnerable when the narrative becomes compromised.

8 | *Structured Subprime Securities*

This chapter brings us to the heart of the contemporary finance sector: the investment banks located on Wall Street, New York, and to a lesser extent in the City of London, with their vast assets and their vast influence over the contemporary financial economy and governments. These banks are at the centre of a web of institutions and practices that has been built up (and constantly remodelled) for hundreds of years, and they continue to exploit and manipulate that context to invent new kinds of financial assets in their constant search for ever-increasing profit. Unlike the advocates of Bitcoin, they do not need to create narratives of value and the corresponding asset circles from scratch. Unlike venture capitalists, they do not need to engage the services of those higher up the financial food chain to secure buyers for their latest creations. As we will see in this chapter, they are able, at least where the discursive and regulatory environment is favourable, to stretch and reshape existing institutions, narratives and asset circles to create a market for the new assets that they invent.

This chapter focuses on an interconnected set of financial assets that I will call *structured subprime securities*. These were introduced in the 1990s and 2000s to parcel up and resell the loan repayment commitments of mostly poorer residential property buyers in the United States. To put it simply, *structured* securities (generally created by financial institutions like investment banks) promise the investor a return calculated from the returns on other simpler assets such as corporate loans or, in the cases we are concerned with here, calculated from the returns on subprime mortgage lending. These structured securities include asset backed securities (ABSs) packaging up subprime mortgages, collateralised debt obligations (CDOs) built on these ABSs, credit default swaps (CDSs) taken out against them and synthetic CDOs funded by the income from these CDSs (I will explain all of these terms in the next section). Collectively, these constituted a massive "pyramid of promises" (Wolf, 2010, p. 10) built on the shaky foundation of the repayments from subprime mortgages.

This pyramid collapsed spectacularly in 2007–2009, bringing about a global financial crisis, and it is precisely because these promises proved so unreliable that I have selected them to discuss in this chapter. Not out of some sense of *schadenfreude*, but rather because it is in cases where we can observe financial constructions being invented and then falling apart that we can learn most about the underlying processes. For this purpose, it helps that the crisis has been widely studied, so there is a great deal of well-documented empirical material about it. My objective here is not to add to that stock or create new interpretations of the crisis itself, but rather to show the implications of what happened for the larger argument of the book. The crisis, in other words, is not the topic of the chapter, but the story of structured subprime securities that *is* its topic is inextricably bound up with the story of the crisis.

In examining that story, I will be asking how these new products were developed, how they were fitted to the existing institutional and discursive environment and what work was done to manipulate that environment to fit them. I will also examine how these products were constructed as having value. In particular, what was the principle of valuation that was employed and how was it established with potential buyers? Which financial actors were brought into the asset circles for them and how, and what other factors contributed to making these assets saleable – or *valuable*?

The chapter begins with an explanation of the history and structure of these new types of securities. My aim is for this to be as brief and transparent an explanation as possible given the need for some understanding of these instruments if the rest of the chapter is to make sense (readers familiar with these securities could skip this section). Then we turn to the processes by which they were constructed as having value, stressing the central role played by the ratings agencies in constructing what I will call *asset sets*: groups of assets that investors come to think of as equivalent to each other, so that investors who are part of the asset circle for existing assets in the set are smoothly inducted into the asset circle for further assets simply by inserting these new assets into the set. These developments were made possible by wider discursive framings of risk, which are covered next, and finally the chapter turns to the lessons that we can draw for the thesis of this book from the collapse of many of these securities in the financial crisis and the related collapse and reconfiguration of the asset circles for them, as the asset sets they had been inserted into started to fragment.

The Products

Structured subprime securities are types of what are known as fixed-income securities, or debt instruments. Fixed-income securities are created by lending money in return for a legal commitment to repay both regular interest over the period of the loan and the outstanding capital at or by the end of the period of the loan – it is the entitlement to receive this series of payments that makes them an asset. They differ from traditional bank loans in that they are negotiable – the asset can be transferred by the original lender (sometimes known as the originator of the loan) to another party in return for a payment. Traditionally, fixed-income securities were created by lending to governments or large stable corporations, and these are known as government or corporate *bonds*. The original lender in effect creates the bond by lending money to the borrower, but the lender can then sell the bond on to others, and when they do so the new owner of the bond is entitled to the income stream entailed by the debt. This could either be a fixed amount, or a variable interest rate pegged to a public index. While the income is fixed in the sense that it cannot be varied from the agreed formula, it is also somewhat risky, as the original borrower could default on their payments, although most governments rarely or never do so (MacKenzie, 2011, p. 1781).

Historically, mortgage lending for private buyers of residential property was done by lenders who then kept the loan on their own books until it was paid off. From time to time, however, lenders have sold on mortgage loans as fixed-income securities (Carruthers, 2010, p. 160). From the late 1930s the US Federal agency Fannie Mae started to buy and then sell on good quality mortgages where other government sponsored bodies had acted as the original lender (MacKenzie, 2011, p. 1790). This developed a step further in the late 1960s and early 1970s when Fannie Mae and its new competitor Freddie Mac started to securitise these loans to create mortgage-backed securities (MBS) (Fligstein & Goldstein, 2010, p. 29; MacKenzie, 2011, p. 1791). The trouble with selling on individual loans was that the buyer not only received the income stream but also carried the risk that the original borrower might default, although in these early cases, many of the mortgages were insured against default and so the main risk was prepayment: that the borrower would pay back the loan early when interest rates for new mortgages fell below the rate they were paying on their existing mortgage, thus depriving the buyer of the higher rate income stream they had expected (and paid for) when they took over the loan (Lewis, 2011, p. 7). It was therefore more attractive to potential buyers for the agency to bundle a number of loans together in one package or pool then divide that package up into lots (i.e. securities) which could be sold on – as illustrated in Figure 8.1. The buyer of each security received a share of the income stream generated by all the loans in the pool and carried an equivalent share of the risk, with the expectation being that they would lose a small percentage of the capital they had invested (rather than all or nothing) but would be compensated for this by the overall rate of return.

The next step (illustrated in Figure 8.2) was known as *tranching*, which meant that not all of the securities issued against a given pool of mortgages had the same rights. Some received a higher income stream, but they also took a higher share of the risk. Typically the riskiest tranches were known as the *junior* or *equity* tranches, and these were the first to lose capital when borrowers defaulted; the next layer were known as *mezzanine* tranches; and the safest layer (but also the layer with the lowest rate of interest) were known as *senior* tranches (for a very clear worked example see Milne, 2009, pp. 129–135). From the late 1970s, private commercial banks that made mortgage loans started to issue these tranched mortgage-backed securities, primarily in order to lower the cost of financing their mortgages. They could achieve this because the very low – effectively zero – default rates anticipated on the senior tranches made them very safe investments, even safer than bonds issued by the bank. Because bond interest rates are closely related to the risk of default, they could be sold on with a lower rate of interest payable to the buyer than alternative financing strategies whose cost was determined by the bank's own credit standing, such as issuing their own corporate bonds (Milne, 2009, pp. 136–137). Indeed, the banks typically kept the riskiest "equity" tranches themselves (another version of this practice is known as over-collateralisation: see Rona-Tas & Hiss, 2010, p. 127), and even if the tranches they had sold to investors suffered defaults, it was common for the bank to cover these losses, in order to maintain their reputation

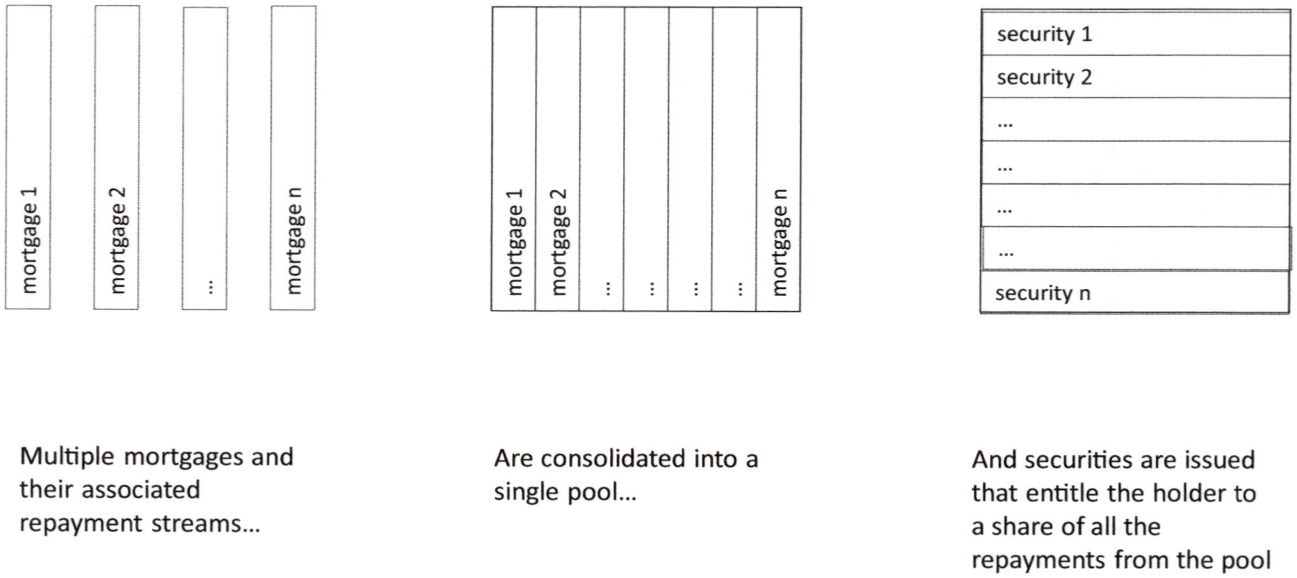

security 1
security 2
...
...
...
...
security n

And securities are issued that entitle the holder to a share of all the repayments from the pool

mortgage n
...
...
...
...
mortgage 2
mortgage 1

Are consolidated into a single pool...

mortgage 1
mortgage 2
...
mortgage n

Multiple mortgages and their associated repayment streams...

Figure 8.1 Mortgage securitisation

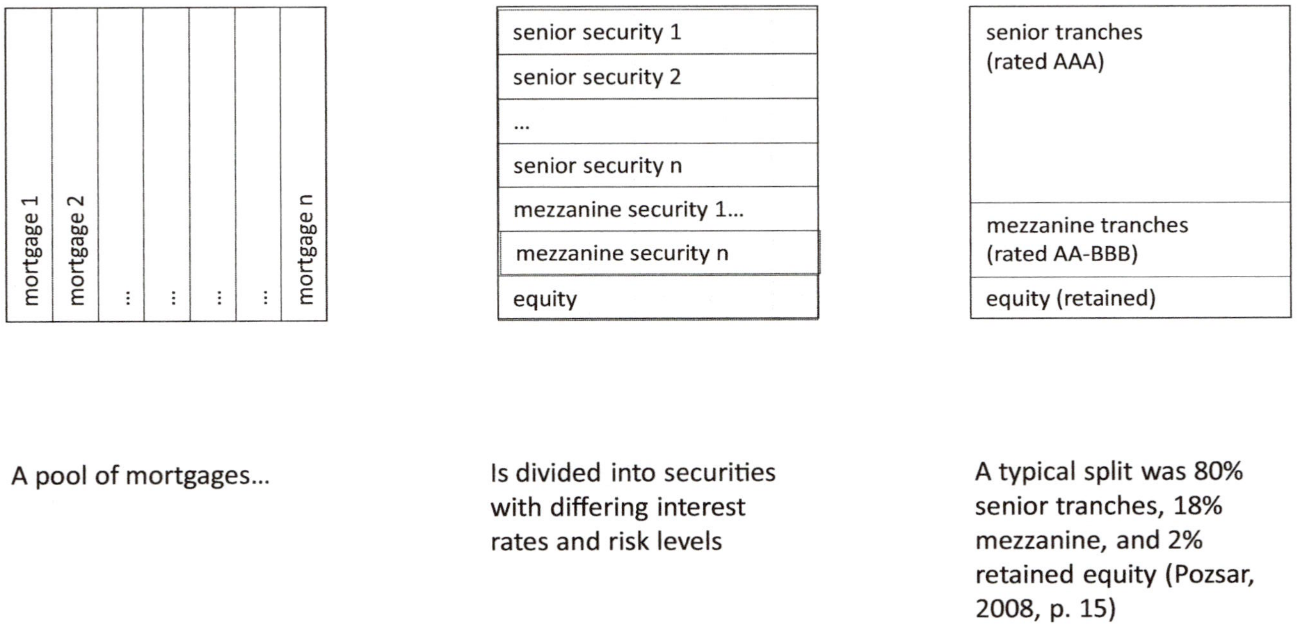

A pool of mortgages...

| mortgage 1 |
| mortgage 2 |
| ... |
| ... |
| ... |
| mortgage n |

Is divided into securities with differing interest rates and risk levels

| senior security 1 |
| senior security 2 |
| ... |
| senior security n |
| mezzanine security 1... |
| mezzanine security n |
| equity |

A typical split was 80% senior tranches, 18% mezzanine, and 2% retained equity (Pozsar, 2008, p. 15)

| senior tranches (rated AAA) |
| mezzanine tranches (rated AA-BBB) |
| equity (retained) |

Figure 8.2 Tranching of securities

and thus continue to be able to borrow cheaply in the future (Milne, 2009, p. 139).

So far, so good. When these institutions issued mortgages, they were generally careful only to make loans that they could be reasonably confident would be paid back, and it was in their own interest to do so, as they ultimately carried most of the risk of default. Securitisation was a technique designed to improve returns a little while providing good quality securities that had very little chance of defaulting.

Things started to change, however, in the 1990s, when a thriving market developed in *subprime* mortgages, mostly made by new lenders with lower standards than the traditional lenders. Subprime mortgages are home loans made to borrowers with a much higher risk of default. They might have a history of missing payments or defaulting completely on earlier mortgages or other loans for example, or low credit scores, court judgments against them, recent bankruptcy or an income that could not realistically support the payments required on the mortgage (Fligstein & Goldstein, 2010, p. 54). As the subprime boom developed, lenders also became increasingly incautious about the terms on which loans were handed out. Some loans were "100 percent nonrecourse mortgage[s]", in which the homeowner did not have to supply any capital at all, and could walk away from the mortgage with no penalty, giving them a large incentive to do so if the house fell into negative equity. Others were launched with "teaser rates" – low rates of interest for the first few years, that would then rise, in the expectation that the borrower would then refinance the house with a new teaser mortgage, but also in the knowledge that if refinancing was not available the borrower would be unable to meet their commitments (Stiglitz, 2010, p. 85). Some had "negative amortisation" – the borrower didn't even have to pay off the full amount of interest each month, but just added it to the loan, and some were issued without seeing any documentation to prove the borrower had the capacity to repay – or with documents that overstated their income, sometimes even overstated by the loan officers themselves (Stiglitz, 2010, p. 86). These were vastly more risky than traditional mortgages, both for the borrower and for whoever ended up holding the risk of default, but there were two factors that assuaged doubts. First, because of the higher risk of default, lenders charged much higher interest rates to subprime borrowers and believed that the profits to be made from those higher rates outweighed the risks of default, and second, US house prices were rising almost every year, so it was expected that borrowers could tap the profits of a rising house price by remortgaging to cover their payments.

Who, one might ask, would be foolish enough to fund this kind of borrowing on the huge scale that occurred during the run-up to the financial crisis? Ultimately, when the crisis hit, we all did through the taxes that funded government bailouts. But until then, it was funded through the complex set of structured subprime securities that are the main topic of this chapter. The simplest products were essentially the same as tranched MBSs although when the mortgages were subprime (and also when they were built on other kinds of loans such as vehicle loans) these were known instead as asset backed securities (Lewis, 2011, p. 99). However, their place in the ecosystem of finance was rather different. The loans were originated by a variety of mortgage issuers and brokers, who often did not hold the mortgages on their own books, but sold them on, typically to the Wall Street investment banks. When they were selling on the whole package, they had no real exposure to the risk of default, which undermined their diligence over the quality of loans; these companies were effectively earning fees for originating loans for the investment banks, rather than taking on credit risk themselves, so they had no incentive to ensure that the borrowers would be able to repay them. The investment banks then packaged the loans into ABSs, and sold on as many of these securities as they could (often through shadowy subsidiaries known as SPVs and SIVs), although it later emerged that they had retained many of the senior tranches, and sometimes also some of the riskiest tranches, believing that they were managing the risk adequately (Fligstein & Goldstein, 2010, p. 30; Goldstein & Fligstein, 2017). Unlike the earlier model of mortgage securitisation run mostly by the commercial (also known as "retail" or "high street") banks, this model was not designed to lower borrowing costs but rather to realise a short-term profit by selling on the securities at a higher price than the banks had paid for the loans in the first place (Milne, 2009, p. 144) – we will see how this was possible shortly. One accounting benefit was that instead of receiving an income stream over a number of years, the banks were able to realise a one-off payment and therefore bring forward profits, making the bank look more profitable (Das, 2012, pp. 389–390). Unlike the commercial banks, they generally sought to sell on the riskiest tranches, passing on the risk from the portfolio to the buyers (or so they thought). For a number of years, the model appeared to be extremely successful, providing finance to many buyers who would otherwise have been unable to purchase their own home, and substantial profits to those involved in funding the process (Gorton, 2009, p. 13).

This model was drawn in part from similar financial products known as collateralised debt obligations, which were also tranched securities, but usually based on other kinds of debt – often corporate debt, particularly loans made to private equity buyout firms. After the Basel Accord, an international agreement on banking practice, banks started to use CDOs to remove debts from their balance sheets so that they did not need to hold as much capital to provide a reserve against possible losses (MacKenzie, 2011, p. 1800; Pozsar, 2008, p. 13). Then they realised that they could make a profit from repackaging these loans and started to actively buy them to securitise (MacKenzie, 2011, p. 1801). Subprime mortgages, for the banks, were just more fuel to feed into the fire of securitisation.

Things became more complex, though, when the banks realised that the same fuel could be used more than once. One way of doing so was to take tranches of ABSs that they were unable to sell, particularly the riskier tranches that they were keen to offload (which were already securitised subprime mortgages), and to securitise them again, by creating CDOs from a pool of these ABS tranches, as illustrated in Figure 8.3 (MacKenzie, 2011, p. 1808). The banks then sold on these new CDOs of ABSs at a premium price and made a further profit on the deal. Milne has estimated that during this period "about $400 billion of ABS-CDOs were created to hold the lower-rated tranches of mortgage-backed securities and consumer ABS" (Milne, 2009, p. 163; also see Pozsar, 2008, p. 15). Some were even recycled further, into CDOs-squared, which were CDOs backed by a pool of other CDOs, sometimes including ABS-CDOs (Milne, 2009, p. 163; Pozsar, 2008, p. 16; Tett, 2010, p. 110).

Another technique was to use credit default swaps to create *synthetic* CDOs (this is the most complex of the structures I will discuss, so let's take it a step at a time). A credit default swap was essentially an insurance policy, although the industry avoided calling them that in order to avoid the regulations around insurance (Das, 2012, pp. 316–317). The core idea was that a bank would buy a CDS from an investor, making a continuing stream of payments, in return for

senior tranches (rated AAA) (80%)	composed of mezzanine securities	senior AAA tranches (62%)
		junior AAA tranches (14%)
mezzanine tranches (rated AA-BBB) (18%)		mezzanine tranches (rated AA-BBB) (20%)
equity (retained) (2%)		equity (retained) (4%)

A tranched pool of mortgage backed securities, used as input for...

A mezzanine ABS CDO composed entirely of securities rated AA-BBB...

Which is also tranched, with over 70% of the securities rated AAA

Figure 8.3 ABS-CDOs (based on Pozsar, 2008, p. 15, Table 1)

which the investor would reimburse the bank for the losses on a particular asset if the income stream from it dried up (Das, 2012, p. 316). Say, for example, the bank had made a loan to a corporation and took out a CDS with an investor (insurer) to cover the risk of default on the loan. If the corporation then collapsed and could not pay its debt (i.e. it defaulted on the credit that had been advanced to it), then the seller of the CDS would be obliged to cover the loss that would otherwise have been incurred by the bank by buying the loan at face value (this is the swap: in the event of a credit default, the seller of the CDS – the insurer, in effect – has to swap cash for the now devalued or even worthless loan). Investment banks used CDSs heavily to cover themselves against the risk of default on the tranches of ABSs and CDOs that they had retained on their own books, initially buying their CDSs from the insurance company AIG, until AIG became worried about the level of risk it was taking on itself (Lewis, 2011, pp. 68–72, 90).

One crucial difference between CDSs and insurance policies was that you could take out a CDS on an asset you didn't actually own, known as a *naked CDS*, and this made them a vehicle for speculation. If a speculator believed that a corporation's debt was worthless, for example, because she expected the corporation to go bankrupt, she could speculate against it by buying a CDS on that debt even though she did not hold any loans from the corporation herself. If the company did then collapse, she could buy up some of its debt at a rock-bottom price and then use it to claim the swap her CDS contract entitled her to, receiving the face value of the debt from the seller of the CDS and pocketing the difference. In the later phases of the subprime bubble, a number of hedge funds (and then some of the investment banks themselves) started to use CDSs in this way to bet against structured subprime securities (Lewis, 2011). Without owning ABSs or CDOs of ABSs themselves, they bought CDSs that would pay out if those ABSs or CDOs of ABSs defaulted (MacKenzie, 2011, p. 1824). The hedge funds bought these CDSs from the investment banks themselves (initially making the banks further exposed if the underlying securities failed) but the banks then generally made balancing transactions: In the earlier cases the bank bought a matching CDS, say from AIG, but at a lower premium, so that they made a profit from the deal. But later they found another way to profit from selling CDSs: the *synthetic CDO*.

The key to making sense of synthetic CDOs is that when a bank sold a CDS on a set of subprime securities, this gave it a revenue stream – the continuing pseudo-insurance payments made by the buyer of the CDS – which would last for the same lifetime as the underlying subprime securities. They were therefore able to do exactly the same thing with this revenue stream as they had done with the subprime mortgage payments that it mimicked: securitise it (Lewis, 2011, p. 76). If an investor bought an ABS, they would receive a cut of the continuing interest payments made by the underlying mortgage borrowers, while if some of the mortgages underlying their share of the income defaulted, they would lose an equivalent amount of their capital. If the investor bought a synthetic CDO instead, they would receive a cut of the continuing payments made by the buyer of the CDS, while if some of the corresponding mortgages from the ABS on which the CDS was based defaulted, they would also lose an equivalent amount of their capital (MacKenzie, 2011, pp. 1806, 1824). These CDOs were synthetic in the sense that the income stream on which they depended came from a CDS rather than from the mortgages that they were tied to, but they were just the same as an ABS or a CDO of ABSs in other respects.

Synthetic CDOs therefore magnified the potential consequences of a default in the underlying mortgage payments: if a certain set of mortgages had both an ABS and a synthetic CDO based on them, then any default would hit two sets of investors, not just one (although a further set of investors, the sellers of the CDSs, would profit correspondingly). But the banks loved them because they could turn another margin by securitisation and they also had tax advantages (Engelen et al., 2011, p. 53). Hence they positively encouraged the growth of CDSs that they could turn into synthetic CDOs (Lewis, 2011, p. 143). In at least one of the more risky categories of subprime lending (loans with BBB ratings) figures from the Federal Reserve suggest that synthetic CDOs were drawn against around half of the original ABSs issued in 2005, and over 90 per cent of those issued in 2006 (Pozsar, 2008, p. 15). The market for subprime based securities could therefore continue to expand even when the number of new mortgages being issued started to slow (Engelen et al., 2011, pp. 57–58).

The Wall Street banks depended on fixed-income securities for the bulk of their revenue (Lewis, 2011, p. 25), and the business of securitising mortgage lending became their biggest single source of income

(Fligstein & Goldstein, 2010, p. 44), particularly as fees could be earned at several steps along the chain (Engelen et al., 2011, p. 57). By the end of 2007 the volume of structured finance securities issued in the United States had reached a total of over 11 trillion dollars (Orléan, 2014, p. 261). The IMF gives similar figures for 2008, which includes corporate loans, commercial real estate lending and non-property consumer loans as well as mortgage-based lending. Prime mortgages (and MBSs built on them) came to $3.8 trillion, and subprime and Alt-A (similar to subprime) mortgages to $900 billion while ABSs amounted to $1.1 trillion and ABS CDOs to $400 billion (IMF, 2008, p. 15).

Ratings and Asset Sets

So far in this book, I have argued that the creators of new financial assets need to establish asset circles for them: groups of people and/or organisations who are prepared to buy the asset, if the price is right. But the creators of structured subprime securities did not build new asset circles; they introduced these new securities to an *existing* asset circle which accepted them remarkably readily as if they were simply more instances of an existing kind of security. When J.P. Morgan, for example, introduced the first synthetic CDOs (which they called a *Bistro* at the time) in 1997, they were able to sell $700 million worth within a few days (Tett, 2010, pp. 59–65). They were also able to use the existing infrastructures for ownership and exchange of fixed interest securities. True, these new securities required some explanation, but resistance proved to be minimal. The concept of asset circles helps us to make sense of how this otherwise extraordinary outcome was possible.

The heart of the explanation was that many of the institutional buyers of fixed-income securities effectively regarded them all as equivalent to each other. The source of the underlying revenue was of relatively little interest to them. What mattered was, to simplify a little, two numbers: the rate of return offered by the security (known as the *spread* or *yield*), and the level of risk associated with it, which was measured by the credit rating agencies on a standardised scale. As MacKenzie puts it, "[E]valuation practices crystallized in ratings reduce a difficult problem of evaluation ... to a simple one, by establishing a rough equivalence among debt instruments of different kinds" (MacKenzie, 2011, p. 1784). Existing buyers of fixed-income securities did not need to be persuaded that a new product was a potentially valuable financial asset, as long as it had a rating from a credit agency, and the level of credit rating determined both whether they would be interested in buying it and what level of return would be required to persuade them to buy it (MacKenzie, 2011, p. 1785).

The market for debt instruments, in other words, was rather different from the market for equities that the venture capitalists were selling into. Buyers of stocks and shares had to be persuaded that the particular company whose stocks they were being asked to buy had a good prospect of making future profits, or at least of rising in price on the market, and only those investors who had been persuaded of this were potential buyers of the stock. To put it another way, there was a separate asset circle for each company's shares. But in the fixed-income market, it was essentially the rating attached to a security that potential buyers cared about, and in effect there was only one asset circle for a whole group of related securities – all the securities with a given credit rating. Let me call the group of securities relating to a single asset circle an *asset set*. All that was required to establish a market for a fixed-income security was to get it past the gatekeepers of the appropriate asset set: the agencies who assigned the credit ratings.

For over a century, there have been agencies in the United States that assess the creditworthiness of potential borrowers, and in particular of businesses (for their early history, see Carruthers, 2013). By the late twentieth century, this business was dominated by three agencies: Moody's, Standard & Poor's and Fitch, and all three used variants of a single scale with which to indicate their assessments. Standard & Poor's scale, for example, starts at AAA – which indicates the safest class of borrowers, or of securities – and goes down through AA, A, BBB, BB, B, CCC, CC and C to D – the lowest possible grade, indicating a borrower who is already in default (there are also finer gradations; for the full list see MacKenzie, 2011, p. 1785). They have gradually extended the kinds of debt to which these gradings are applied, so that today they include not only business loans but also, for example, government borrowing (by both nations and municipalities), corporate bonds and all the various kinds of fixed-income securities developed on Wall Street. As Carruthers points out, the use of a single rating schema for all of these different kinds of debt has helped to make them "commensurable" in the sense that the differences between them have come to be seen "as quantitative (involving more-or-less risk) rather than qualitative" (Carruthers, 2010, p. 171). However different the borrowers concerned, and however different in character the types of risks that they faced, investors came to regard any two securities with the same risk rating as equivalent. Credit ratings have become proxies for the more detailed knowledge about a particular debt instrument that one might otherwise expect a sophisticated investor to require before taking the risk of investing in it.

Ratings also became embedded in a set of related institutions. For example, many pension funds put rules in place that constrained the investments their investment managers could purchase, based on these ratings, and many investment laws and regulations, known as *prudential regulations*, also refer to them. One survey found that over 70 per cent of investment managers were only allowed to buy assets at or above a particular minimum rating (Cantor Gwilym & Thomas, 2007). Even potential buyers who were not directly subject to such rules were often part of a community of professional investors, and thus strongly aware of the significance of credit ratings (Carruthers, 2010, pp. 167–168). Although different investors might have different rules about which investments they could purchase, securities rated BBB or higher are typically known as *investment grade* while those with lower ratings are known as non-investment grade or speculative grade securities (Fitch Ratings, 2021). This set of institutional structures created a sense of equivalence between very different investments across the financial community so that the asset circles for securities, of whatever type, that shared the same credit rating were merged into one. But they also installed the ratings agencies in a position of significant power as the gatekeepers of these asset circles.

Originally, the credit rating agencies earned revenue by selling subscriptions to the investors who made use of their ratings, but from the 1970s they started charging the issuers of debt instruments to rate them (Carruthers, 2010, p. 157). This created a conflict of interest that became particularly acute when the agencies were faced with a new sector where a small number of powerful customers controlled the vast majority of the business. With the rise of structured securities, the agencies faced a stream of requests from a handful of investment banks to rate new securities. The banks shopped around to find the ratings agency that would give their new products the best ratings (Fligstein & Goldstein, 2010, p. 29) and "constantly threatened to boycott the agencies if they failed to produce the wished-for ratings"

(Tett, 2010, p. 119). A rating for a CDO could command a fee of a hundred thousand dollars or more (Tett, 2010, p. 119), and given that each of these banks commanded a steady stream of such fees, they were in a position to put considerable pressure on the agencies. It is striking, for example, that Fitch made relatively little revenue from these securities (MacKenzie, 2011, p. 1812), which Engelen and his co-authors attribute to it using a model that produced less favourable ratings for them and therefore to the banks switching to the other agencies (Engelen et al., 2011, p. 56). The agencies' internal process for rating these securities always concluded with a management review of the recommended rating, and there is clear evidence that in the run-up to the financial crisis managers at some agencies consistently prevented ratings staff from downgrading subprime backed securities (Besedovsky, 2018, p. 76; Lewis, 2011, p. 102; Rona-Tas & Hiss, 2010, p. 130). There were even cases where banks asked (successfully) for analysts who they thought would rate their products less favourably to be removed from the team rating their securities (Besedovsky, 2018, p. 76). Both Standard & Poor's and Moody's subsequently paid enormous settlements (though without admitting guilt) to the US authorities over their ratings of mortgage-backed securities during this period (Reuters, 2017).

The banks also found other ways to get even more favourable ratings for their products. One was to do their own estimation of the rating that an agency would give a product – which was made easier because Moody's posted its model publicly (Tett, 2010, p. 118). The bank could then tweak the design of the product – for example by changing the division of the securities to be issued between different tranches – to maximise the number of securities that would receive the highest ratings (Carruthers, 2010, p. 161; MacKenzie, 2011, p. 1786; Tett, 2010, p. 119).

The consequence was that a remarkably high proportion of the structured securities built on subprime mortgages ended up with AAA or other very high ratings from the agencies. Given the institutional and discursive context, this "anointment" (Tett, 2010, p. 118), this consecration of value, immediately short-circuited the process of finding an asset circle for the new security and inserted it into an established asset set – and also as a consequence connected it to a valuation convention. A rating alone made an asset buyable by members of the existing asset circles for debt instruments of the allocated grade, and led those potential buyers to value it equivalently to those other debt instruments. CDOs, for example, would have been unpurchaseable for most institutional investors without a credit rating, but they became "a safe investment with well-defined risk features" (Carruthers, 2010, p. 162), regardless of their internal complexity, as soon as they were given an investment grade credit rating. With no access to the internal processes of the rating agencies, investors assumed they were applying scientific quantitative methods to make objective judgements and accepted those judgements as equating complex new securities to older types of asset that they knew and understood. Furthermore, these markets were so well established that there was a going rate at any one time for a security of a given rating: the valuation convention was simply that a buyer would expect a security of a given rating to offer the same rate of return as other securities of the same rating.

These ratings were also the key that enabled banks to profit from the securitisation process. At first sight, it is hard to see how an issuer could profit by taking one set of loans, repackaging them and selling them as another set of loans. Given that one would expect the new loans to be as risky as the old loans one would also expect the bank to pay as much interest on the new loans as they received on the old ones, leaving no margin to make the operation profitable. But because the ratings agencies could be persuaded to give many tranches of the new securities higher ratings than the original debt, it was possible to make a profit from securitisation (Carruthers, 2010, p. 161; MacKenzie, 2011, p. 1786). It was possible, for example, to construct a set of mortgage-backed securities from a set of subprime mortgages, and have 80 per cent of the new securities rated AAA – the highest possible grade of fixed-income security, higher even than most government debt – even though a significant number of the underlying mortgages were likely to default. And it was even possible to recycle the lower tranches produced by this exercise into a "Mezzanine ABS CDO" based entirely on BBB securities, and have 76 per cent of the new CDOs rated AAA (Pozsar, 2008, p. 15, Table 1). The first issuer (of the ABS) could pay a lower rate of interest on the first set of AAA securities than they received from the original mortgages, the second issuer (of the ABS CDO) could pay a lower rate of interest on the second set of AAA securities than on the intermediate BBB securities, and both issuers could realise the difference as profit.

The ratings issued by the agencies, then, not only gave access to a certain group of buyers by inserting the securities concerned into an asset set, but also generated opportunities for investment banks to make huge profits from what came to be known as *ratings arbitrage* – taking debt and shifting it to a higher rating in order to make a margin from the reduced rate of interest required to sell it on. It was the existence of this opportunity that led the banks to issue such huge quantities of these securities, drawing in vast amounts of investment that was funnelled into ever-increasing subprime mortgage lending and helping to inflate the housing bubble further as a consequence (Fligstein & Goldstein, 2010, pp. 46–47).

While the ratings agencies thus played a central role in the rise of structured subprime securities, none of this could have occurred without a series of other developments, some of which were actively pursued by the investment banks, although others were a product of the broader economic and political context. The central theme of these developments was a transformation in the treatment of risk by the financial sector.

The Risk Game

For much of the twentieth century, a carefully constructed regulatory regime forced much of the US finance sector to avoid taking major risks. In the early years of the twenty-first century, however, the Wall Street investment banks embraced risk, believing they could manipulate it, manage it and profit from it (Besedovsky, 2018, pp. 61–62). Structured securities were their preferred technology for making money out of risk.

The rise of structured securities was only possible, however, because of the transformation of the regulatory environment that had previously constrained the banks. The banks themselves played a role in this process, but they were pushing at a door that had already been partially opened by the rise of neoliberal discourse in the preceding decades, and in particular neoliberalism's mantra of allowing the market to function as freely as possible, which had been embraced by the Clinton administration. In finance, this mantra was propagated most aggressively by academic economists whose "relentless propagandizing ... for financial deregulation" (Orléan, 2014, p. 258) made it difficult for regulators to hold back the tide, and restrictions on the banks' activities were steadily swept away in the 1980s and 1990s. The investment banks themselves, however, were also active lobbyists. In the 1990s, for example, the International Swaps and Derivatives Association, led by a Hayekian banker from J.P. Morgan, successfully resisted at least four different bills before Congress that sought to regulate credit default swaps and related derivatives (Tett, 2010, pp. 36, 44–46).

By the early 2000s the mantra had even been adopted by the regulators themselves. Most significantly, Alan Greenspan, as governor of the Federal Reserve and thus the chief regulator of the US financial sector, actively resisted not only new regulations but also the application of old regulations to restrict the sale of subprime mortgages and securities based on them (Fligstein & Goldstein, 2010, p. 30). Greenspan believed that the banks were best placed to regulate their own behaviour and would avoid taking on excessive risk themselves without the need for any external regulatory intervention (Fligstein & Goldstein, 2010, p. 47). Greenspan himself later recognised that this had been an error (Tett, 2010, p. 297), but it was not a politically innocent error: it was the product of a discursive environment which encouraged the belief that the market could be relied on to regulate itself, and that discursive environment was in turn at least in part the product of the lobbying of the very firms that believed they could benefit from a relaxation of regulation.

The banks, meanwhile, had started to look at risk differently. They came to believe that new kinds of financial derivatives gave them tools for protecting themselves against risk by hedging – effectively buying insurance, such as CDSs, to cover potential defaults. They also, for a period, believed their own stories about securitisation: that it allowed risk to be dispersed around the financial system, where the most significant risks would be picked up by investors who were willing to take the riskiest tranches in return for higher rates of interest, while the highly rated tranches really were as safe as houses – or rather, safer. New financial technologies, they argued, had tamed risk, removing the need for regulation, and opening up a range of other benefits such as making finance available for new investment and to previously excluded classes of borrowers – the subprime mortgagees (Engelen et al., 2011, p. 44). As Besedovsky puts it, these new practices "suggest a high level of control over risk, and imply that knowledge about risk is sufficient to render it unproblematic" (Besedovsky, 2018, p. 61). Risk, to the investment banks, no longer felt like a threat. Now it smelled like an opportunity to make money.

This shift of orientation was also made more attractive to the bankers by a shift of organisational structure. Until the 1980s Wall Street's investment banks were organised as partnerships, which meant that their top managers were also the owners of the business: they earned a personal share of any profits but were also liable for a personal share of any losses. As a consequence, they were fairly risk averse, and oriented to the long term which meant that they were sensitive not only to financial risk but to activities that might be seen as damaging their reputation, upon which they depended for future business (Lewis, 2011, pp. 257–259). During the 1980s, however, these banks were all converted into public limited companies, with the consequence that the owners of the business – the people with an interest in preventing losses and in the long-term health of the business – were now a widely dispersed set of shareholders, with no control over day-to-day decisions and little information about what decisions were being made. Remarkably, in a period where the *agency problem* was prominent in financial discourse – the problem that managers of businesses could not be trusted to follow the interests of their owners (Jensen & Meckling, 1976) – the Wall Street banks moved away from a solution that prevented the problem.

A common response was to demand measures that supposedly aligned managers' interests with the creation of *shareholder value*, such as introducing bonuses linked to profits, and the inclusion of stock awards and stock options in compensation packages. The banks were enthusiastic adopters of this principle, but the consequences were perverse. The staff who set up securitisation deals and their managers raked off anything up to 50 per cent of the profits from these deals (and strongly influenced how those profits were calculated) but they had no exposure to the consequences of making major losses – the worst that would usually happen was that they might wipe out their bonus for the year, while still taking home a lucrative salary, and the very worst was that they might lose their job, but never the bonuses they had earned in previous years (Das, 2012, p. 176). There was therefore a massive incentive to take risks: "If they win then they get a share of the winnings. If they lose, then the bank picks up the loss" (Das, 2012, p. 176). Nor did their managers have much incentive to limit the risks, as they also picked up a share of the profits made by their staff.

Superficially these bonuses were justified by the delivery of profits to shareholders, but this was accompanied by what Curran calls *"risk illusion,* in which [a] massive amplification of risk is registered as an increase in the long-term value of an investment" (Curran, 2015, p. 398). The risk built into the banks' portfolios, in other words, was responsible for their apparent success, but also remained hidden to those viewing summary financial statements.

Both regulatory and institutional obstacles to the creation of risky new securities were thus swept away. But a further factor was that many of the investment banks failed to understand just how risky the securities they created actually were. The models used by the banks and the ratings agencies to estimate risk were all based on the Gaussian copula model, which, it turned out, systematically underestimated the likelihood of extreme events (Carruthers, 2010, p. 168; Das, 2012, pp. 187–189; MacKenzie, 2011, p. 1804). In particular, their models made conservative assumptions about the degree of correlation between the failures of different loans (MacKenzie, 2011, pp. 1813–1814). In normal circumstances, this was reasonable – the occasional mortgage default in one city, for example, would have little effect on the likelihood of a mortgage defaulting somewhere else. But occasionally, housing markets crash at the national scale, and mortgage defaults then contribute to a feedback loop: as more houses are repossessed and placed onto the market for resale, house prices fall further, and this pushes more borrowers into default (Tett, 2010, p. 235) – for example borrowers who needed to refinance their loans at the end of a teaser rate and now found their house was worth less than the outstanding finance on it.

Nor do most of the actors in this drama seem to have realised that the quality of the raw material being fed into their structured securities was steadily deteriorating. The proportion of conventional mortgage lending gradually fell, with subprime lending exceeding conventional mortgages for the first time by the end of 2004, and rising to 70 per cent of all mortgage loans at their peak in 2006 (Fligstein & Goldstein, 2010, p. 47). The quality of subprime loans themselves also gradually deteriorated as mortgage lenders relaxed their standards and even helped their customers to "game" their credit ratings (Rona-Tas & Hiss, 2010, pp. 133–137).

When the subprime housing bubble inevitably ran out of steam many more mortgages defaulted than the risk models had predicted.

The consequences will mostly be covered in the next section, but one is significant here: not only the junior but also the mid-ranking or mezzanine tranches of ABSs built on subprime mortgages started to default, and this meant that the mezzanine ABS CDOs described in the previous section also failed, including their supposedly AAA tranches (MacKenzie, 2011, p. 1817). The trick of tranching securities, it turned out, did not eliminate risk in the way that the banks, the ratings agencies, the regulators and the purchasers had all believed.

This was particularly unfortunate for those investment banks that had held on to huge quantities of the senior tranches of these securities themselves in the belief that they were extremely safe investments (Fligstein & Goldstein, 2010, p. 30; Pozsar, 2008, p. 16; Tett, 2010, p. 115). It turned out that, rather than having been dispersed by the new securitisation technologies, much of the risk had been concentrated in the banks themselves (and in some cases the insurers who had issued CDSs on these securities) (Engelen et al., 2011, pp. 59–60; MacKenzie, 2011, p. 1826). In the most spectacular individual case to come to public attention a senior trader at Morgan Stanley sold CDSs on 16 billion dollars' worth of supposedly safe AAA-rated CDOs. When the crisis hit, Morgan Stanley took a 9 billion dollar loss on the deal (Lewis, 2011, pp. 200–216).

When Asset Circles Break Down

A central element of the 2007–2009 crisis was the collapse of the market for many of the subprime based securities that I have been discussing in this chapter. This took the form of a breakdown in the asset circles for highly rated fixed-interest securities. As the crisis developed investors gradually realised that not all AAA rated fixed-income securities were equal. What had been a single asset circle for a single set of assets divided into multiple asset circles as the grouping of the assets into a single set dissolved, but this was not a neat straightforward process. This section traces the process through which this asset circle broke down and was reconfigured.

By late 2007, an increasing number of US subprime borrowers were defaulting on their mortgages, particularly those who had taken out loans in 2005 and 2006 when the property market had been at its peak (Tett, 2010, p. 234). When they relinquished their homes to the lenders, they often stripped them of anything of value before they left and at the same time resale prices were falling, particularly in the areas where many subprime borrowers were concentrated. The result was that when lenders defaulted, borrowers were only able to recover a much smaller percentage of their original loans than the risk models had assumed (Tett, 2010, p. 235). The combination of increasing numbers of defaults and reduced recovery rates from the sale of repossessed properties had tipped losses on subprime lending beyond the points that had seemed possible when many of the subprime based securities had been designed.

When the losses in the pool of mortgages behind a set of ABSs "have been big enough to cause the pool's total value to fall below the aggregate face value of the securities making up the CDO's topmost tranches (those initially rated AAA)", the holders of those senior securities could take control of the entire cashflow or even sell off the assets in the pool (MacKenzie, 2011, pp. 1818–1819). In these circumstances, the value of the lower tranches would be completely wiped out, as well as that of any CDOs of ABSs built from them (even the AAA tranches, as mentioned earlier). Indeed, the AAA tranches of the initial ABSs were also likely to be reduced in value as defaults moved beyond the point at which the income of the AAA tranches was also affected. MacKenzie reports that

Events of default have been declared in around 30% of ABS CDOs issued in 2005; in over 40% of those issued in the first half of 2006; in over 70% of deals from the second half of 2006; and in over 80% of deals from 2007 (Sakoui 2009). By March 2010, events of default had been declared in 418 CDOs totaling $371.6 billion, the vast majority of them ABS CDOs (MacKenzie, 2011, p. 1819).

The ratings agencies finally realised that these securities were far less safe than their models had predicted. Having steadily *increased* the initial ratings they gave to subprime based securities from 2003 to 2007 (Fligstein & Goldstein, 2010, pp. 48–49), they then started to downgrade those ratings. Around half of the securities issued in 2004 were downgraded by at least two notches (e.g. from AAA to A), and over 80 per cent of those issued in 2006 (Fligstein & Goldstein, 2010, p. 49). Those securities issued in 2006 and subsequently downgraded were moved down on average by more than 4.5 steps (e.g. from AAA to B) (Fligstein & Goldstein, 2010, p. 50).

The fragmentation of the asset circle, however, began before these public downgrades. As early as May 2005, some hedge funds started buying CDSs against subprime securities (Lewis, 2011, pp. 49–52), not to protect themselves against a loss of value of securities they already owned, but rather to speculate on the possibility of a price fall – they were *shorting* these securities. Shorting a security bears an intriguing relationship to the concept of an asset circle. While there are different ways of going short on a security, the basic model is the *put option*: you buy the right to sell the security at a given price (the strike price) at or before a certain point in the future. Buying a put option (or a CDS) for speculative reasons implies that you might want to buy the security in the future if its market price falls below the strike price so that you can then exercise the option to sell the security on to the party that sold you the put option at an immediate profit (though options are some-times settled for cash, making the intermediate purchase unnecessary). Shorting is a vote of no confidence in the current price of a security but also a statement that you might be willing to enter the market for it under certain future conditions. There is a sense, then, in which shorting makes the buyer of the option a member of the asset circle for the underlying security.

By November 2005, these hedge funds had been joined by some of the banks themselves (Lewis, 2011, pp. 58–59) but on the whole the motivation of these banks was slightly different from the hedge funds at this stage: they had started to realise that they were exposed to price falls on these securities, and wanted to hedge against this risk. Again, this implies a willingness to be in the market for these securities, but concern about the price. Still, some of the banks eventually sought ways to get out of the market altogether, with both J.P. Morgan and Goldman Sachs doing so sometime between late 2006 and early 2007 (Lewis, 2011, p. 209). Extraordinarily, some of the banks were still building and selling new CDOs – 50 billion dollars' worth between February and June 2007 (Lewis, 2011, pp. 164–165). It has even been alleged that some banks carried on selling them to customers while going short on the same types of securities themselves (Engelen et al., 2011, p. 56).

While one might still consider these banks and speculators to be part of an asset circle for subprime based securities, it is clear that they no longer regarded them as equivalent to other securities with the same ratings. They no longer, for example, classed AAA-rated ABS CDOs as being in the same asset set as other AAA rated securities or believed that the same valuation convention applied to them, because they no longer believed that they would receive the revenue flows that were officially attached to them. At this point two valuation conventions or lay theories of value came into conflict: the convention that the value of a bond could be determined by its credit rating and the convention that it depended on the expected revenue stream. Ultimately the credit rating convention was a proxy for the expected revenue convention, but as soon as some buyers doubted that the future revenue streams were as secure as the credit rating implied, a gap emerged between those who were applying one convention and those applying the other. This generated opportunities for arbitrage between the two – and thus those cases where banks reputedly sold securities to customers while simultaneously shorting the same securities themselves.

The banks' declining confidence was reflected in the increasing price of credit default swaps to cover the risk of default on these securities. As the demand for CDSs to cover ABS and CDO risk increased and the supply fell, the price rose, and this became public information through a set of price indices for these securities known as ABX. The ABX spread for BBB rated securities hit 10 per cent in March 2007 and over 25 per cent by November, implying that the market expected that proportion of their value to be written off, and even the index for the supposedly super-safe AAA rated securities rose to 5 per cent in November (Orléan, 2014, p. 287). Indeed by mid-2008, the BBB spread had risen to over 90 per cent and the AAA spread to almost 60 per cent (IMF, 2008, p. 13) One consequence was that it became public knowledge that major players doubted the creditworthiness of these instruments (MacKenzie, 2011, p. 1825).

From around June 2007, the credit agencies started to respond by downgrading securities publicly, and in some cases radically (Orléan, 2014, p. 289). This sparked a chain reaction. Owners of these securities lost confidence in them and sought to dispose of them. Many institutions found themselves obliged to sell because their rules (or legal constraints, in some cases – prudential regulations) did not allow them to hold lower-rated securities in their portfolios (Das, 2012, p. 384). They remained members of the asset circle for AAA rated securities, but the downgraded securities had been removed from the corresponding asset set.

Just as significantly, though, many of these buyers started to doubt the prospects of other, not yet downrated, subprime based securities. Nominally, these remained AAA rated, but who knew for how long? The consequence was that these securities, too, fell out of the set that these institutions were willing to hold. In other words, the asset circle or rather the asset set for AAA rated securities had started to fragment: now the asset circle willing to buy or hold subprime structured securities, even AAA rated ones, became a different group than the asset circle willing to buy or hold AAA rated fixed-income securities more generally. The market experienced a "flight to quality", or to put it differently, a reclassification of what counted as a quality investment and thus a flight away from assets that had been perceived as "quality" only a little earlier.

In these circumstances, prices went into freefall. At one point, sellers found that "AAA tranches were quoted (if you could find a quote!) at around 60% of face value. AA and A were lower again" (Das, 2012, p. 384). It seemed highly likely that most of these securities would return a much higher share than that of the original income projections, but no one was willing to buy them (Das, 2012, p. 384; Milne, 2009, pp. 13, 128; Tett, 2010, pp. 268–269). There was at least one obvious reason: unless you were an expert on the subprime mortgage market, it was impossible to tell which securities were at risk of dropping from a category that the market believed had a 10 per cent risk of default loss to one with a 30 per cent or greater risk. Structured subprime securities had become highly illiquid – it became impossible to sell them at what their holders thought of as a reasonable price – and this fed into the collapse of the asset circle since even those who still thought of them as potentially worthwhile investments were wary of buying them because of the risk of subsequently being unable to sell them.

Orléan argues that the reason for the collapse of this market was that "in August 2007, the valuation convention that had prevailed up until then was discarded without a new one being installed in its place, with the result that market participants no longer knew what a subprime loan was worth" (Orléan, 2014, p. 289). This is partly true. Although the valuations of other AAA rated securities were also shaken due to fears of contagion, and a cascade of doubt in the ratings system, ultimately it was not the convention as such that disappeared but its application to subprime based securities. A new convention was required for this asset set that reflected new knowledge about these securities, but inevitably it took some time for confidence to be established in alternative theories of value when hundreds of billions of dollars' worth of assets were involved. The carnage in the market meant that for the moment the beauty contest convention took over, and because investors had very little idea of how attractive other investors were going to find these securities they were generally unwilling to take the risk of buying them.

Conclusion

This chapter has examined how the value of structured subprime securities was constructed – invented – in the years running up to the financial crisis of 2007–2009 and how that construction fell apart when the crisis hit. Unlike the cases discussed in the previous two chapters, the creators of these securities did not need to create new asset circles or infrastructures for them. They were able to exploit their position at the heart of the web of established financial institutions to slot these new securities into the asset sets of existing asset circles, and thus to align them with a set of existing valuation conventions.

The banks expended considerable effort on shaping the discursive and institutional environment to allow them to create these securities unhindered by prudential regulations, although in doing so they took advantage of the wider discursive hegemony of neoliberal ideas. Having established the capacity to create such securities, they then expended further effort, and took advantage of their market power, to have them legitimated as belonging to an existing category of securities. This was achieved through the ratings agencies, who had the discursive authority to align new securities to existing categories: they were the gatekeepers of these asset sets. While the ratings agencies were more than willing to respond to the commercial incentives offered by the banks, the banks pushed the envelope further by tweaking the design of these securities to give them exactly the characteristics that aligned them maximally with the most advantageous categories. Arguably, there was also an element of concealment of the deteriorating quality of the raw materials bundled up in these assets, although it is by no means clear who was most responsible for the ratings agencies' ignorance of the unreliability of their ratings, and it seems likely that for some time none of the players were aware of the scale of the risks they were creating. The discursive authority of the ratings agencies was unquestioned in the wider investment community, with the result that once a security was assigned a rating it was readily accepted by the corresponding asset circle and valued according to the corresponding principle: the spread or yield expected for assets in that rating class.

In financial inventions we can often trace the development of socially constructed institutions that later come to be taken for granted. The principles of valuation of these securities were taken sufficiently for granted for investors to buy hundreds of billions of dollars' worth of them, and yet in this case we can also trace the collapse of the construction. As the financial crisis unfolded, the value of structured subprime securities was increasingly called into question, and their alignment with other securities accorded the same credit ratings started to unwind. Privately at first, and then in an increasingly unruly public process, these securities were detached from the asset sets into which they had been placed and effectively dumped in a newly separate asset set with a much smaller asset circle and no clear and broadly accepted principle of valuation. This application of the asset circles model developed in this book therefore helps us to make sense of the chaotic process that occurred in the markets for structured subprime securities as the crisis developed.

The impact of the resulting crisis has been widely documented. By October 2008, for example, the IMF estimated that the financial sector would need to write off $1.4 trillion of assets, including $210 billion of ABSs and $290 billion of ABS CDOs (IMF, 2008, p. 15). But the crisis did not only have direct costs for the financial sector. It also produced a major recession in the wider economy, with the result that production of new goods and services was lost. The chief economist at the Bank of England estimated that this foregone output amounted to 6.5 per cent of world GDP in 2009 – at a value of 4 trillion dollars. But this impact is not confined to a single year. His most conservative estimate is that in the long term the world has lost an entire year's worth of output, valued at 60 trillion dollars (Haldane, 2010).

These are some of the consequences of incautious inventions of financial value by institutions with enormous concentrations of power.

Such concentrations of power are always vulnerable to the temptation to overreach. If the banks had not stretched the risk model so thin, or pumped so much funding into inflating the bubble in subprime lending, they might have avoided the worst of the crisis. But unhindered competition in the service of profit maximisation does not know moderation.

9 | *Conclusion*

This chapter summarises the key points of the book's argument and then opens out to consider their wider implications for the study of the economy and the politics of finance.

Reinventing the Theory of Value

Neither the commodity economy nor the asset economy can function without persuading purchasers that their products have value. Although these sectors do not constitute our whole economy (Elder-Vass, 2016), they are the foundations of capitalism and the enormous power and influence it generates for contemporary corporations. If we are to understand the basis of that power we must therefore investigate – among other things – how value works and how it influences economic outcomes. But neither the marginalist tradition that dominates mainstream economics nor the Marxist tradition that dominates critical political economy has a viable understanding of value. Hence this book aims to reconstruct the theory of value, both to contribute to a better explanatory understanding of the commodity and asset economies and to support a more coherent critical politics of the economy.

The starting point is to recognise that value in the economic sense of the word is both subjective – it is a person's beliefs about what a thing is worth in monetary terms – and socially constructed – it depends on shared beliefs about how we should judge what things are worth. I have called these shared beliefs *lay theories of value*, a concept that overlaps heavily with the idea of a *valuation convention*. Lay theories of value are norms, ranging from quite simple and familiar norms like the convention that the price of an item should be lower if it is damaged to far more complex and specialised norms like the formulae that are sometimes used to calculate prices for some financial instruments. Like all norms, they are effective only to the extent that they are backed by a group of social actors that is willing to endorse and enforce them: a norm circle. Norm circles are social phenomena and thus are open to social influence, with the result that the range of actors supporting any given norm is constantly subject to change. In particular, norms about value have become the target of what we may call *value entrepreneurs*: social actors with an interest in advancing one theory of value rather than others, and in having those theories of value applied to particular commodities or assets. Typically, value entrepreneurs are the producers or sellers of the commodities and assets whose value they are seeking to influence. One striking example is the industry that has grown up around luxury goods, which depends on value norms that favour goods that are considered to have a higher social status by some group that we identify with. The most recent varieties of this particular structure are organised around concepts of heritage and craft, which are supposed to confer extra value on the products with which they are associated, regardless of their actual historical provenance (Boltanski & Esquerre, 2016; Thurnell-Read, 2019). The producers of these goods also invest in developing and sustaining the narratives of heritage, craft, luxury and so on that are used to confer extra value on them, through a broad range of marketing and advertising.

One important implication of this argument is that the profits of contemporary capitalists depend as much on their discursive power to influence beliefs related to their products as they do on more traditional forms of economic power. To put it in the terms developed in my previous book *Profit and Gift in the Digital Economy*, the discursive construction of value is an essential component of the complex of appropriative practices that many contemporary capitalists enact in order to generate profits (e.g. Elder-Vass, 2016, pp. 123–129).

Lay theories of value play a significant role in the determination of prices because they influence what potential purchasers are willing to pay (and indeed what potential sellers are willing to accept in payment). Prices, however, like all events in open systems, are influenced by many interacting causal factors and so cannot be explained purely in terms of a single mechanism, such as the market equilibration framework of mainstream economics or the extraction of surplus value upon which the Marxist tradition places so much weight. Each of these explanatory accounts dimly reflects one set of real influences on some prices – the responsiveness of demand and supply in some circumstances to price changes and the influence of labour costs on prices – but it leads to massive distortion to see either of them as the only or dominant determinant of what happens in the commodity economy. By contrast, I do not suggest that lay theories of value wholly determine prices, but rather that they interact with many other influences including some of the factors underlying mainstream and Marxist theories. The argument developed here transforms the theory of price determination, not by rejecting entirely the influence of demand, supply or labour costs, but by rejecting single-mechanism models like price equilibration and the labour theory of value. Instead, we must recognise the many and varied ways in which different mechanisms interact in the process of price determination. Once we do that it is clear that the lay theories of value that shape what prices buyers are willing to pay and what prices sellers are willing to accept will always play a central role in the explanation.

The argument necessarily becomes more complex when we turn to the financial sector and the value of financial assets. The value of a commodity like a chair or a haircut may be socially constructed, but the chair and the haircut themselves exist or occur independently (in a certain sense) of what we think of them. Financial assets are different. Not only is their value socially constructed, but so are the assets themselves. An asset is only an asset if people believe that it is and only remains an asset as long as they continue to believe it. To make sense of how assets can exist at all we have to recognise both that they depend on technical and institutional infrastructures and that their very existence as assets depends on them being resaleable. They thus exist only in the context of, and as a result of, larger socio-technical structures that I have called asset complexes, which consist on the one hand of the infrastructures that make it possible to register ownership and exchange of assets, and on the other hand of asset circles for the assets concerned: groups of social actors that are open to buying them.

Just as commodity producers invest heavily in shaping lay theories of value related to their products, asset producers are also value entrepreneurs. They invest not only in shaping theories of value and their application to their products, but also in establishing asset circles for their products. In the most extreme case of a brand-new asset type like Bitcoin, the asset circle must be built from scratch. In a market like that for equities, an asset circle must be carved out for each new equity by its value entrepreneurs, such as the VCs and investment bankers who launch unicorns onto the stock market. In the bond market, structured subprime securities were made comparable to existing fixed-income securities by bringing them into the set of assets rated by credit rating agencies and manipulating their risk ratings, thus inserting them into the existing structure of valuation conventions and asset circles for those securities.

These processes depend on the deployment of power. The establishment of Bitcoin was a long slow process, led at first by a group with little existing power, although they started to accumulate financial power as the value of the currency rose and narrative power as the reach of their discourses extended out beyond the small community of cryptographers to which they were originally confined. Venture capitalists, by contrast, start with control over substantial amounts of capital and in many cases with an established reputation for making profits for investors: symbolic capital that they can deploy to enrol a web of allies with existing valuation power. They must also guide their portfolio investments through a process of building a business with a plausible narrative about future returns, but their economic and discursive power gives them a massive advantage over independent businesses seeking to make their own way through similar processes. On the other hand, they must use some of their monetary power to buy the services of yet more powerful actors: the investment banks that control the marketing of new securities to the large investing institutions in the IPO process. Those banks can also act on their own account, deploying their power to establish new securities like CDOs. CDOs slipped smoothly into the asset portfolios of major investors with relatively little discursive work because the banks were able to use their reputations to underpin the plausibility of the new securities and their economic power to, in effect, buy favourable risk ratings for them. This power could not ultimately suppress the inherent instability of the underlying revenue streams, although their capacity to enrol governmental support did protect most of them from the most serious consequences of the crisis that resulted. But it did give them an extraordinary capacity to sell those unreliable revenue streams so easily and in such huge quantities in the first place.

One of the lessons of this book, then, is that value is socially constructed but not by anonymous, amorphous, discursive or linguistic forces (Elder-Vass, 2012). Value, rather, is actively invented through the self-interested actions of powerful economic actors. This is one of the mechanisms through which they tilt the playing field in their favour and thus extract profits from the sale of both commodities and assets. One consequence is that the value that is attributed to these commodities and assets is not a simple reflection of their usefulness to their purchasers or indeed the amount of labour expended in producing them, but rather is heavily skewed by those sellers who are able to exercise their discursive power to influence the assessments of value made by potential purchasers.

How to Study Value and the Economy

The approach I have adopted roots constructionism in a causal analysis that recognises the importance of structural power. But it also requires focus on the more micro-level mechanisms that underpin that power and on the specific interactions of human individuals, other material objects and social structures that produce particular events. This approach arises from a critical realist understanding of the ontology of the social world and the appropriate methods for studying it. Many of the components of the resulting analysis are potentially compatible with other approaches, but it is hard to see how they could be brought together coherently outside the critical realist framework.

By contrast with the marginalist and Marxist frameworks, critical realism liberates us from the "one ring to rule them all" approach that makes one specific mechanism, whether price equilibration or the extraction of surplus value, overwhelmingly dominant in every explanation of economic events. Economic events are like any other event in the sense that they depend on unique configurations of interacting causal forces, with no pre-ordained priority between them. They occur in open systems and must be approached with open minds. For any given event or set of similar events, we must investigate what combination of causal forces has contributed to it – retrodiction. But we must also examine the mechanisms that lie behind each type of causal force before we can plausibly explain how it contributes to the interaction of forces in any given event – retroduction. This is not to say that we cannot generalise our explanations. As I have argued, our retrodictive explanations may sometimes be framed in a way that applies to a range of similar events, and our retroductions of mechanisms may sometimes be generalisable to explain a similar causal power of a range of similar entities or structures. But all such generalisation requires caution and judgement to ensure that we do not extend it beyond the range of cases to which it legitimately applies due to relevant similarities in the cases and structures concerned.

Causal explanations are inevitably incomplete – there are always more causal influences that could be investigated, and we can only focus on a few mechanisms in the depth required to make sense of how they work and interact with particular others. The contribution of this book has been to theorise some of the mechanisms that lie behind valuations of commodities and assets, and to show how those theoretical developments can help improve our understanding of some important cases. The related concepts of lay theories of value, asset circles and asset sets provide new tools for explaining the construction of financial value. In the case of venture capital, the book has gone beyond the existing literature by showing that the venture capital process is heavily oriented to building an asset circle for the stock of the portfolio company. In the case of Bitcoin, these concepts enable us to explain the progression of Bitcoin's price as the product primarily of a series of expansions of its asset circle, each driven by the application of new lay theories of value, whereas existing accounts tend to dismiss this trend as merely a symptom of the madness of the Bitcoin crowd. In the case of structured subprime securities, the addition of the concept of asset sets helps to make sense of why it was so easy for the investment banks to secure buyers for these innovative and risky instruments, but also of how the markets reacted when these assets were downgraded during the financial crisis.

Inevitably there are always more angles that could be pursued, more causal mechanisms that could be investigated and introduced into our explanations. There is always a trade-off, however, between being more comprehensive and maintaining a clear focus. Hence, we must always draw a line beyond which the analysis will stop, with the result that there will always be issues one must neglect. To give only one example from the host of mechanisms that I have largely neglected, the value of financial assets also depends on macro-economic forces such as the enormous flows of funds into investment markets during the period in which the cases studied occurred, under the influence of the neoliberal privatisation of pension provision (Blackburn, 2011; Froud, Johal & Williams, 2002). I intend to return to this, and related issues, in future work.

By contrast with the pragmatist and actor-network theory approaches that have influenced recent sociological studies of value and finance, critical realism insists that we recognise the roles played by structural forms of power in bringing about social events. This includes powerful institutions such as governments, investment banks and venture capital firms but also interactive structures like discursive norm circles and asset circles. The neglect of the former, organisational, structures in any analysis of the finance sector would be incomprehensible, and the persistence of discourses that claim to deny structural influence of this sort while depending on it in practice is an obstacle to serious analysis of the economy. The neglect of the latter, interactive, structures is the consequence of ontologies and epistemologies that are oblivious to the need to look beneath the empirical surface of events to analyse the unobservable mechanisms that lie behind them.

More generally, the effacement of structures from explanations of the economy and the finance sector has the effect of eliminating or misdirecting the critical potential of those explanations. When we recognise the structural power of major financial institutions and the ways in which they deploy it in pursuit of narrow sectional interests we create space for questioning that power and those uses of it; when we deny that structures have power, as actor-network theory and some version of pragmatism do, we eliminate that space. The rise of performativity theory has sometimes provided another route for blunting this kind of critique: the suggestion that academics and their work shape the economy seems to redirect responsibility for the failings of finance away from those powerful institutions and towards academic discourse. Where performativity analysis broadens out to the analysis of wider discourses such as the rise of neoliberalism and economic reason it becomes more critical again, but arguably by losing the features that are characteristic of performativity theory in the first place, blending it with something like Foucauldian discourse theory and opening it up to the influence of structural forces (e.g. Roscoe, 2015).

While the classic Marxist approach to critique does address structural power from a critical perspective, in other respects it is no more satisfactory. The Marxist theory of value is not an explanatory theory but ethics masquerading as explanation (Elder-Vass, 2016, pp. 49–51, 61–70). It begins from the assumption that workers deserve the entire product of the process of production and conceals this ethical assumption at the heart of a theory of value that purports to explain the fundamental dynamics of the capitalist economy. It then claims to draw political conclusions from its economic analysis, without acknowledging that the conclusions were built into the analysis from the very beginning. The result is both an economic analysis and a politics that are dominated by a single ethical argument which is itself never stated explicitly or critically examined.

This book represents a different approach to critique in which, on the one hand, structural power is identified as an important object of critique, and on the other, critical positions are recognised as inherently ethical and as requiring clarity about their ethical assumptions. It identifies structures that are clearly implicated in the appropriation of benefits: benefits in the form of extraordinary profits, wages and bonuses derived from activities that often produce no benefit, or even substantial harms, for the rest of the population. And it calls for a reconsideration of the finance sector that is driven by concern for the long-term needs of the population as a whole.

The Politics of Finance

The typical mainstream response to arguments like this one is that the market merely rewards businesses that meet social needs. Adam Smith's invisible hand and the principle of Pareto optimality are cited to support the argument that if you can sell something to a willing buyer then the production of that thing must have been socially desirable. For marginalist economists and the liberal and neoliberal traditions of politics that have drawn on the marginalist argument, the market automatically calls forth the optimal combination of products that people need because it produces what people are willing to pay for and the magic of supply and demand does the rest. We saw some of the many flaws in this argument in Chapter 2, but it remains a mainstay of the contemporary politics of the economy. Most strikingly, it is built into the notions of national income and GDP that purport to measure the health of our economies. Anything that is sold, regardless of its real social value, is counted as a positive contribution to the national income, and nothing else appears in the reckoning (even government services appear only at cost – reducing them to the price of what is sold to governments).

Yet this argument bases the politics of the economy on a model that simply encodes the ideology of commodity production. Its ideological character is apparent from the continuing employment of the argument despite its manifest falsity: much of what is sold does not benefit us as much as its price suggests, for example when its production creates pollution, and much of what is not sold benefits us in ways that national income figures completely ignore, for example the work that is done by volunteers to help others. This book has stressed one more reason to reject the argument. Value entrepreneurs do not only produce things to be sold but also shape the discourses that lead potential buyers to value them. Hence, we cannot take those valuations, and therefore "demand" and the prices realised for these products, as untainted estimates of even the individual value of a product to its purchaser, let alone any further considerations of its wider social value. This is increasingly true of consumer products such as so-called luxury goods, but as we have seen it is also true of financial assets.

In the case of financial assets, valuation has increasingly become focused on the essentially speculative question of what other investors would be willing to pay for an asset in the future, and this in turn is increasingly shaped by the narrative work done by financial sector actors. Given the socially constructed nature of assets and their value, this work often "works", in the sense that the narratives succeed in persuading investors of valuations that have little other basis than the belief that others will go along with them. But those valuations can persist only as long as the narratives hold, and so the belief, implicit in the ideology of the market, that the price an investor is willing to pay for an asset reflects the social value of the asset is an illusion.

The unjustifiable and unsustainable inflation of asset prices that results undermines the idea that prices are a reliable guide to the value of an asset, even for investors. The cases discussed in this book illustrate this point nicely, but they also illustrate what is ultimately a more important point. Both the inflation and the collapse of asset prices bring wider social consequences than their impacts on the wealth of value entrepreneurs and investors. Even the price inflation phase is problematic, notably when venture capitalists hype up the value of platform economy companies in order to attract further investment, then drive existing operators out of business by using vast amounts of private capital to undercut their prices. This has consequences in the form of lost jobs, degraded quality of jobs, evasion of the regulations that protect service users and the misallocation of social resources to businesses that may never deliver a socially useful service at a price that covers its costs. The collapse phase is even more damaging. When the internet bubble generated by venture capital burst at the beginning of the twenty-first century, and even more so when the subprime bubble generated by the investment banks burst a few years later, it was not only the finance sector that suffered. The collapse of financial values fed through into the rest of the economy and destroyed millions of jobs and billions of dollars' worth of incomes, with the burden carried disproportionately by the 99 per cent, and in particular the more marginalised sections of it, who had no hand in causing the crises in the first place.

We cannot continue, then, to treat the market process as unremit- tingly benevolent, particularly in the case of financial markets, on the basis of the ideological framework of marginalist economics. Just as we must reject the covert one-dimensional ethics of the Marxist theory of value, we must reject the thoroughly dishonest ethics of market fundamentalism that simply glosses the pursuit of personal enrichment with an ever-thinner coat of claims to serve the common good.

Decisions about how our economy should work are ethical decisions with enormously important consequences for the whole population, and they should be based on open and explicit ethical principles that the people affected can accept (Elder-Vass, 2010a, 2016, pp. 51–53). The first of those ethical principles should surely be that what happens in the economy should benefit the population in general – that it should deliver social value, in the terms I attributed to Mazzucato in Chapter 2. One consequence is that maximising "national income" must cease to be the ultimate object of economic policy. Many of the things that contribute to national income as it is currently understood, including much of the income appropriated in and through the finance sector, make no real contribution to the welfare of the larger popula- tion, whereas many things that are ignored in the national income, such as production in the non-monetary sectors of the provisioning economy, make a much more significant contribution. We need to shift economic policy to encouraging those things that genuinely improve people's lives, rather than those things that only improve corporations' bottom lines, and we must shift policy to ensuring that the economy provides the possibility of a decent life to the whole population rather than vast amounts of money to the few. That also means recognising the potential environmental benefits of reducing some forms of eco- nomic growth and the human benefits of redirecting our focus from ever-increasing quantities of goods to the personal and social quality of life (Abbott & Wallace, 2012; Gasper, 2011).

This entails, among other things, that the finance sector must be treated very differently: it must become the servant of the people and not our master. We need to ask "what is the finance sector good for?" and reorient it to doing those things, rather than allowing it to massively distort our economy for the benefit of the finance sector itself. We have enough experience, for example, of the disastrous consequences of so-called financial innovation to understand by now that when new financial assets are invented by those who profit from them and then marketed to those who do not fully understand them, there can be no presumption that they will serve the needs of the population as a whole. Currently many new financial assets serve the interests of financial institutions rather than the interests of society more broadly. Financial assets therefore need to be carefully regulated when they genuinely support the creation of wider social value and outlawed entirely when they do not.

These arguments point towards a mixed economy oriented towards basic human needs and social value: a commodity system regulated and restricted to activities that are compatible with these needs and values, alongside both a positive productive role for the state and support for the enormous non-commercial economy (Elder-Vass, 2016, pp. 22–41). Achieving this sort of humanised politics in turn depends on restoring a system of political power with meaningful democracy, as opposed to the steady slide towards finocracy – the rule of money – we have experienced in recent times.

There is a place for some of the services provided by the finance sector in a model like this, but it seems likely to be a radically reduced place. As Engelen and colleagues have argued, the complexity of finance is also a major obstacle to its effective regulation and simplification of the sector would help to make it more manageable (Engelen et al., 2011, p. 36). Considerable work is required to develop plausible plans for what a reformed finance might look like and how to address the enormous political and transitional challenges this scale of reform might raise. It is already clear, however, that it is not only the theory of value and financial value that needs to be reinvented: so does the financial sector itself.

References

Abbott, P., & Wallace, C. (2012). Social quality: A way to measure the quality of society. *Social Indicators Research*, *108*(1), 153–167.

Aliaj, O., Mackenzie, M., & Fletcher, L. (2021, February 6). Melvin Capital, GameStop and the road to disaster. *Financial Times*. Retrieved from https://www.ft.com/content/3f6b47f9-70c7-4839-8bb4-6a62f1bd39e0

Andreou, A. (2013, November 20). The rise of money trading has made our economy all mud and no brick. *The Guardian*. Retrieved from http://www.theguardian.com/commentisfree/2013/nov/20/money-trading-econ omy-foreign-exchange-markets-economy

Appadurai, A. (1988). Introduction: Commodities and the politics of value. In A. Appadurai (Ed.), *The social life of things: Commodities in cultural perspective* (pp. 3–63). Cambridge University Press.

Archer, M. S. (1995). *Realist social theory: The morphogenetic approach*. Cambridge University Press.

Archer, S. (2017, August 8). Snap slips as traders ready for next week's lock-up expiration. *Markets Insider*. Retrieved from http://markets .businessinsider.com/news/stocks/snap-stock-price-slips-a-week-ahead-of-next-lock-up-period-2017-8-1002241262

Ardalan, K. (2019). Equity home bias: A review essay. *Journal of Economic Surveys*, *33*(3), 949–967.

Arthur, C. J. (2001). The spectral ontology of value. In A. Brown, S. Fleetwood, & J. Roberts (Eds.), *Critical Realism and Marxism* (pp. 215–233). Routledge.

Aspers, P. (2009). Knowledge and valuation in markets. *Theory and Society*, *38*(2), 111.

Aspers, P., & Beckert, J. (2010). Value in markets. In J. Beckert & P. Aspers (Eds.), *The worth of goods* (pp. 3–38). Oxford University Press.

Assa, J. (2018). Finance, social value, and the rhetoric of GDP. *Finance and Society*, *4*(2), 144–158.

Austin, J. L. (1962). *How to do things with words*. Oxford University Press.

Barbrook, R., & Cameron, A. (1995). The Californian ideology. *Mute*, *1*(3).

Barman, E. (2015). Of principle and principal: Value plurality in the market of impact investing. *Valuation Studies*, *3*(1), 9–44.

(2016). *Caring capitalism: The meaning and measure of social value.* Cambridge University Press.

BBC News. (2011, November 21). Thousands 'told Sid' 25 years ago. Retrieved from http://www.bbc.co.uk/news/business-15792873

(2014, December 30). Xiaomi most valuable tech start-up. Retrieved from https://www.bbc.co.uk/news/business-30629883

(2017, December 11). Bitcoin futures trading begins in Chicago. Retrieved from http://www.bbc.co.uk/news/business-42304657

Beckert, J. (2013). Capitalism as a system of expectations toward a sociological microfoundation of political economy. *Politics & Society, 41*(3), 323–350.

(2016). *Imagined futures.* Harvard University Press.

Bell, R. G., Filatotchev, I., & Aguilera, R. V. (2014). Corporate governance and investors' perceptions of foreign IPO value: An institutional perspective. *Academy of Management Journal, 57*(1), 301–320.

Bernstein, B. (2018, January 8). Weathering the Altcoin Storm (and investing for the next). *CoinDesk.* Retrieved from https://www.coindesk.com/weathering-altcoin-shitstorm-investing-next-one/

Besedovsky, N. (2018). Financialization as calculative practice: The rise of structured finance and the cultural and calculative transformation of credit rating agencies. *Socio-Economic Review, 16*(1), 61–84.

Beunza, D., & Garud, R. (2007). Calculators, lemmings or frame-makers? The intermediary role of securities analysts. In M. Callon, Y. Millo, & F. Muniesa (Eds.), *Market devices* (pp. 13–39). Blackwell.

Bhaskar, R. (1975). *A realist theory of science.* Leeds Books.

Birch, K. (2017). Rethinking value in the bio-economy: Finance, assetization, and the management of value. *Science, Technology, & Human Values, 42*(3), 460–490.

Birch, K., & Muniesa, F. (Eds.). (2020a). *Assetization: Turning things into assets in technoscientific capitalism.* MIT Press.

Birch, K., & Muniesa, F. (2020b). Introduction: Assetization and technoscientific capitalism. In K. Birch & F. Muniesa (Eds.), *Assetization: Turning things into assets in technoscientific capitalism* (pp. 1–41). MIT Press.

Bitcoin Core. (2018). Team. Retrieved from https://bitcoincore.org/en/team/

Bitcoin Wiki. (2016, July 22). Value overflow incident. Retrieved from https://en.bitcoin.it/wiki/Value_overflow_incident

Bitcoin.org. (2018). Frequently asked questions. Retrieved from https://bitcoin.org/en/faq

BitInfoCharts. (2018, January 31). Bitcoin average transaction fee chart. Retrieved from https://bitinfocharts.com/comparison/bitcoin-transactionfees.html

(2020, May 28). Bitcoin average transaction fee chart. Retrieved from https://bitinfocharts.com/

Blackburn, R. (2011). *Age shock: How finance is failing us.* Verso.

Bloomberg.com. (2017, November 29). Bitcoin 'ought to be outlawed,' Nobel Prize Winner Stiglitz Says. Retrieved from https://www .bloomberg.com/news/articles/2017-11-29/bitcoin-ought-to-be-outlawed-nobel-prize-winner-stiglitz-says-jal10hxd

Boltanski, L., & Esquerre, A. (2016). The economic life of things. *New Left Review,* (98), 31–54.

Boltanski, L., Esquerre, A., & Muniesa, F. (2015). Grappling with the economy of enrichment. *Valuation Studies, 3*(1), 75–83.

Boltanski, L., & Thévenot, L. (2006). *On justification: Economies of worth.* Princeton University Press.

Bourdieu, P. (1984). *Distinction: A social critique of the judgement of taste.* Routledge & Kegan Paul.

(1993). *The field of cultural production.* Polity Press.

Bradbury, D. (2014, November 9). How can we make bitcoin mainstream? *CoinDesk.* Retrieved from https://www.coindesk.com/can-make-bitcoin-mainstream/

Bradley, D. J., Jordan, B. D., Ritter, J. R., & Wolf, J. G. (2004). The IPO quiet period revisited. *Journal of Investment Management, 2*(3), 1–11.

Bullock, N., & Kuchler, H. (2017, March 6). Snap drops 12% to close below Thursday's opening price. *Financial Times.* Retrieved from https://www .ft.com/content/a4b645ee-02b2-11e7-aa5b-6bb07f5c8e12

Burniske, C., & Tatar, J. (2017). *Cryptoassets: The innovative investor's guide to bitcoin and beyond.* McGraw-Hill Education.

Callon, M. (1998). Introduction: The embeddedness of economic markets in economics. In M. Callon (Ed.), *The laws of the markets* (pp. 1–57). Blackwell/The Sociological Review.

Callon, M., Méadel, C., & Rabeharisoa, V. (2002). The economy of qualities. *Economy and Society, 31*(2), 194–217.

Cantor, R., Gwilym, O. A., & Thomas, S. H. (2007). The use of credit ratings in investment management in the U.S. and Europe. *The Journal of Fixed Income, 17*(2), 13–26.

Carruthers, B. G. (2010). Knowledge and liquidity: Institutional and cognitive foundations of the subprime crisis. In M. Lounsbury & P. M. Hirsch (Eds.), *Markets on trial: The economic sociology of the U.S. financial crisis* (pp. 155–180). Emerald.

(2013). From uncertainty toward risk: The case of credit ratings. *Socio-Economic Review, 11*(3), 525–551.

Carruthers, B. G., & Babb, S. (1996). The color of money and the nature of value. *American Journal of Sociology, 101*(6), 1556–1591.

Carruthers, B. G., & Kim, J.-C. (2011). The sociology of finance. *Annual Review of Sociology, 37*(1), 239–259.

Cassidy, J. (2002). *Dot.Con.* Allen Lane.

(2010). *How markets fail: The logic of economic calamities* (New.). Penguin.

Chamberlin, E. (1956). *The theory of monopolistic competition* (7th ed.). Harvard University Press.

Chemmanur, T. J., & Krishnan, K. (2012). Heterogeneous beliefs, IPO valuation, and the economic role of the underwriter in IPOs. *Financial Management, 41*(4), 769–811.

Chiapello, E. (2015). Financialisation of valuation. *Human Studies, 38*(1), 13–35.

Chicago Board Options Exchange. (2000). *Market Statistics 1999*.

Ciaian, P., Rajcaniova, M., & Kancs, D. (2016). The digital agenda of virtual currencies: Can BitCoin become a global currency? *Information Systems and E-Business Management, 14*(4), 883–919.

CNBC. (2018, February 27). BTC – Stock Quote and News – CNBC. *CNBC*. Retrieved from https://www.cnbc.com/quotes/?symbol=BTC=

Coinmarketcap.com. (2019a). Cryptocurrency market capitalizations. Retrieved from https://coinmarketcap.com/currencies/bitcoin/historical-data/

(2019b). Historical data for bitcoin. Retrieved from https://coinmarketcap .com/currencies/bitcoin/historical-data/

Curran, D. (2015). Risk illusion and organized irresponsibility in contemporary finance: Rethinking class and risk society. *Economy and Society, 44*(3), 392–417.

(2018). From performativity to representation as intervention: Rethinking the 2008 financial crisis and the recent history of social science. *Journal for the Theory of Social Behaviour, 48*(4), 492–510.

Cutler, T., Hindess, B., Hussain, A., & Hirst, P. Q. (1977). *Marx's capital and capitalism today* (Vol. 1). Routledge & Kegan Paul.

Damodaran, A. (2018). *The dark side of valuation: Valuing young, distressed, and complex businesses* (3rd ed.). Pearson FT Press.

Das, S. (2012). *Traders, guns and money* (3rd ed.). Pearson Education.

Davies, G. (1994). *A history of money*. University of Wales Press.

De Long, J. B., Shleifer, A., Summers, L. H., & Waldmann, R. J. (1990). Noise trader risk in financial markets. *Journal of Political Economy, 98* (4), 703–738.

Dealbook. (2017, March 16). The people From 'Government Sachs.' *The New York Times*. Retrieved from https://www.nytimes.com/2017/03/ 16/business/dealbook/goldman-sachs-goverment-jobs.html

Debreu, G. (1959). *Theory of value: An axiomatic analysis of economic equilibrium*. Wiley.

Delmestri, G., & Greenwood, R. (2016). How Cinderella became a queen: Theorizing radical status change. *Administrative Science Quarterly, 61* (4), 507–550.

Diaz-Bone, R. (2017). Classifications, quantifications and quality conventions in markets. *Historical Social Research, 42*(1), 238–262.

Dodd, N. (1994). *The sociology of money.* Continuum.

(2014). *The social life of money.* Princeton University Press.

Doganova, L., & Muniesa, F. (2015). Capitalization devices: Business models and the renewal of markets. In M. Kornberger, L. Justesen, A. K. Madsen, & J. Mouritsen (Eds.), *Making things valuable* (pp. 109–125). Oxford University Press.

Dolfsma, W. (1997). The social construction of value. *The European Journal of the History of Economic Thought, 4*(3), 400–416.

Downward, P., & Lee, F. (2001). Post Keynesian pricing theory 'Reconfirmed'? A critical review of 'Asking about Prices.' *Journal of Post Keynesian Economics, 23*(3), 465–483.

Edgecliffe-Johnson, A., & Badkar, M. (2019, September 30). WeWork to formally withdraw IPO filing. *Financial Times.* Retrieved from https://www.ft.com/content/a18aa1a0-e390-11e9-b112-9624ec9edc59

Ehrbar, H. (2007). The relation between Marxism and critical realism. In J. Frauley & F. Pearce (Eds.), *Critical realism and the social sciences: Heterodox elaborations* (pp. 224–239). University of Toronto Press.

Elder-Vass, D. (2007). A method for social ontology. *Journal of Critical Realism, 6*(2), 226–249.

(2010a). Realist critique without ethical naturalism or moral realism. *Journal of Critical Realism, 9*(1), 33–58.

(2010b). *The causal power of social structures.* Cambridge University Press.

(2011). The causal power of discourse. *Journal for the Theory of Social Behaviour, 41*(2), 143–160.

(2012). *The reality of social construction.* Cambridge University Press.

(2014). Social entities and the basis of their powers. In J. Zahle & F. Colin (Eds.), *Rethinking the individualism-holism debate* (pp. 39–54). Springer.

(2016). *Profit and gift in the digital economy.* Cambridge University Press.

(2017a). Material parts in social structures. *Journal of Social Ontology, 3* (1), 89–105.

(2017b). Materialising social ontology. *Cambridge Journal of Economics, 41*(5), 1437–1451.

(2020). Pragmatism, critical realism and financial value. Presented at the SASE Annual Conference, Online.

Elson, D. (1979). The value theory of labour. In D. Elson (Ed.), *Value: The representation of labour in capitalism* (pp. 115–180). CSE Books.

Engelen, E., Ertürk, I., Froud, J., Johal, S., Leaver, A., Moran, M., ... Williams, K. (2011). *After the great complacence: Financial crisis and the politics of reform.* Oxford University Press.

Engelskirchen, H. (2007). Why is this labour value? In J. Frauley & F. Pearce (Eds.), *Critical realism and the social sciences: Heterodox elaborations* (pp. 202–223). University of Toronto Press.

Evans, D. S., & Schmalensee, R. (2005). *Paying with plastic.* MIT Press.

Eymard-Duvernay, F. (2011). Le travail dans l'entreprise: pour une démocratisation des pouvoirs de valorisation. In R. Baudoin (Ed.), *L'entreprise, formes de la propriété et responsabilités sociales* (pp. 162–226). Éditions Lethielleux.

Fama, E. F. (1965). *Random walks in stock-market prices.* Graduate School of Business, University of Chicago.

(1970). Efficient capital markets: A review of theory and empirical work. *The Journal of Finance, 25*(2), 383–417.

(1991). Efficient capital markets: II. *Journal of Finance, 46*(5), 1575–1617.

Faulkner, P. (2007). Closure. In M. Hartwig (Ed.), *Dictionary of critical realism* (pp. 56–57). Routledge.

Favereau, O. (2008). The unconventional, but conventionalist, legacy of Lewis's 'Convention.' *Topoi, 27*(1–2), 115–126.

(2017). Hommage à François Eymard-Duvernay. *Revue Française de Socio-Économie, 18*, 5–12.

Fehr, E., & Gächter, S. (2000). Fairness and retaliation: The economics of reciprocity. *Journal of Economic Perspectives, 14*(3), 159–181.

Feng, H., Froud, J., Johal, S., Haslam, C., & Williams, K. (2001). A new business model? The capital market and the new economy. *Economy and Society, 30*(4), 467–503.

Feuer, A. (2013, December 14). The bitcoin ideology. *The New York Times.* Retrieved from https://www.nytimes.com/2013/12/15/sunday-review/the-bitcoin-ideology.html

Financial Times. (2015, December 27). Sorting truth from myth at technology unicorns. Retrieved from https://www.ft.com/content/89f8deda-a3f7-11e5-8218-6b8ff73aae15

Finzi, E. (2007). Gli Italiani e la grappa: 25 anni di rapida evoluzione. In C. D. G. L. Bonollo (Ed.), *Grappa e consumatore.* Centro Documentazione Grappa Luigi Bonollo.

Fitch Ratings. (2021). Rating definitions. Retrieved from https://www.fitchratings.com/products/rating-definitions

Fleetwood, S. (2001). Causal laws, functional relations and tendencies. *Review of Political Economy*, 13(2), 201–220.

Fligstein, N., & Goldstein, A. (2010). The anatomy of the mortgage securitization crisis. In M. Lounsbury & P. M. Hirsch (Eds.), *Markets on trial: The economic sociology of the U.S. financial crisis* (pp. 29–70). Emerald.

Foley, D. K. (2000). Recent developments in the labor theory of value. *Review of Radical Political Economics*, 32(1), 1–39.

Fourcade, M. (2011). Cents and sensibility: Economic valuation and the nature of 'Nature.' *American Journal of Sociology*, 116(6), 1721–77.

Frank, T. (2000). *One market under god: Extreme capitalism, market populism, and the end of economic democracy*. Doubleday Books.

Franssen, T., & Velthuis, O. (2016). Making materiality matter. *Socio-Economic Review*, 14(2), 363–381.

Freeman, J. (2005). Venture capital and modern capitalism. In V. Nee & R. Swedberg (Eds.), *The economic sociology of capitalism* (pp. 145–167). Princeton University Press.

Froud, J., Johal, S., & Williams, K. (2002). Financialisation and the coupon pool. *Capital & Class*, 26(3), 119–151.

Fuldner, G. (2012, May 8). How does an IPO roadshow not violate SEC 'quiet period' rules? *Quora*. Retrieved from https://www.quora.com/How-does-an-IPO-roadshow-not-violate-SEC-quiet-period-rules

GameKyuubi. (2013, December 18). I AM HODLING. *bitcointalk.org*. Retrieved from https://bitcointalk.org/index.php?topic=375643.0

Gasper, D. (2011). The human and the social: A comparison of the discourses of human development, human security and social quality. *International Journal of Social Quality*, 1(1), 91–108.

Gerard, D. (2017). *Attack of the 50 foot blockchain: Bitcoin, blockchain, ethereum & smart contracts*. CreateSpace.

Geras, N. (1985). The controversy about Marx and justice. *New Left Review*, (150), 47–85.

Gilbert, M. (1990). *Walking Together: Midwest Studies in Philosophy*, XV, 1–14.

Goede, M. D. (2005). *Virtue, fortune, and faith: A genealogy of finance*. University of Minnesota Press.

Goldstein, A., & Fligstein, N. (2017). Financial markets as production markets: The industrial roots of the mortgage meltdown. *Socio-Economic Review*, 15(3), 483–510.

Golumbia, D. (2015). Bitcoin as politics: Distributed right-wing extremism. In G. Lovink, N. Tkacz, & P. De Vries (Eds.), *MoneyLab reader: An intervention in digital economy* (pp. 117–131). Institute of Network Cultures.

Gompers, P., & Lerner, J. (2006). *The venture capital cycle.* MIT Press.

Gorton, G. (2009). The subprime panic. *European Financial Management,* *15*(1), 10–46.

Gregory, C. A. (2000). Value switching and the commodity-free zone. In A. Vandevelde (Ed.), *Gifts and interests* (pp. 95–113). Peeters.

Habermas, J. (1996). *Between facts and norms.* Polity.

Haldane, A. G. (2010, March 30). The $100 billion question. Presented at the Institute of Regulation and Risk, Hong Kong.

Hall, S. (1973). Encoding and decoding in the television discourse. Presented at the Council Of Europe Colloquy on 'Training In the critical reading of televisual language,' Leicester: Centre for Cultural Studies, University of Birmingham.

Hann, C. (2010). Moral economy. In K. Hart, J.-L. Laville, & A. D. Cattani (Eds.), *The human economy* (pp. 187–198). Polity Press.

Harrington, B. (2008). *Pop finance: Investment clubs and the new investor populism.* Princeton University Press.

Harvey, D. (2011). *The enigma of capital: And the crises of capitalism.* Profile Books.

Harvey, M., & Geras, N. (2013). *Marx's economy and beyond.* CRESI, University of Essex.

Heilbroner, R. L. (1988). *The problem of value: In behind the veil of economics* (pp. 104–133). Norton.

Helgesson, C.-F., & Muniesa, F. (2013). For what it's worth. *Valuation Studies, 1*(1), 1–10.

Hellmann, T., & Puri, M. (2002). Venture capital and the professionalization of start-up firms: Empirical evidence. *The Journal of Finance, 57*(1), 169–197.

Hern, A. (2014, June 16). Bitcoin currency could have been destroyed by '51%' attack. *The Guardian.* Retrieved from http://www.theguardian.com/technology/2014/jun/16/bitcoin-currency-destroyed-51-attack-ghash-io

Hochberg, Y. V. (2012). Venture capital and corporate governance in the newly public firm. *Review of Finance, 16*(2), 429–480.

Hook, L. (2015, November 10). Unicorns face end of the 'steroid era.' *Financial Times.* Retrieved from https://www.ft.com/content/6ad992e6-8792-11e5-9f8c-a8d619fa707c

(2016, September 6). Investors' need for start-up knowledge spurs new breed of analyst. *Financial Times.* Retrieved from https://www.ft.com/content/61de9980-7093-11e6-9ac1-1055824ca907

(2017, March 9). Airbnb completes $1bn fundraising to support expansion. *Financial Times.* Retrieved from https://www.ft.com/content/0fde09e0-04ef-11e7-ace0-1ce02ef0def9

Hornby, C. (2007, August 1). German household investors hug sidelines. *Reuters*. Retrieved from https://uk.reuters.com/article/lifestyle-germany-stocks-risk-dc-idUKL1978588820070801

Howells, T., & Morgan, E. (2020). *Gross domestic product by industry fourth quarter and year 2019* (News release). Bureau of Economic Analysis, US Department of Commerce.

IMF. (2008). *IMF Global Financial Stability Report – October 2008*.

Ingham, G. (2004). *The nature of money*. Polity.

International Valuation Standards Council. (2013). *International Valuation Standards 2013: Framework and Requirements*.

Jagd, S. (2007). Economics of convention and new economic sociology: Mutual inspiration and dialogue. *Current Sociology*, *55*(1), 75–91.

Jensen, M. C., & Meckling, W. H. (1976). Theory of the firm: Managerial behavior, agency costs and ownership structure. *Journal of Financial Economics*, *3*(4), 305–360.

Johnson, R. (1993). Editor's introduction. In P. Bourdieu, *The field of cultural production: Essays on art and literature* (pp. 1–25). Polity Press.

Kaelberer, M. (2007). Trust in the Euro. *European Societies*, *9*(4), 623–642.

Kahneman, D., Knetsch, J. L., & Thaler, R. (1986). Fairness as a constraint on profit seeking: Entitlements in the market. *The American Economic Review*, *76*(4), 728–741.

Karlstrøm, H. (2014). Do libertarians dream of electric coins? The material embeddedness of Bitcoin. *Distinktion: Journal of Social Theory*, *15*(1), 23–36.

Karpik, L. (2010). *Valuing the unique: The economics of singularities* (N. Scott, Trans.). Princeton University Press.

Keen, S. (2011). *Debunking economics* (Revised and expanded.). Zed Books.

Kenney, M., & Zysman, J. (2019). Unicorns, Cheshire cats, and the new dilemmas of entrepreneurial finance. *Venture Capital*, *21*(1), 35–50.

Keynes, J. M. (1973). *The general theory of employment, interest and money*. Macmillan.

Kirman, A. P., & Vriend, N. J. (2000). Learning to be loyal: A Study of the Marseille Fish Market. In D. D. Gatti, M. Gallegati, & A. P. Kirman (Eds.), *Interaction and market structure* (pp. 33–56). Springer, Berlin, Heidelberg.

Kliman, A. J., & McGlone, T. (1999). A temporal single-system interpretation of Marx's value theory. *Review of Political Economy*, *11*(1), 33–59.

Kovach, S. (2021, February 8). Tesla buys $1.5 billion in bitcoin, plans to accept it as payment. *CNBC*. Retrieved from https://www.cnbc.com/2021/02/08/tesla-buys-1point5-billion-in-bitcoin-in-bitcoin.html

Kuchler, H. (2017, July 11). Snap downgraded by lead IPO underwriter as shares fall. *Financial Times*. Retrieved from https://www.ft.com/content/a10f4b28-663c-11e7-9a66-93fb352ba1fe

Kuchler, H., & Bullock, N. (2017, March 2). Snapchat owner closes up 44% for $28.3bn valuation. *Financial Times*. Retrieved from https://www.ft.com/content/89f1a01a-ff55-11e6-96f8-3700c5664d30

Lamont, M. (2012). Toward a comparative sociology of valuation and evaluation. *Annual Review of Sociology*, 38(1), 201–221.

Langley, P., & Leyshon, A. (2017). Platform capitalism: The intermediation and capitalization of digital economic circulation. *Finance and Society*, 3(1), 11–31.

Lapavitsas, C. (2013). *Profiting without producing: How finance exploits us all*. Verso Books.

Lawrence, C. J., & Mudge, S. L. (2019). Movement to market, currency to property: the rise and fall of Bitcoin as an anti-state movement, 2009–2014. *Socio-Economic Review*, 17(1), 109–134.

Lawson, T. (1997). *Economics and reality*. Routledge.

(2003). *Reorienting economics*. Routledge.

(2006). The nature of heterodox economics. *Cambridge Journal of Economics*, 30(4), 483–505.

(2019). *The nature of social reality: Issues in social ontology*. Routledge.

Lehdonvirta, V. (2017, December 6). Bitcoin isn't a currency – and unless it becomes one it could be worthless. *The Conversation*. Retrieved from http://theconversation.com/bitcoin-isnt-a-currency-and-unless-it-becomes-one-it-could-be-worthless-88656

Lewis, M. (2011). *The Big Short: Inside the Doomsday Machine*. Penguin.

Lex. (2017a, March 27). Snap: Evanescent analysts. *Financial Times*. Retrieved from https://www.ft.com/content/56f1620e-1332-11e7-b0c1-37e417ee6c76

(2017b, August 11). Snap: Hangdog billionaire. *Financial Times*. Retrieved from https://www.ft.com/content/8c1dd068-7e1f-11e7-ab01-a13271d1ee9c

Liu, X., & Ritter, J. R. (2011). Local underwriter oligopolies and IPO underpricing. *Journal of Financial Economics*, 102(3), 579–601.

Lohmann, L. (2010). Neoliberalism and the calculable world: The rise of carbon trading. In K. Birch & V. Mykhnenko (Eds.), *The rise and fall of neoliberalism: The collapse of an economic order?* (pp. 77–94). Zed Books.

Lowry, M., Officer, M. S., & Schwert, G. W. (2010). The variability of IPO initial returns. *The Journal of Finance*, 65(2), 425–465.

Lustig, C., & Nardi, B. A. (2015). Algorithmic authority: The case of bitcoin. Presented at the 2015 48th Hawaii International Conference on System Sciences.

MacKenzie, D. (2006). *An engine, not a camera: How financial models shape markets.* MIT Press.

(2009). *Material markets: How economic agents are constructed.* Oxford University Press.

(2011). The credit crisis as a problem in the sociology of knowledge. *American Journal of Sociology, 116*(6), 1778–1841.

MacKenzie, D., & Millo, Y. (2003). Constructing a market, performing theory: The historical sociology of a financial derivatives exchange. *American Journal of Sociology, 109*(1), 107–145.

MacKenzie, Donald, Muniesa, F., & Siu, L. (2007). Introduction. In *Do economists make markets?* (pp. 1–19). Princeton University Press.

Marx, K. (1954). *Capital, Volume 1.* Lawrence & Wishart.

(1959). *Capital, Volume 3.* Lawrence & Wishart.

Mazzucato, M. (2018). *The value of everything: Making and taking in the global economy.* Allen Lane.

McGuigan, J. (2009). *Cool capitalism.* Pluto Press.

McLellan, D. (1980). *The thought of Karl Marx.* Macmillan.

Megginson, W. L., & Weiss, K. A. (1991). Venture capitalist certification in initial public offerings. *The Journal of Finance, 46*(3), 879–903.

Metrick, A., & Yasuda, A. (2010). *Venture capital and the finance of innovation* (2nd revised edition.). John Wiley & Sons.

MicroStrategy. (2020, December 21). MicroStrategy announces over $1B in total bitcoin purchases in 2020. Retrieved from https://www .microstrategy.com/en/company/company-videos/microstrategy-announces-over-1b-in-total-bitcoin-purchases-in-2020

Milne, A. (2009). *The fall of the house of credit: What went wrong in banking and what can be done to repair the damage?* Cambridge University Press.

(2017, May 18). *Cryptocurrencies from an Austrian perspective.* SSRN.

Mirowski, P. (1991). *More heat than light.* Cambridge University Press.

Mirowski, P., & Nik-Kah, E. (2007). Markets made flesh. In D. MacKenzie, F. Muniesa, & L. Siu (Eds.), *Do economists make markets?* (pp. 190–224). Princeton University Press.

Mohun, S., & Veneziani, R. (2017). *Value, price and exploitation: The logic of the transformation problem* (Working paper No. 813). School of Economics and Finance, QMUL.

Moore, T., & Christin, N. (2013). Beware the middleman: Empirical analysis of bitcoin-exchange risk. In Ahmad-Reza Sadeghi (Ed.), *Financial Cryptography and Data Security* (pp. 25–33). Springer, Berlin, Heidelberg.

Morgan, J. (2008). *Private equity finance: Rise and repercussions.* Palgrave Macmillan.

Muniesa, F. (2011). A flank movement in the understanding of valuation. *The Sociological Review*, *59*, 24–38.

Muniesa, F., Doganova, L., Ortiz, H., Pina-Stranger, A., Paterson, F., Bourgoin, A., ... Yon, G. (2017). *Capitalization: A cultural guide*. (C. Méadel, Ed.). Presses des Mines.

Nakamoto, S. (2008a, October). Bitcoin: A Peer-to-Peer Electronic Cash System.

(2008b, November 14). Re: Bitcoin P2P e-cash paper.

Neate, R. (2019, December 4). End of an era as Google founders step down from parent company. *The Guardian*. Retrieved from http://www .theguardian.com/technology/2019/dec/04/end-of-an-era-as-google-found ers-step-down-from-parent-company

Nicholas, T. (2019). *VC: An American history*. Harvard University Press.

Orléan, A. (2014). *The empire of value: A new foundation for economics*. (M. B. Debevoise, Trans.). MIT Press.

Ouma, S. (2018). This can('t) be an asset class: The world of money management, "society", and the contested morality of farmland investments: *Environment and Planning A: Economy and Space*.

Pagliery, J. (2014). *Bitcoin: And the future of money*. Triumph Books.

Partington, R. (2017, December 2). Bitcoin: Is it a bubble waiting to burst or a good investment? *The Guardian*. Retrieved from http://www .theguardian.com/business/2017/dec/02/bitcoin-is-it-a-bubble-waiting-to-burst-or-a-good-investment

Pistor, K. (2019). *The code of capital*. Princeton University Press.

Platt, E., & Fontanella-Khan, J. (2019, September 16). WeWork postpones IPO after chilly response from investors. *Financial Times*. London. Retrieved from https://www.ft.com/content/b869bc42-d8d9-11e9-8f9b-77216ebe1f17

Popper, N. (2015). *Digital gold: The untold story of bitcoin*. Allen Lane.

Pozsar, Z. (2008, July). The Rise and Fall of the Shadow Banking System. Moody's Economy.com.

Redshaw, T. (2017). Bitcoin beyond ambivalence: Popular rationalization and Feenberg's technical politics. *Thesis Eleven*, *138*(1), 46–64.

Reuters. (2017, January 14). Moody's $864m penalty for ratings in run-up to 2008 financial crisis. *The Guardian*. Retrieved from http://www .theguardian.com/business/2017/jan/14/moodys-864m-penalty-for-ratings-in-run-up-to-2008-financial-crisis

Rhodes, C. (2019). *Financial services: Contribution to the UK economy* (Briefing Paper No. 6193). House of Commons Library.

Ritter, J. R. (2011). *Equilibrium in the IPO Market* (SSRN Scholarly Paper No. ID 1822542). Social Science Research Network.

Rona-Tas, A., & Hiss, S. (2010). The role of ratings in the subprime mortgage crisis. In M. Lounsbury & P. M. Hirsch (Eds.), *Markets on trial: The economic sociology of the U.S. financial crisis* (pp. 113–153). Emerald Group Publishing Limited.

Roscoe, P. (2015). *A richer life: How economics can change the way we think and feel.* Penguin.

Rutzou, T., & Elder-Vass, D. (2019). On assemblages and things: Fluidity, stability, causation stories, and formation stories. *Sociological Theory, 37*(4), 401–424.

Sahlman, W. A. (1990). The structure and governance of venture-capital organizations. *Journal of Financial Economics, 27*(2), 473–521.

Salzman, A. (2021, February 11). Not just Tesla: Why big companies are buying into Crypto-Mania. *Barron's.* Retrieved from https://www .barrons.com/articles/not-just-tesla-why-big-companies-are-buying-into-crypto-mania-51613069805

Sayer, A. (2000). *Realism and social science.* Sage.

(2015). *Why we can't afford the rich.* Policy Press.

Searle, J. R. (1995). *The construction of social reality.* Allen Lane.

Shaxson, N. (2018). *The finance curse: How global finance is making us all poorer.* Bodley Head.

Shiller, R. J. (1990). Market volatility and investor behavior. *The American Economic Review, 80*(2), 58–62.

(2015). *Irrational exuberance* (3rd ed.). Princeton University Press.

Simmel, G. (1955). *Conflict and the web of group affiliations.* Free Press.

Simon, H. (1972). Theories of bounded rationality. In C. B. McGuire & R. Radner (Eds.), *Decision and organization* (pp. 161–176). Elsevier Science Publishing Co Inc., U.S.

Singer, D. (2018, March 1). Anniversary of Snap IPO to Trigger Final Lockup Expiration. *Bloomberg.Com.* Retrieved from https://www .bloomberg.com/news/articles/2018-03-01/anniversary-of-snap-ipo-to-trigger-final-lockup-expiration

Smart, E. (2016, August 13). 6 Cards Battle for Bitcoin Supremacy, Bitcoin Debit Card Comparison Test. *Cointelegraph.* Retrieved from https://cointelegraph.com/news/6-cards-battle-for-bitcoin-supremacy-bitcoin-debit-card-comparison-test

Smith, C. (2010). *What is a person?* University of Chicago Press.

Smith, C. W. (1999). *Success and survival on Wall Street: Understanding the mind of the market.* Rowman & Littlefield.

(2010). Coping with contingencies in equity option markets. In J. Beckert & P. Aspers (Eds.), *The worth of goods: Valuation and pricing in the economy* (pp. 272–294). Oxford University Press, U.S.A.

Snap Inc. (2017). *Snap Inc. S-1 Registration Statement.* US Securities and Exchange Commission.

Solari, L. (2007). Entrepreneurship at the margins of society: Founding dynamics in gray (sex shops) and black markets (Mafia). In M. Ruef & M. Lounsbury (Eds.), *Research in the sociology of organizations* (Vol. 25, pp. 337–368). Emerald.

Song, J. (2017, December 20). Bring on the FUD: 2017 Was The Year Bitcoin Became Anti-Fragile. *CoinDesk.* Retrieved from https://www.coindesk.com/bring-fud-2017-year-bitcoin-became-anti-fragile/

Sotirakopoulos, N. (2017). Cryptomarkets as a libertarian counter-conduct of resistance. *European Journal of Social Theory, 21*(2), 189–206.

Spaven, E. (2015, June 17). EBA: 51% attack remains bitcoin's biggest problem. *CoinDesk.* Retrieved from https://www.coindesk.com/eba-51-attack-remains-bitcoins-biggest-problem/

Srnicek, N. (2016). *Platform capitalism.* Polity Press.

Stark, D. (2011). *The sense of dissonance: Accounts of worth in economic life.* Princeton University Press.

Statista. (2021). Bitcoin market cap 2013–2021. Retrieved from https://www.statista.com/statistics/377382/bitcoin-market-capitalization/

Steuart, J. (1767). *An Inquiry into the Principles of Political Economy.*

Stewart, E. (2018, November 19). Mark Zuckerberg is essentially untouchable at Facebook. *Vox.* Retrieved from https://www.vox.com/technology/2018/11/19/18099011/mark-zuckerberg-facebook-stock-nyt-wsj

Stewart, I. (2012). *Seventeen equations that changed the world.* Profile Books.

Stiglitz, J. (2010). *Freefall: Free markets and the sinking of the global economy.* Penguin.

Strebel, P., & Cantale, S. (2014, June 17). Is your company addicted to value extraction? *MIT Sloan Management Review.*

Stross, R. (2000). *EBoys: The first inside account of venture capitalists at work.* Crown Publications.

Swartz, L., & Maurer, B. (2014, May 22). The future of money-like things. *The Atlantic.*

Talmud, I., & Darr, A. (2014). Ilan Talmud interviewed by Asaf Darr. *Economic Sociology – The European Electronic Newsletter, 16*(1), 28–30.

Tett, G. (2010). *Fool's gold: How unrestrained greed corrupted a dream, shattered global markets and unleashed a catastrophe.* Abacus.

Thompson, E. P. (1971). The moral economy of the English crowd in the eighteenth century. *Past & Present,* (50), 76–136.

Thrift, N. (2001). "It's the romance, not the finance, that makes the business worth pursuing": Disclosing a new market culture. *Economy and Society, 30*(4), 412–432.

Thurnell-Read, T. (2018). The embourgeoisement of beer: Changing practices of "Real Ale" consumption. *Journal of Consumer Culture, 18*(4),
539–557.

Thurnell-Read, T. (2019). A thirst for the authentic: Craft drinks producers
and the narration of authenticity. *The British Journal of Sociology, 70*
(4), 1448–1468.

Varian, H. R. (2010). *Intermediate microeconomics: A modern approach*
(8th International student edition.). W. W. Norton & Company.

Veblen, T. (1899). *The theory of the leisure class.* Macmillan.

Waters, R. (2017, August 17). Uber crafts share sale plan to prop up
valuation. *Financial Times.* Retrieved from https://www.ft.com/con
tent/51d97262-82da-11e7-94e2-c5b903247afd

Webb, M. S. (2018, January 19). I told you investing in bitcoin was a bad
idea. *Financial Times.* Retrieved from https://www.ft.com/content/
42822ebe-fc4a-11e7-9b32-d7d59aace167

Weber, B. (2016). Bitcoin and the legitimacy crisis of money. *Cambridge
Journal of Economics, 40*(1), 17–41.

Weber, M. (1978). *Economy and society* (Vol. 1). University of California
Press.

Wikipedia. (2020, September 29). List of public corporations by market
capitalization.

Williams, J. W. (2020). Recidivists, rough sleepers, and the unemployed as
financial assets: Social impact bonds and the creation of new markets in
social services. In K. Birch & F. Muniesa (Eds.), *Assetization: Turning
things into assets in technoscientific capitalism* (pp. 287–312). MIT
Press.

Witko, C. (2016, March 29). How Wall Street became a big chunk of the
U.S. economy – and when the Democrats signed on. *Washington Post.*
Retrieved from https://www.washingtonpost.com/news/monkey-cage/wp/
2016/03/29/how-wall-street-became-a-big-chunk-of-the-u-s-economy-and-
when-the-democrats-signed-on/

Wolf, M. (2010). *Fixing global finance* (Expanded edition.). Yale University
Press.

Yenkey, C. (2010). Selling value in Nairobi's stock exchange. In J. Beckert &
P. Aspers (Eds.), *The worth of goods: Valuation and pricing in the
economy* (pp. 247–271). Oxford University Press.

Yermack, D. (2014). *Is bitcoin a real currency? An economic appraisal*
(Working Paper No. 19747). National Bureau of Economic Research.

Yu, S., & Kynge, J. (2021, February 17). Virtual control: The agenda behind
China's new digital currency. *Financial Times.* Retrieved from https://
www.ft.com/content/7511809e-827e-4526-81ad-ae83f405f623

Zajac, E. J., & Westphal, J. D. (2004). The social construction of market value: Institutionalization and learning perspectives on stock market reactions. *American Sociological Review*, *69*(3), 433–457.

Zuckerman, E. W. (1999). The categorical imperative: Securities analysts and the illegitimacy discount. *American Journal of Sociology*, *104*(5), 1398–1438.

(2012). Construction, concentration, and (Dis)Continuities in social valuations. *Annual Review of Sociology*, *38*(1), 223–245.

Zuckerman, M. J. (2018, February 16). Japan's financial regulator to conduct inspections of 15 unregistered crypto exchanges. *Cointelegraph*. Retrieved from https://cointelegraph.com/news/japans-financial-regulator-to-conduct-inspections-of-15-unregistered-crypto-exchanges

Index

For EU product safety concerns, contact us at Calle de José Abascal, 56–1°,
28003 Madrid, Spain or eugpsr@cambridge.org.

www.ingramcontent.com/pod-product-compliance
Ingram Content Group UK Ltd.
Pitfield, Milton Keynes, MK11 3LW, UK
UKHW020353140625

459647UK00020B/2450